Autodesk
AutoCAD Architecture 2022
Fundamentals

Elise Moss

SDC
PUBLICATIONS

SDC Publications
P.O. Box 1334
Mission, KS 66222
913-262-2664
www.SDCpublications.com
Publisher: Stephen Schroff

ISBN-13: 978-1-63057-427-7
ISBN-10: 1-63057-427-9

Printed and bound in the United States of America.

Preface

No textbook can cover all the features in any software application. This textbook is meant for beginning users who want to gain a familiarity with the tools and interface of AutoCAD Architecture before they start exploring on their own. By the end of the text, users should feel comfortable enough to create a standard model, and even know how to customize the interface for their own use. Knowledge of basic AutoCAD and its commands is helpful but not required. I do try to explain as I go, but for the sake of brevity I concentrate on the tools specific to and within AutoCAD Architecture.

The files used in this text are accessible from the Internet from the book's page on the publisher's website: www.SDCpublications.com. They are free and available to students and teachers alike.

We value customer input. Please contact us with any comments, questions, or concerns about this text.

Elise Moss
elise_moss@mossdesigns.com

Acknowledgments from Elise Moss

This book would not have been possible without the support of some key Autodesk employees.

The effort and support of the editorial and production staff of SDC Publications is gratefully acknowledged. I especially thank Stephen Schroff for his helpful suggestions regarding the format of this text.

Finally, truly infinite thanks to Ari for his encouragement and his faith.

- Elise Moss

About the Author

Elise Moss has worked for the past thirty years as a mechanical designer in Silicon Valley, primarily creating sheet metal designs. She has written articles for Autodesk's Toplines magazine, AUGI's PaperSpace, DigitalCAD.com and Tenlinks.com. She is President of Moss Designs, creating custom applications and designs for corporate clients. She has taught CAD classes at Laney College, DeAnza College, Silicon Valley College, and for Autodesk resellers. Autodesk has named her as a Faculty of Distinction for the curriculum she has developed for Autodesk products. She holds a baccalaureate degree in Mechanical Engineering from San Jose State.

She is married with three sons. Her husband, Ari, is retired from a distinguished career in software development.

Elise is a third-generation engineer. Her father, Robert Moss, was a metallurgical engineer in the aerospace industry. Her grandfather, Solomon Kupperman, was a civil engineer for the City of Chicago.

She can be contacted via email at elise_moss@mossdesigns.com.

More information about the author and her work can be found on her website at www.mossdesigns.com.

Autodesk
Certified Instructor

Other books by Elise Moss
Autodesk Revit Architecture 2022 Basics
AutoCAD 2022 Fundamentals

Table of Contents

Preface i

Acknowledgments i

About the Author ii

Lesson 1:
Desktop Features

Exercise 1-1: 1-5
Setting the Template for QNEW

Exercise 1-2: 1-24
Creating a New Geometric Profile

Exercise 1-3: 1-28
Creating a New Visual Style

Exercise 1-4: 1-30
Creating an Autodesk Cloud Account

Exercise 1-5: 1-32
Creating a New Wall Style

Exercise 1-6: 1-40
Tool Palettes

Exercise 1-7: 1-43
Copying a Style to a Template

Exercise 1-8: 1-52
Exploring the Display Manager

Exercise 1-9: 1-56
Creating a Text Style

Exercise 1-10: 1-57
Project Settings

Quiz 1

Lesson 2:
Site Plans

Exercise 2-1: 2-2
Creating Custom Line Types

Exercise 2-2: 2-4
Creating New Layers

Exercise 2-3: 2-8
Creating a Site Plan

Exercise 2-4:
Creating a Layer User Group   2-22

Quiz 2

Lesson 3:
Floor Plans

Exercise 3-1:
Going from a 2D to 3D Floor Plan   3-2

Exercise 3-2:
Importing a PDF into ACA   3-10

Exercise 3-3:
Creating Walls   3-13

Exercise 3-4:
Creating a Floor Plan Using an Image   3-16

Exercise 3-5:
Adding Doors   3-31

Exercise 3-6:
Create an Arched Opening Tool   3-41

Exercise 3-7:
Adding an Opening   3-43

Exercise 3-8:
Add Window Assemblies   3-47

Exercise 3-9:
Place a Grid   3-53

Exercise 3-10:
Convert to Grid   3-55

Exercise 3-11:
Place a Curtain Wall   3-57

Quiz 3

Lesson 4:
Space Planning

Exercise 4-1:
Creating AEC Content   4-1

Exercise 4-2:
Furnishing the Common Areas   4-8

Exercise 4-3:
Adding to the Service Areas   4-11

Exercise 4-4:   4-17
Adding Components to the Bathrooms

Quiz 4

Lesson 5:
Roofs

Exercise 5-1:   5-4
Creating a Roof Using Existing Walls

Exercise 5-2:   5-7
Roof Slabs

Exercise 5-3:   5-10
Modify Roof Line

Exercise 5-4:   5-13
Trimming Roof Slabs

Exercise 5-5:   5-20
Adding a Hole to a Roof

Exercise 5-6:   5-23
Add a Gabled Roof

Exercise 5-7:   5-26
Modifying a Hole in a Roof Slab

Exercise 5-8:   5-28
Add Walls to a Gabled Roof

Exercise 5-9:   5-32
Roof Slab Styles

Exercise 5-10:   5-35
Applying a Roof Slab Style

Quiz 5

Lesson 6:
Structural Members

Exercise 6-1:   6-4
Creating Member Styles

Exercise 6-2:   6-5
Creating Member Shapes

Exercise 6-3:   6-7
Adding Structural Members

Quiz 6

Lesson 7:
Floors, Ceilings, and Spaces

Exercise 7-1:
Creating Slab Styles — 7-2

Exercise 7-2:
Create Slab from Linework — 7-10

Exercise 7-3:
Create Slab from Boundary — 7-12

Exercise 7-4:
Create Ceiling Grid — 7-14

Exercise 7-5:
Add Lights to Ceiling Grid — 7-18

Exercise 7-6:
Add a Space — 7-20

Exercise 7-7:
Add a Ceiling and Floor to a Space — 7-21

Exercise 7-8:
Add a Lighting Fixture to a Ceiling — 7-23

Exercise 7-9:
Creating a Multi-Level Building — 7-25

Exercise 7-10:
Placing a Stair — 7-28

Exercise 7-11:
Placing a Railing — 7-30

Exercise 7-12:
Placing a Stair Tower — 7-32

Quiz 7

Lesson 8:
Rendering & Materials

Exercise 8-1:
Modifying the Material Browser Interface — 8-5

Exercise 8-2:
Copy a Material from a Library to a Drawing — 8-10

Exercise 8-3:
Adding Color to Walls — 8-14

Exercise 8-4:
Reference Manager — 8-19

Exercise 8-5: — 8-22

Camera View

Exercise 8-6:   8-28
Create Rendering

Exercise 8-7:   8-34
Render in Cloud

Exercise 8-8:   8-38
Create an Animation

Exercise 8-9:   8-42
Using the Sun & Sky

Exercise 8-10:   8-46
Applying Materials

Exercise 8-11:   8-54
Applying Materials to Furniture

Exercise 8-12:   8-59
Replace a Block

Exercise 8-13:   8-61
Using Artificial Light

Exercise 8-14:   8-64
Mapping Materials

Quiz 8

Lesson 9:
Documentation

Exercise 9-1:   9-2
Creating a Custom Titleblock

Exercise 9-2:   9-13
Creating Elevation Views

Exercise 9-3:   9-16
Creating Layouts

Exercise 9-4:   9-20
Copy a Layout

Exercise 9-5:   9-23
Loading a Linetype

Exercise 9-6:   9-24
Applying a Fire Rating Line

Exercise 9-7:   9-30
Assigning Fire Ratings to Wall Properties

Exercise 9-8:   9-32
Creating a Schedule Tag

Exercise 9-9:
Creating a Schedule Tag tool on the Document
Palette
9-35

Exercise 9-10:
Modify a Dimension Style
9-39

Exercise 9-11:
Dimensioning a Floor Plan
9-41

Exercise 9-12:
Create a Wall Section
9-49

Exercise 9-13:
Add Keynotes
9-52

Exercise 9-14:
Add Keynote Legend
9-56

Exercise 9-15:
Copy and Paste between Drawings
9-63

Exercise 9-16:
Create a Section View
9-65

Exercise 9-17:
Add a Door Elevation
9-69

Exercise 9-18:
Add a Door Details Layout
9-72

Exercise 9-19:
Add a Callout
9-74

Exercise 9-20:
Creating Space Styles
9-82

Exercise 9-21:
Adding Spaces
9-84

Exercise 9-22:
Modifying Spaces
9-87

Exercise 9-23:
Create a Room Tag
9-90

Exercise 9-24:
Create a Room Tag Tool
9-99

Exercise 9-25:
Adding Room Tags
9-101

Exercise 9-26:
Adding Door Tags
9-103

Exercise 9-27:
Create a Door Schedule
9-107

Exercise 9-28:   9-110
Create a Door Schedule Style

Exercise 9-29:   9-116
Create a Room Schedule

Exercise 9-30:   9-124
Creating a PDF Document

Exercise 9-31:   9-126
Create Door Symbols for a Legend

Exercise 9-32:   9-132
Convert Images to Blocks

Exercise 9-33:   9-138
Create a Door Legend

Quiz 9

Notes:

Lesson 1:
Desktop Features

AutoCAD Architecture (ACA) enlists object-oriented process systems (OOPS). That means that ACA uses intelligent objects to create a building. This is similar to using blocks in AutoCAD. Objects in AutoCAD Architecture are blocks on steroids. They have intelligence already embedded into them. A wall is not just a collection of lines. It represents a real wall. It can be constrained, has thickness and material properties, and is automatically included in your building schedule.

AEC is an acronym for Architectural/Engineering/Construction.
BID is an acronym for Building Industrial Design.
BIM is an acronym for Building Information Modeling.
AIA is an acronym for the American Institute of Architects.
MEP is an acronym for Mechanical/Electrical/Plumbing.

The following table describes the key features of objects in AutoCAD Architecture:

Feature Type	Description
AEC Camera	Create perspective views from various camera angles. Create avi files.
AEC Profiles	Create AEC objects using polylines to build doors, windows, etc.
Anchors and Layouts	Define a spatial relationship between objects. Create a layout of anchors on a curve or a grid to set a pattern of anchored objects, such as doors or columns.
Annotation	Set up special arrows, leaders, bar scales.
Ceiling Grids	Create reflected ceiling plans with grid layouts.
Column Grids	Define rectangular and radial building grids with columns and bubbles.
Design Center	Customize your AEC block library.
Display System	Control views for each AEC object.
Doors and Windows	Create custom door and window styles or use standard objects provided with the software.
Elevations and Sections	An elevation is basically a section view of a floor plan.
Layer Manager	Create layer standards based on AIA CAD Standards. Create groups of layers. Manage layers intelligently using Layer Filters.
Masking Blocks	Store a mask using a polyline object and attach to AEC objects to hide graphics.
Model Explorer	View a model and manage the content easily. Attach names to mass elements to assist in design.
Multi-view blocks	Blocks have embedded defined views to allow you to easily change view.

Feature Type	Description
Railings	Create or apply different railing styles to a stair or along a defined path.
Roofs	Create and apply various roof styles.
Floorplate slices	Generate the perimeter geometry of a building.
Spaces and Boundaries	Spaces and boundaries can include floor thickness, room height, and wall thickness.
Stairs	Create and apply various stair types.
Tags and Schedules	Place tags on objects to generate schedules. Schedules will automatically update when tags are modified, added, or deleted.
Template Files	Use templates to save time. Create a template with standard layers, text styles, linetypes, dimension styles, etc.
Walls	Create wall styles to determine material composition. Define end caps to control opening and end conditions. Define wall interference conditions.

AutoCAD Architecture sits on top of AutoCAD. It is helpful for users to have a basic understanding of AutoCAD before moving to AutoCAD Architecture. Users should be familiar with the following:

- ❑ AutoCAD toolbars and tab on the ribbons
- ❑ Zoom and move around the screen
- ❑ Manage blocks
- ❑ *Draw* and *Modify* commands
- ❑ *Model* and *Paper space* (layout)
- ❑ Dimensioning and how to create/modify a dimension style

If you are not familiar with these topics, you can still move forward with learning AutoCAD Architecture, but you may find it helpful to have a good AutoCAD textbook as reference in case you get stuck.

The best way to use AutoCAD Architecture is to start your project with massing tools (outside-in design) or space planning tools (inside-out design) and continue through to construction documentation.

The AEC Project Process Model

Conceptual Design

In the initial design phase, you can assemble AutoCAD Architecture mass elements as simple architectural shapes to form an exterior model of your building project. You can also lay out interior areas by arranging general spaces as you would in a bubble diagram. You can manipulate and consolidate three-dimensional mass elements into massing studies.

Later in this phase, you can create building footprints from the massing study by slicing floorplates, and you can begin defining the structure by converting space boundaries into walls. At the completion of the conceptual design phase, you have developed a workable schematic floor plan.

Design Development

As you refine the building project, you can add more detailed information to the schematic design. Use the features in AutoCAD Architecture to continue developing the design of the building project by organizing, defining, and assigning specific styles and attributes to building components.

Construction Development

After you have fully developed the building design, you can annotate your drawings with reference marks, notes, and dimensions. You can also add tags or labels associated with objects. Information from the objects and tags can be extracted, sorted, and compiled into schedules, reports, tables, and inventories for comprehensive and accurate construction documentation.

Presentations

A major part of any project is presenting it to the client. At this stage, you develop renderings, animations, and perspective views.

If you use the **QNEW** tool, it will automatically use the template set in the Options dialog.

ExClick Tools

ExClick Tools are installed with AutoCAD Architecture. If you do not see ExClick Tools on the menu bar, try typing EXCLICKTOOLS to see if that loads them.

Exercise 1-1:

Setting the Template for QNEW

Drawing Name: New
Estimated Time: 15 minutes

This exercise reinforces the following skills:

- ❑ Use of templates
- ❑ Getting the user familiar with tools and the ACA environment

1.   Launch ACA.

2.   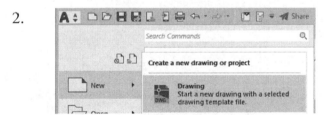   Select the drop-down arrow next to the large A to access the Application Menu.

Select **New→Drawing**.

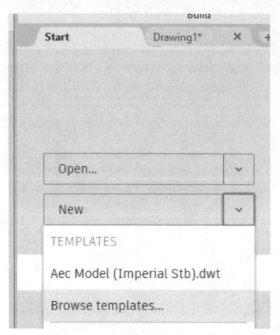

You can also select **New** from the Start tab.

Click the down arrow next to New and select **Browse templates…**

3.

Browse to the *Template* folder under *ProgramData/Autodesk/ACA 2022/enu*.

4.

Right click on the left panel of the dialog.

Select **Add Current Folder**.

This adds the template folder to the palette.

5.

Select the desired template to use.

Each template controls units, layers, and plot settings.

Select *Aec Model (Imperial.Ctb)*.

This template uses Imperial units (feet and inches and a Color Table to control plot settings).

Click **Open.**

6. Place your cursor on the command line.

7. Right click the mouse.

Select **Options** from the short-cut menu.

8. Select the **Files** tab.
Locate the *Template Settings* folder.

9. Click on the + symbol to expand.
Locate the Default Template File Name for QNEW.

10.   → None   Highlight the path and file name listed or None (if no path or file name is listed) and select the **Browse** button.

11. Browse to the *Template* folder or select it on the palette if you added it.

This should be listed under *Program Data/Autodesk/ ACA 2022/enu*

12. Locate the *Aec Model (Imperial Ctb).dwt [Aec Model (Metric Ctb).dwt]* file.

Click **Open**.

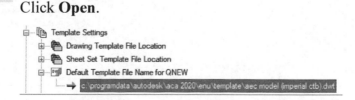

Note that you can also set where you can direct the user for templates. This is useful if you want to create standard templates and place them on a network server for all users to access.

You can also use this setting to help you locate where your template files are located.

13. Click **Apply** and **OK**.

14. Select the **QNEW** tool button.

15. Note that you have tabs for all the open drawings.

You can switch between any open drawing files by selecting the folder tab. You can also use the + tab to start a new drawing. The + tab acts the same way as the QNEW button and uses the same default template.

16. Select the **Model** tab of the open drawing.

17. Type **units** on the *Command* line.

Notice how you get a selection of commands as you type.

Click ENTER to select UNITS.

18. Note that the units are in Architectural format.

The units are determined by the template you set to start your new drawing.

19. Close the drawing without saving.

Templates can be used to preset layers, property set definitions, dimension styles, units, and layouts.

AEC Drawing Options

Menu	Tools→Options
Command line	Options
Context Menu→Options	Place mouse in the graphics area and right click
Shortcut	Place mouse in the command line and right click

Access the Options dialog box.

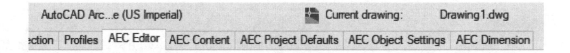

ACA's Options include five additional AEC specific tabs.
They are AEC Editor, AEC Content, AEC Project Defaults, AEC Object Settings, and AEC Dimension.

AEC Editor

Diagnostic Messages	All diagnostic messages are turned off by default.
Similar-Purpose Dialogs	Options for the position of dialog boxes and viewers.
Use Common Position	Sets one common position on the screen for similar dialog boxes, such as door, wall, and window add or modify dialog boxes. Some dialog boxes, such as those for styles and properties, are always displayed in the center of the screen, regardless of this setting.
Use Common Viewer Position and Sizes	Sets one size and position on the screen for the similar-purpose viewers in AutoCAD Architecture. Viewer position is separately controlled for add, modify, style, and properties dialog boxes.
Optimize for Speed	Options for display representations and layer loading in the Layer Manager dialog.
Object Snap	Enable to limit certain display representations to respond only to the Node and Insert object snaps. This setting affects stair, railing, space boundary, multi-view block, masking block, slice, and clip volume result (building section) objects.
Apply Common Property Sets to New Objects	Property sets are used for the creation of schedule tables. Each AEC object has embedded property sets, such as width and height, to be used in its schedule. AEC properties are similar to attributes. Size is a common property across most AEC objects. Occasionally, you may use a tool on an existing object and the result may be that you replace the existing object with an entirely different object. For example, if you apply the tool properties of a door to an existing window, a new door object will replace the existing window. When enabled, any property sets that were assigned to the existing window will automatically be preserved and applied to the new door provided that the property set definitions make sense.
Solution Tips	Users can set whether they wish a solution tip to appear while they are drafting or plotting. A solution tip identifies a drafting error and suggests a solution.
Dynamic Dimensions Linetype	Set the linetype to be used when creating dynamic dimensions. This makes it easier to distinguish between dynamic and applied dimensions. You may select either continuous or dot linetypes.

Export to AutoCAD	Enable Bind Xrefs.
☐ *Export to AutoCAD* ☑ Bind xrefs ☑ Use Insert Method when Binding xrefs Filename Prefix: Filename Suffix: [ACAD-] [ ]	If you enable this option, the xref will be inserted as a block and not an xref. Enable Use Insert Method when binding Xrefs if you want all objects from an xref drawing referenced in the file you export to be automatically exploded into the host drawing. If you enable this option, the drawing names of the xref drawings are discarded when the exported drawing is created. In addition, their layers and styles are incorporated into the host drawing. For example, all exploded walls, regardless of their source (host or xref) are located on the same layer. Disable Use Insert Method when binding Xrefs if you want to retain the xref identities, such as layer names, when you export a file to AutoCAD or to a DXF file. For example, the blocks that define walls in the host drawing are located on A-Wall in the exploded drawing. Walls in an attached xref drawing are located on a layer whose name is created from the drawing name and the layer name, such as Drawing1|WallA. Many architects automatically bind and explode their xrefs when sending drawings to customers to protect their intellectual property. Enter a prefix or a suffix to be added to the drawing filename when the drawing is exported to an AutoCAD drawing or a DXF file. In order for any of these options to apply, you have to use the Export to AutoCAD command. This is available under the Files menu.
Unselected Grip Colors	Assign the colors for each type of grip.

Units for Legacy Drawings	Determines the units to be used when opening an AutoCAD drawing in AutoCAD Architecture.
	    Automatic – uses the current AutoCAD Architecture
	       units setting
	    Imperial – uses Imperial units
	    Metric – uses Metric units

Option Settings are applied to your current drawing and saved as the default settings for new drawings. Because AutoCAD Architecture operates in a Multiple Document Interface, each drawing stores the Options Settings used when it was created and last saved. Some users get confused because they open an existing drawing and it will not behave according to the current Options Settings.

AEC Content

| 3D Modeling | Selection | Profiles | AEC Editor | AEC Content | AEC Project Defaults | AEC Object Settings | AEC Dimension |

Architectural / Documentation / Multi-Purpose Object Style Path:
C:\ProgramData\Autodesk\ACA 2020\enu\Styles\Imperial   Browse...

AEC DesignCenter Content Path:
C:\ProgramData\Autodesk\ACA 2020\enu\AEC Content   Browse...

Tool Catalog Content Root Path:
C:\ProgramData\Autodesk\ACA 2020\enu\   Browse...

IFC Content Path:
C:\ProgramData\Autodesk\ACA 2020\enu\Styles\   Browse...

Detail Component Databases: Add/Remove...

Keynote Databases: Add/Remove...

☑ Display Edit Property Data Dialog During Tag Insertion

Architectural/Documentation/Multipurpose Object Style Path	Allows you to specify a path of source files to be used to import object styles; usually used for system styles like walls, floors, or roofs.
AEC DesignCenter Content Path	Type the path and location of your content files or click Browse to search for the content files.
Tool Catalog Content Root Path	Type the path and location of your Tool Catalog files or click Browse to search for the content files.

IFC Content Path	Type the path and location of your Tool Catalog files or click Browse to search for the content files.
Detail Component Databases	Select the **Add/Remove** button to set the search paths for your detail component files.
Keynote Databases	Select the **Add/Remove** button to set the search paths for your keynote database files.
Display Edit Schedule Data Dialog During Tag Insertion	To attach schedule data to objects when you insert a schedule tag in the drawing, this should be ENABLED.

IFC Content is an object-based building data model that is non-proprietary. It uses open-source code developed by the IAI (International Alliance for Interoperability) to promote data exchange between CAD software. IFC Content might be created in Autodesk Revit, Inventor, or some other software for use in your projects.

Using AEC Content

AutoCAD Architecture uses several pre-defined and user-customizable content including:

- Architectural Display Configurations
- Architectural Profiles of Geometric Shapes
- Wall Styles and Endcap geometry
- Door styles
- Window styles
- Stair styles
- Space styles
- Schedule tables

Standard style content is stored in the AEC templates subdirectory. You can create additional content, import and export styles between drawings.

AEC Object Settings

Wall Settings	
Autosnap New Wall Justification Lines	Enable to have the endpoint of a new wall that is drawn within the Autosnap Radius of the baseline of an existing wall automatically snap to that baseline.
	If you select this option and set your Autosnap Radius to 0, then only walls that touch clean up with each other.
Autosnap Grip Edited Wall Justification Lines	Enable to snap the endpoint of a wall that you grip edit within the Autosnap Radius of the baseline of an existing wall.
	If you select this option and set your Autosnap Radius to 0, then only walls that touch clean up with each other.
Autosnap Radius	Enter a value to set the snap tolerance.
Do not display opening end cap styles	Enable Do Not Display Opening Endcap Styles to supClick the display of endcaps applied to openings in walls.
	Enabling this option boosts drawing performance when the drawing contains many complex endcaps.

Stair Settings	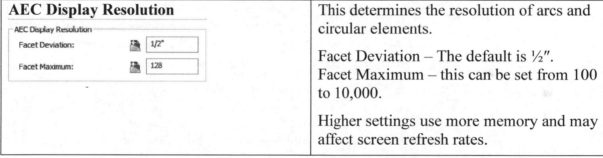
Presentation Format (No Cut Lines or Path)	If this is enabled, a jagged line and directional arrows will not display.
Node Osnap	Determines which snap is enabled when creating stairs: 　　Vertical Alignment 　　Flight and Landing Corners
Measure Stair Height	Rough floor to floor – ignore offsets Finished floor to floor – include top and bottom offsets
Calculator Limits	Strict – stair will display a defect symbol when an edit results in a violation of the Calculation rules. Relaxed – no defect symbol will be displayed when the stair violates the Calculation rules. The Calculation rules determine how many treads are required based on the riser height and the overall height of the stairs.

AEC Display Resolution	This determines the resolution of arcs and circular elements.
AEC Display Resolution Facet Deviation: 1/2" Facet Maximum: 128	Facet Deviation – The default is ½". Facet Maximum – this can be set from 100 to 10,000. Higher settings use more memory and may affect screen refresh rates.

Space Settings	If *Automatically update associative spaces* is enabled, AutoCAD Architecture will automatically determine which spaces are adjacent to each other and update their association accordingly.
	The Maximum Gap Size is the allowable distance between spaces.
	The Maximum Automatic Adjacency sets the gap allowance between spaces for spaces to be considered adjacent.
	The Floor Boundary Thickness sets the value of the Floor Boundary Thickness.
	The Calculation Standard determines how the space values are calculated.
AEC Property Set Definitions	Enable Automatically Attach to attach property set data to objects that you want to include in a schedule table or link to schedule tags.
	By default, this option is disabled, which means you would have to manually attach property set data to elements when the property set data is modified or created.
Property Override	Provides the ability to control visibility and order of properties assigned to AEC elements.

AEC Dimension

General	
Update Added/Removed points immediately	Enable to update the display every time you add or remove a point from a dimension chain.
Make Manual Dimension Points Associative	Enable if you want the dimension to update when the object is modified.
Override Display of Undefined Text	Enable to automatically underline each manually overridden dimension value.
Underline All	Enable to manually underline overridden dimension values.
Underline None	Enable to not underline any overridden dimension value.
Units	
Dimension in:	Select the desired units from the drop-down list.
Use Superscript mm	If your units are set to meters or centimeters, enable superscripted text to display the millimeters as superscript. 4.34²⁵

Trailing Zero SupClickion for Superscript	To supClick zeros at the end of superscripted numbers, select Trailing Zeros SupClickion for Superscript. You can select this option only if you have selected Use Superscript mm and your units are metric. 4.12^3
Automatic Scale of AutoCAD Dimstyles	Select the dimstyles you would like to automatically scale when units are reset.
Elevation Labels	Select the unit in which elevation labels are to be displayed. This unit can differ from the drawing unit.
Display +/- for 0.00 Values	
Display + for Positive Values	
Dimension Label Prefixes	Dimension Label Prefixes are set based on the object selected from the drop-down. You can set label prefixes for Doors, Windows, Openings, and Stairs. Select the object, and then set the prefix for each designation. The designations will change based on the object selected.

AEC Project Defaults

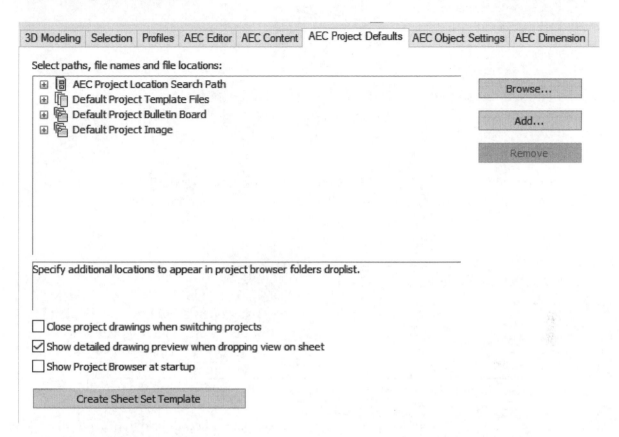

Most BID/AEC firms work in a team environment where they divide a project's tasks among several different users. The AEC Project Defaults allow the CAD Manager or team leader to select a folder on the company's server to locate files, set up template files with the project's title blocks, and even set up a webpage to post project information.

To add a path, simply expand the folder and use the Browse button to locate the desired folder.

You can add more than one path to the AEC Project Location Search Path. All the other folders only allow you to have a single location for template files, the project bulletin board, and the default project image.

I highly recommend that you store any custom content in a separate directory as far away from AutoCAD Architecture as possible. This will allow you to back up your custom work easily and prevent accidental erasure if you upgrade your software application.

You should be aware that AutoCAD Architecture currently allows the user to specify only ONE path for custom content, so drawings with custom commands will only work if they reside in the specified path.

☐ Close project drawings when switching projects	If enabled, when a user switches projects in the Project Navigator, any open drawings not related to the new project selected will be closed. This conserves memory resources.
☑ Show detailed drawing preview when dropping view on sheet	If enabled, then the user will see the entire view as it is being positioned on a sheet. If it is disabled, the user will just see the boundary of the view for the purposes of placing it on a sheet.
☐ Show Project Browser at startup	If enabled, you will automatically have access to the Project Browser whenever you start AutoCAD Architecture.

Architectural Profiles of Geometric Shapes

You can create mass elements to define the shape and configuration of your preliminary study, or mass model. After you create the mass elements you need, you can change their size as necessary to reflect the building design.

- **Mass element**: A single object that has behaviors based on its shape. For example, you can set the width, depth, and height of a box mass element, and the radius and height of a cylinder mass element.

Mass elements are parametric, which allows each of the shapes to have very specific behavior when it comes to the manipulation of each mass element's shape. For example, if the corner grip point of a box is selected and dragged, then the width and depth are modified. It is easy to change the shape to another form by right-clicking on the element and selecting a new shape from the list.

Through Boolean operations (addition, subtraction, intersection), mass elements can be combined into a mass group. The mass group provides a representation of your building during the concept phase of your project.

- **Mass group**: Takes the shape of the mass elements and is placed on a separate layer from the mass elements.
- **Mass model**: A virtual mass object, shaped from mass elements, which defines the basic structure and proportion of your building. A marker appears as a small box in your drawing to which you attach mass elements.

As you continue developing your mass model, you can combine mass elements into mass groups and create complex building shapes through addition, subtraction, or intersection of mass elements. You can still edit individual mass elements attached to a mass group to further refine the building model.

To study alternative design schemes, you can create a number of mass element references. When you change the original of the referenced mass element, all the instances of the mass element references are updated.

The mass model that you create with mass elements and mass groups is a refinement of your original idea that you carry forward into the next phase of the project, in which you change the mass study into floor plates and then into walls. The walls are used to start the design phase.

Mass Elements are accessed from the Home tab on the ribbon.

Mass Elements that can be defined from the Home tab include Arches, Gables, Cones, etc.

The Style Manager

Access the Style Manager from the Manage tab on the ribbon.

The Style Manager is a Microsoft® Windows Explorer-based utility that provides you with a central location in Autodesk AutoCAD Architecture where you can view and work with styles in drawings or from Internet and intranet sites.

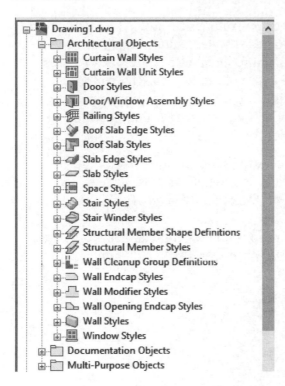

Styles are sets of parameters that you can assign to objects in Autodesk AutoCAD Architecture to determine their appearance or function. For example, a door style in Autodesk AutoCAD Architecture determines what door type, such as single or double, bi-fold or hinged, a door in a drawing represents. You can assign one style to more than one object, and you can modify the style to change all the objects that are assigned that style.

Depending on your design projects, either you or your CAD Manager might want to customize existing styles or create new styles. The Style Manager allows you to easily create, customize, and share styles with other users. With the Style Manager, you can:

- Provide a central point for accessing styles from open drawings and Internet and intranet sites

- Quickly set up new drawings and templates by copying styles from other drawings or templates

- Sort and view the styles in your drawings and templates by drawing or by style type

- Preview an object with a selected style

- Create new styles and edit existing styles

- Delete unused styles from drawings and templates

- Send styles to other Autodesk AutoCAD Architecture users by email

Objects in Autodesk AutoCAD Architecture that use styles include 2D sections and elevations, AEC polygons, curtain walls, curtain wall units, doors, endcaps, railings, roof slab edges, roof slabs, schedule tables, slab edges, slabs, spaces, stairs, structural members, wall modifiers, walls, window assemblies, and windows.

Additionally, layer key styles, schedule data formats, and cleanup group, mask block, multi-view block, profile, and property set definitions are handled by the Style Manager.

Most of the objects in Autodesk AutoCAD Architecture have a default Standard style. In addition, Autodesk AutoCAD Architecture includes a starter set of styles that you can use with your drawings. The Autodesk AutoCAD Architecture templates contain some of these styles. Any drawing that you start from one of the templates includes these styles.

You can also access the styles for doors, end caps, spaces, stairs, walls, and windows from drawings located in *ProgramData\Autodesk\ACA 2022\enu\Styles*.

Property set definitions and schedule tables are located in the *ProgramData\Autodesk\ACA 2022\enu\AEC Content* folder.

Exercise 1-2:
Creating a New Geometric Profile

Drawing Name: New
Estimated Time: 15 minutes

This exercise reinforces the following skills:

- ❑ Use of AEC Design Content
- ❑ Use of Mass Elements
- ❑ Use of Views
- ❑ Visual Styles
- ❑ Modify using Properties

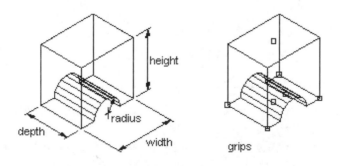

Creating an arch mass element

1. Start a New Drawing.

2. Select the QNEW tool from the Standard toolbar.

3. Because we assigned a template in Exercise 1-1, a drawing file opens without

prompting us to select a template.

All the massing tools are available on the **Home** tab on the ribbon in the Build section.

4.   Select the **Arch** tool from the Massing drop down list.

5. Expand the **Dimensions** section on the Properties palette.

Set Specify on screen to **No**.
Set the Width to **6'** [**183**].
Set the Depth to **6"** [**15**].
Set the Height to **6' 8"** [**203**].
Set the Radius to **2'** [**61**].

Units in brackets are centimeters.

You need to enter in the ' and " symbols.

6. Pick a point anywhere in the drawing area.

Click ENTER to accept a Rotation Angle of 0 or right click and select **ENTER**.

Click **ENTER** to exit the command.

7. Switch to an isometric view.

To switch to an isometric view, simply go to **View** panel on the Home tab. Under the Views list, select **SW Isometric**.

Or select the Home icon next to the Viewcube.

Our model so far.

8.   Select **Visual Styles, Realistic** on the View panel on the Home tab to shade the model.

You can also type **SHA** on the command line, then **R** for Realistic.

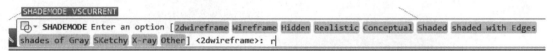

9. To change the arch properties, select the arch so that it is highlighted.
If the properties dialog doesn't pop up automatically, right click and select **Properties**.

10.

Dimensions	▼
Width	6'-0"
Depth	6"
Height	6'-8"
Radius	9"
Volume	20 CF

Change the Radius to **9″** [**15**].

Pick into the graphics window and the arch will update.

11. Click **ESC** to release the grips on the arc.

12. Save the drawing as *ex1-2.dwg*.

If you see this dialog, it means that the mass element just created (the arch) cannot be saved as a previous version file.

Click **Close**.

  Visual Styles are stored with the drawing.

Visual Styles

Visual styles determine the display of edges, lighting, and shading in each viewport.

You can choose a predefined visual style in the upper-left corner of each viewport. In addition, the Visual Styles Manager displays all styles available in the drawing. You can choose a different visual style or change its settings at any time. ACA comes with several pre-defined visual styles or you can create your own.

Exercise 1-3:
Creating a New Visual Style

Drawing Name: visual_style.dwg
Estimated Time: 15 minutes

This exercise reinforces the following skills:

- ❑ Workspaces
- ❑ Use of Visual Styles
- ❑ Controlling the Display of Objects

1.   Open *visual_style.dwg*.

2. Activate the **View** tab on the ribbon.

3. 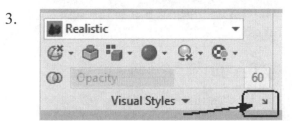 Launch the Visual Styles Manager.

To launch, select the small arrow in the lower right corner of the Visual Styles panel.

4. 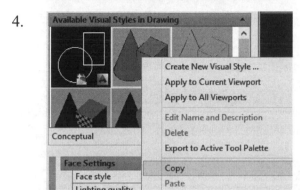 Highlight the **Conceptual** tool.

Right click and select **Copy**.

5. 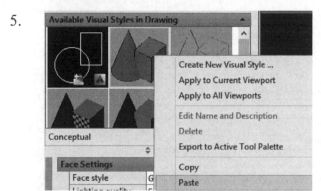 Right click and select **Paste**.

6. 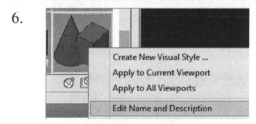 Highlight the copied tool.
Right click and select **Edit Name and Description**.

7. 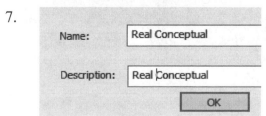 Change the name and description to **Real Conceptual**.

Click **OK**.

8. Under Face Settings:

Set the Face Style to **Realistic**.

Set Material display to **Materials and textures**.

Under Environment Settings:

Set the Backgrounds to **Off**.

Under Edge Settings:

Set the Show to **None**.

9. Verify that the Real Conceptual Style is highlighted/ selected.

Right click and select the **Apply to Current Viewport** tool.

[−][SW Isometric][Real Conceptual]

Note that the active visual style is listed in the upper right corner of the drawing.

10. Save the drawing as *ex1-3.dwg*.

Exercise 1-4:
Creating an Autodesk Cloud Account

Drawing Name: (none, start from scratch)
Estimated Time: 5 Minutes

This exercise reinforces the following skills:

❑   Create an account on Autodesk.

> *You must have an internet connection to access the Autodesk server. Many government agencies do not allow the use of cloud accounts due to security concerns. Autodesk's cloud account is useful for students, home users, and small shops.*

1.   Next to the Help icon at the top of the screen:

Select **Sign In to Autodesk account**.

2.

Sign in

Email

name@example.com

NEXT

NEW TO AUTODESK? CREATE ACCOUNT

If you have an existing Autodesk ID, you can use it.

If not, select the link that says **Create Account.**

You may have an existing Autodesk ID if you have registered Autodesk software in the past. Autodesk's cloud services are free to students and educators. For other users, you are provided a small amount of initial storage space for free.

I like my students to have an on-line account because it will automatically back up their work.

3.

Create account

First name   Last name

Email

Confirm email

Password

☐ I agree to the Autodesk **Terms of Use** and acknowledge the **Privacy Statement**.

CREATE ACCOUNT

Fill in the form to create an Autodesk ID account.

Be sure to write down the ID you select and the password.

4.

Account created

This single account gives you access to all your Autodesk products

☐ I would like to receive email communications from Autodesk

DONE

You should see a confirmation window stating that you now have an account.

5. ⟳ elise_moss ▾ 🅇 ⑦ ▾

You will see the name you selected as your Autodesk ID in the Cloud sign-in area.

Use your Autodesk account to create renderings, back up files to the Cloud so you can access your drawings on any internet-connected device, and to share your drawings.

Exercise 1-5:

Creating a New Wall Style

Drawing Name: New using Imperial [Metric] (ctb).dwt
Estimated Time: 30 minutes

This exercise reinforces the following skills:

- ❑ Style Manager
- ❑ Use of Wall Styles

1. Select the **QNEW** tool from the Quick Access toolbar.

2. Activate the **Manage** tab on the ribbon.

   Select the **Style Manager** from the **Style & Display** panel.

   Style Manager

3. The Style Manager is displayed with the current drawing expanded in the tree view. The wall styles in the current drawing are displayed under the wall style type. All other style and definition types are filtered out in the tree view.

   Locate the wall styles in the active drawing.

4. Highlight Wall Styles by left clicking on the name.
   Right click and select **New**.

5. Change the name of the new style by typing **Brick_Block**.

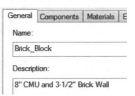

6. In the General tab, type in the description **8″ CMU and 3-1/2″ [200 mm CMU and 90 mm] Brick Wall** in the Description field as shown.

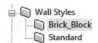

7. Select the Components tab.
    Change the Name to **CMU** by typing in the Name field indicated.

    Click the dropdown arrow next to the Edge Offset Button.
    Set the Edge Offset to 0.

8. A 0 edge offset specifies that the outside edge of the CMU is coincident with the wall baseline.

9. Click the **Width** down arrow button.

    Set the value to **-3″** **[-80]**.

    This specifies that the CMU has a fixed width of 3 inches [80 mm] in the negative direction from the wall baselinc (to the inside).

    You now have one component defined for your wall named CMU with the properties shown.

10. Click the **Add** Component button on the right side of the dialog box.
    Next, we'll add wall insulation.

11. In the Name field, type **Insulation**.

    Set the Priority to 1. (The lower the priority number, the higher the priority when creating intersections.)

    Set the Edge Offset with a value of **0**.

    Set the Component Width as shown, with a value of **1.5″ [38]** and the Base Width set to 0.

This specifies that the insulation has a fixed width of 1.5″ [38 mm] offset in a positive direction from the wall baseline (to the outside).

12. Set the Function to **Non-Structural**.

13. Note that the preview changes to show the insulation component.

14. Now, we add an air space component to our wall. Click the **Add Component** button.

15. Rename the new component **Air Space**.

Set the Edge Offset to **0**.

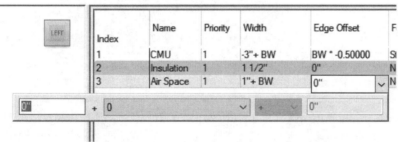

This specifies that the inside edge of the air space is coincident with the outside edge of the insulation.

The width should be set to **1″ [25.4] + Base Width**.

This specifies that the air gap will have a fixed width of 1 inch [25.4 mm] offset in the positive direction from the wall baseline (to the outside).

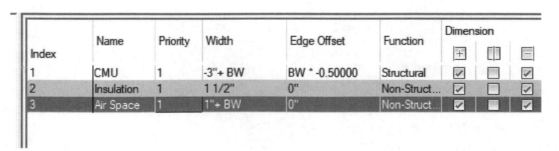

16. Use the **Add Component** tool to add the fourth component.

Index	Name	Priority	Width	Edge Offset	Function	Dimension [+] [‖] [‖]	Bottom Elevation Offset	From	Top Elevation Offset	From
1	CMU	1	-3"+ BW	BW * -0.50000	Structural	☑ ☐ ☑	0"	Wall Bottom	0"	Wall Top
2	Insulation	1	1 1/2"	0"	Non-Struct...	☑ ☐ ☑	0"	Wall Bottom	0"	Wall Top
3	Air Space	1	1"+ BW	0"	Non-Struct...	☑ ☐ ☑	0"	Wall Bottom	0"	Wall Top

Total Width: "VARIES"

The Name should be **Brick**.
The Priority set to **1**.
The Edge Offset set to **2.5″** [**63.5**].
The Width set to **3.5″** [**90**].

The Function should be set to **Structural**.

Index	Name	Priority	Width	Edge Offset	Function
1	CMU	1	-3"+ BW	BW * -0.50000	Structural
2	Insulation	1	1 1/2"	0"	Non-Structural
3	Air Space	1	1"+ BW	0"	Non-Structural
4	Brick	1	3 1/2"	2 1/2"	Structural

Index	Name	Priority	Width	Edge Offset	Function
1	CMU	1	-80.0...	0.00	Structural
2	INSULATION	1	38.00...	0.00	Non-Structural
3	AIR SPACE	1	25.40...	0.00	Non-Structural
4	BRICK	1	90.00...	63.50	Structural

Index	Name	Priority	Width	Edge Offset	Function	Dimension [+] [‖] [‖]	
1	CMU	1	-3"+ BW	BW * -0.50000	Structural	☑ ☑ ☑	0
2	Insulation	1	1 1/2"	0"	Non-Structural	☐ ☐ ☐	0
3	Air Space	1	1"+ BW	0"	Non-Structural	☐ ☐ ☐	0
4	Brick	1	3 1/2"	2 1/2"	Structural	☑ ☑ ☑	0

17. The Dimension section allows you to define where the extension lines for your dimension will be placed when measuring the wall. In this case, we are not interested in including the air space or insulation in our linear dimensions. Uncheck those boxes.

18.   Note how your wall style previews.

If you right click in the preview pane, you can change the preview window by zooming, panning, or assigning a Preset View.

The preview pane uses a DWF-style interface.

19. Select the **Materials** tab.

Highlight the **CMU** component.

Select the **Add New Material** tool.

20. Enter **CMU** in the New Name field and Click **OK**.

21. Use the **Add New Material** tool to assign new materials to each component.

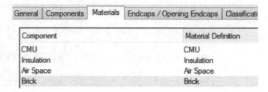

22.

Component	Material Definition
CMU	CMU
Insulation	Insulation
Air Space	Air Space
Brick	Brick
Shrinkwrap	Standard

The shrink-wrap material is automatically added. The shrink-wrap material controls the appearance of the wall. Items inside the wall are not shrink-wrapped, while exterior components are – similar to how walls appear in reality.

23. Highlight the **CMU** Component.

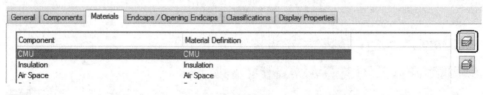

Select the **Edit Material** tool.

24. Select the **Display Properties** tab.

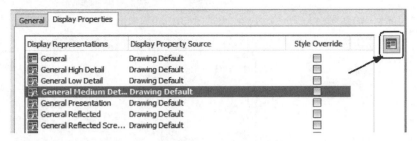

Highlight the **General Medium Detail** Display Representation.

Click on the **Style Override** button.

25. Select the **Hatching** tab.

Highlight **Plan Hatch** and select **Pattern**.

Under Type, select **Predefined**.

Under Pattern Name, select **AR-CONC**.

26. Assign the **AR-CONC** Pattern to all the Display Components.

Set the Angles to **0**.

27. Click **OK** twice to return to the Materials tab of the Wall Properties dialog.

28. 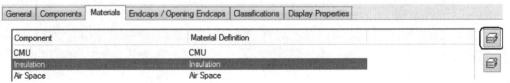 Highlight **Insulation** and select the **Edit Material** tool.

29. Select the **Display Properties** tab.

Click on the **Style Override** button.

Highlight the **General Medium Detail** Display Property.

30. Select the **Hatching** tab.

    Select all the Display Components so they are all highlighted.

31. 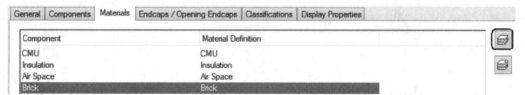 Set the Plan Hatch to the **INSUL** pattern under Predefined type.

    Set the Angle to **0.00**.

32. Verify that a check is placed in the Style Override button.

Display Representations	Display Property Source	Style Override
General	Material Definition Override - Standard	☑
General High Detail	Material Definition Override - Standard	☑
General Low Detail	Material Definition Override - Standard	☑
General Medium Det...	**Material Definition Override - Standard**	☑
General Presentation	Material Definition Override - Standard	☑
General Reflected	Material Definition Override - Standard	☑
General Reflected Scre...	Material Definition Override - Standard	☑
General Screened	Material Definition Override - Standard	☑

33. Click **OK** to return to the previous dialog.

34. Highlight **Brick** and select the **Edit Material** tool.

General | Components | Materials | Endcaps / Opening Endcaps | Classifications | Display Properties

Component	Material Definition
CMU	CMU
Insulation	Insulation
Air Space	Air Space
Brick	Brick

35. Select the **Display Properties** tab.

Highlight the **General Medium Detail** Display Representation.

Click on the **Style Override** button.

Display Representations	Display Property Source	Style Override
General	Drawing Default	☐
General High Detail	Drawing Default	☐
General Low Detail	Drawing Default	☐
General Medium Det...	**Drawing Default**	☐
General Presentation	Drawing Default	☐

36. 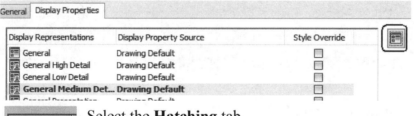 Select the **Hatching** tab.

    Highlight the three display components.

    Select the first pattern.

37. Set the Type to **Predefined**.

38. Select the **Browse** button.

39. Select the **BRSTONE** pattern.

BRSTONE

40. Set the Angle to 0 for all hatches.

Click **OK** twice.

Display Comp...	Pattern	Scale/S...	Angle
Plan Hatch	BRSTONE	24.00000	0.00
Surface Hatch	BRSTONE	24.00000	0.00
Section Hatch	BRSTONE	24.00000	0.00

41.

Index	Name	Priority	Width	Edge Offset
1	CMU	1	-3"	0"
2	Insulation	1	1 1/2"	0"
3	Air Space	1	1"+BW	1"
4	Brick	1	3 1/2"	8 1/2"

Activate the Components tab. Highlight each component and use the << >> arrows to position the component. By shifting each component position, you can see where it is located. Locate the Brick so it is on the Exterior side and the CMU so it is interior.

☑ Auto Calculate Edge Offset

You can also use the Auto Calculate Edge Offset option to ensure all the components are correct.

42. Close the Style Manager.

Click **OK** to exit the Edit dialog.
You can preview how the changes you made to the material display will appear when you create your wall.

43. Save as *ex1-5.dwg*.

Exercise 1-6:
Tool Palettes

Drawing Name: tool_palettes.dwg
Estimated Time: 15 minutes

This exercise reinforces the following skills:

- ❑ Use of AEC Design Content
- ❑ Use of Wall Styles

1.   Open or continue working in *ex1-5.dwg*.

2.   Activate the Home tab on the ribbon.

       Select **Tools→Design Tools** to launch the tool palette.

3.   Right click on the tabs and you will see a list of the tabs available in the Design Tools.

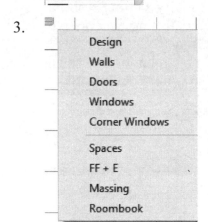

4.   Select the **Walls** palette.

5. On the Walls tool palette:

Select the **Properties** button.

6. Select **View Options**.

7. Adjust the Image Size and select the desired View style.

You can apply the preference to the Current Palette (the walls palette only) or all palettes.

Click **OK**.

8. Verify that the tool palette is open with the Walls palette active.

9. Activate the **Manage** tab on the ribbon.

Select the **Style Manager** tool.

10. Locate the **Brick-Block** wall style you created in the Style Manager.

11.   Drag and drop the wall style onto your Walls palette.

Click **OK** to close the Style Manager.

12.   Highlight the **Brick_Block** tool.
Right click and select **Rename**.

13.   Change the name to **8″ CMU- 3.5″ Brick [200 mm CMU – 90 mm]**.

14. Select the new tool and draw a wall.
You may draw a wall simply by picking two points.
If you enable the ORTHO button on the bottom of the screen, your wall will be straight.

15.   Select the wall you drew.

Right click and select **Properties**.

Note that the wall is placed on the A-Wall Layer and uses the Brick-Block Style you defined.

16. Save your file as ***Styles.dwg***.

The wall style you created will not be available in any new drawings unless you copy it over to the default template.

 To make it easy to locate your exercise files, browse to where the files are located when you save the file. Right click on the left pane and select Add Current Folder.

Exercise 1-7:

Copying a Style to a Template

Drawing Name: Styles1.dwg, Imperial (Metric).ctb.dwt
Estimated Time: 20 minutes

This exercise reinforces the following skills:

- Style Manager
- Use of Templates
- Properties dialog

1. Close any open drawings.

   Go to the Application menu and select
   Close → All Drawings.

   You can also type CLOSEALL.

2. Start a New Drawing using plus tab.

3. 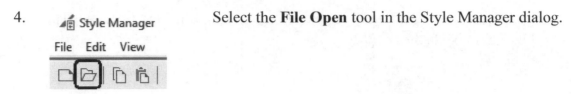 Activate the **Manage** tab on the ribbon.

Select the **Style Manager** tool.

4. Select the **File Open** tool in the Style Manager dialog.

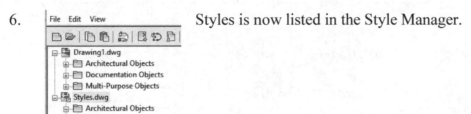

5. Locate the *styles.dwg* you created.
Select **Open**.

Note: Make sure the Files of type is set to dwg or you will not see your files.

6. Styles is now listed in the Style Manager.

7. Select the **File Open** tool.

8. Set the Files of type to ***Drawing Template (*.dwt)***.

You should automatically be directed to the Template folder.

If not, browse to the Template folder.

9. Locate the *AEC Model Imperial (Metric) Ctb.dwt* file.
Click **Open**.

This is the default template we selected for QNEW.

10. You should see files open in the Style Manager.

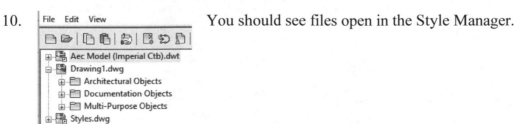

11. Locate the **Brick_Block** Wall Style in the *Styles.dwg*.

12. Right click and select **Copy**.

13. Locate Wall Styles under the template drawing.

Highlight, right click and select **Paste**.

14. You could also just drag and drop the Brick_block style from the Styles file to the template.

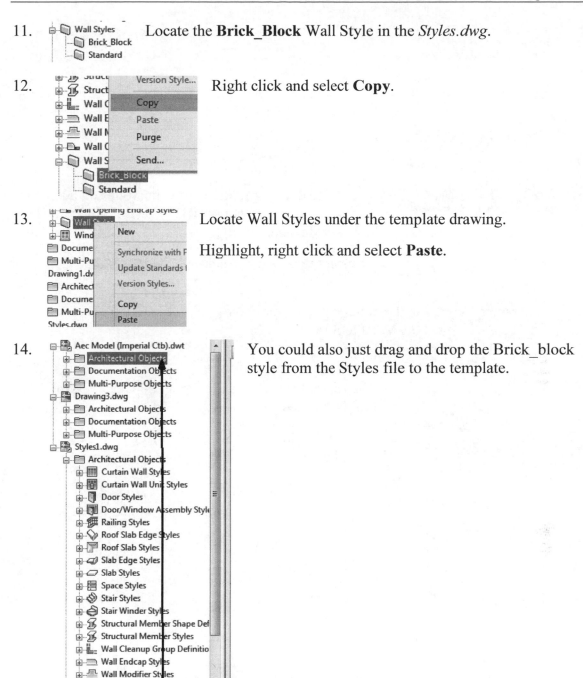

15. Click **Apply**.

16.

> The following drawing has changed.
> C:\ProgramData\Autodesk\ACA
> 2020\enu\Template\Aec Model (Imperial
> Ctb).dwt
>
> Do you wish to save changes to this file?
>
> [Yes] [No]

Click **Yes**.

17. Close the Style Manager.

18.

> Drawing1*   ×

Look at the drawing folder tabs. The Styles.dwg and the template drawing are not shown. These are only open in the Style Manager.

19.

> Start   +

Select the **plus** tab to start a new drawing.

20.

> Home Insert
> Wall ▾
> Door ▾
> Window ▾

Activate the Home tab on the ribbon.
Select the **Wall** tool.

21.

> Search...
> Style   Standard
> Bound spaces   Brick_Block
> Cleanup automati... Standard
> Cleanup group d... Standard

The Properties dialog should pop up when the WallAdd tool is selected.

In the Style drop-down list, note that Brick_Block is available.

If you don't see the wall style in the drop-down list, verify that you set the default template correctly in Options.

22. Click Escape to end the WallAdd command.

23. Close all drawing files without saving.

A fast way to close all open files is to type CLOSEALL on the command line. You will be prompted to save any unsaved files.

Layer Manager

Back in the days of vellum and pencil, drafters would use separate sheets to organize their drawings, so one sheet might have the floor plan, one sheet the site plan, etc. The layers of paper would be placed on top of each other and the transparent quality of the vellum would allow the drafter to see the details on the lower sheets. Different colored pencils would be used to make it easier for the drafter to locate and identify elements of a drawing, such as dimensions, electrical outlets, water lines, etc.

When drafting moved to Computer Aided Design, the concept of sheets was transferred to the use of Layers. Drafters could assign a Layer Name, color, linetype, etc. and then place different elements on the appropriate layer.

AutoCAD Architecture has a Layer Management system to allow the user to implement AIA standards easily.

Layer Manager

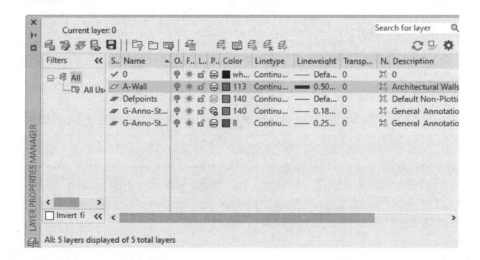

The Layer Manager helps you organize, sort, and group layers, as well as save and coordinate layering schemes. You can also use layering standards with the Layer Manager to better organize the layers in your drawings.

When you open the Layer Manager, all the layers in the current drawing are displayed in the right panel. You can work with individual layers to:

- Change layer properties by selecting the property icons

- Make a layer the current layer

- Create, rename, and delete layers

If you are working with drawings that contain large numbers of layers, you can improve the speed at which the Layer Manager loads layers when you open it by selecting the Layer Manager/Optimize for Speed option in your AEC Editor options.

The Layer Manager has a tool bar as shown.

	Layer Standards You can import Layer Standards from an existing drawing or Export Layer Standards using the current drawing.
	Layer Key Styles – Brings up the Style Manager. A layer key is a map between the AEC object that you draw on screen and a defined layer. When you create an object, the layer key that is associated with the object automatically places that object on the layer to which the layer key is mapped. Using layer keys to automatically place objects on predefined layers is called *layer keying*.

The layer key styles in Autodesk AutoCAD Architecture, Release 3 and above replace the use of LY files. If you have LY files from S8 or Release 1 of AutoCAD Architecture that you want to use, then you can create a new layer key style from an LY file. On the command line enter **-AecLYImport** to import legacy LY files.

	Layer Key Overrides You can apply overrides to any layer keys within a layer key style that is based on a layer standard. The structure of the layer name of each layer that each layer

	key maps an object to is determined by the descriptive fields in the layer standard definition. You can override the information in each field according to the values set in the layer standard definition. You can allow overrides on all the layer keys within a layer key style, or you can select individual layer keys that you want to override. You can also choose to allow all of the descriptive fields that make up the layer name to be overridden, or you can specify which descriptive fields you want to override.
	Load Filter Groups This tool allows you to load a saved filter group.
	Save Filter Groups This tool allows you to save a defined filter group, so that you can use it in other drawings.
	New Property Filter
	New Group Filter
	New Standards Filter
	New Layer Creates a new layer.
	New Layer from Standard Creates a new layer based on an existing layer standard. 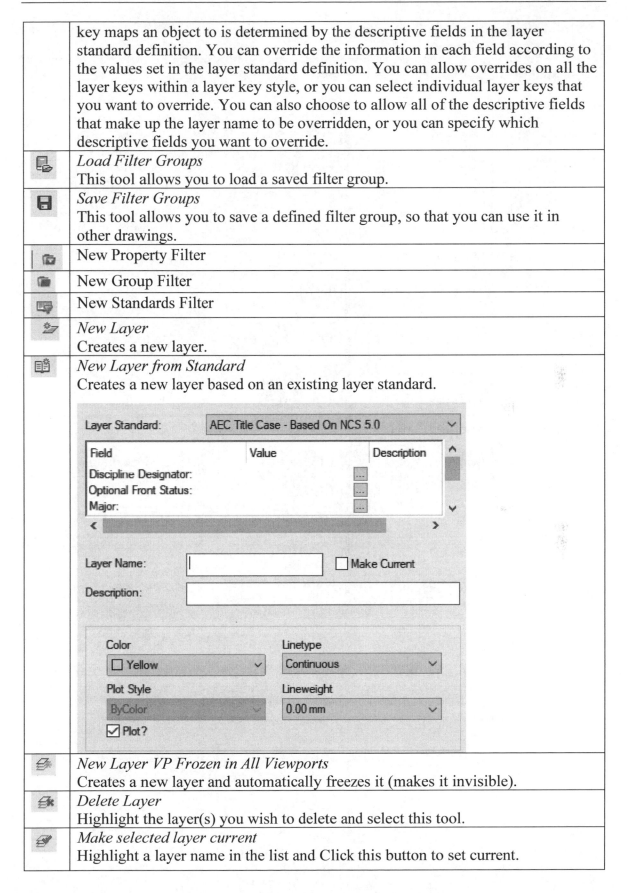
	New Layer VP Frozen in All Viewports Creates a new layer and automatically freezes it (makes it invisible).
	Delete Layer Highlight the layer(s) you wish to delete and select this tool.
	Make selected layer current Highlight a layer name in the list and Click this button to set current.

The following are the default layer keys used by Autodesk AutoCAD Architecture when you create AEC objects.

Default layer keys for creating AEC objects			
Layer Key	**Description**	**Layer Key**	**Description**
ANNDTOBJ	Detail marks	COMMUN	Communication
ANNELKEY	Elevation Marks	CONTROL	Control systems
ANNELOBJ	Elevation objects	CWLAYOUT	Curtain walls
ANNMASK	Masking objects	CWUNIT	Curtain wall units
ANNMATCH	Match Lines	DIMLINE	Dimensions
ANNOBJ	Notes, leaders, etc.	DIMMAN	Dimensions (AutoCAD points)
ANNREV	Revisions	DOOR	Doors
ANNSXKEY	Section marks	DOORNO	Door tags
ANNSXOBJ	Section marks	DRAINAGE	Drainage
ANNSYMOBJ	Annotation marks	ELEC	Electric
APPL	Appliances	ELECNO	Electrical tags
AREA	Areas	ELEV	Elevations
AREAGRP	Area groups	ELEVAT	Elevators
AREAGRPNO	Area group tags	ELEVHIDE	Elevations (2D)
AREANO	Area tags	EQUIP	Equipment
CAMERA	Cameras	EQUIPNO	Equipment tags
CASE	Casework	FINCEIL	Ceiling tags
CASENO	Casework tags	FINE	Details- Fine lines
CEILGRID	Ceiling grids	FINFLOOR	Finish tags

Layer Key	Description	Layer Key	Description
CEILOBJ	Ceiling objects	FIRE	Fire system equip.
CHASE	Chases	FURN	Furniture
COGO	Control Points	FURNNO	Furniture tags
COLUMN	Columns	GRIDBUB	Plan grid bubbles
GRIDLINE	Column grids	SITE	Site
HATCH	Detail-Hatch lines	SLAB	Slabs
HIDDEN	Hidden Lines	SPACEBDRY	Space boundaries
LAYGRID	Layout grids	SPACENO	Space tags
LIGHTCLG	Ceiling lighting	SPACEOBJ	Space objects
LIGHTW	Wall lighting	STAIR	Stairs
MASSELEM	Massing elements	STAIRH	Stair handrails
MASSGRPS	Massing groups	STRUCTBEAM	Structural beams
MASSSLCE	Massing slices	STRUCTBEAMIDEN	Structural beam tags
MED	Medium Lines	STRUCTBRACE	Structural braces
OPENING	Wall openings	STRUCTBRACEIDEN	Structural brace tags
PEOPLE	People	STRUCTCOLS	Structural columns
PFIXT	Plumbing fixtures	STRUCTCOLSIDEN	Structural column tags
PLANTS	Plants - outdoor	SWITCH	Electrical switches
PLANTSI	Plants - indoor	TITTEXT	Border and title block
POLYGON	AEC Polygons	TOILACC	Arch. specialties
POWER	Electrical power	TOILNO	Toilet tags
PRCL	Property Line	UTIL	Site utilities
PRK-SYM	Parking symbols	VEHICLES	Vehicles
ROOF	Rooflines	WALL	Walls
ROOFSLAB	Roof slabs	WALLFIRE	Fire wall patterning
ROOMNO	Room tags	WALLNO	Wall tags
SCHEDOBJ	Schedule tables	WIND	Windows

Layer Key	Description	Layer Key	Description
SEATNO	Seating tags	WINDASSEM	Window assemblies
SECT	Miscellaneous sections	WINDNO	Window tags
SECTHIDE	Sections (2D)		

Display Manager

Exercise 1-8:

Exploring the Display Manager

Drawing Name: display_manager.dwg
Estimated Time: 15 minutes

This exercise reinforces the following skills:

❑   Display Manager

1.   Open *display_manager.dwg*.

2.   Access the **Display Manager** from the Manage tab on the ribbon.

The display system in Autodesk® AutoCAD Architecture controls how AEC objects are displayed in a designated viewport. By specifying the AEC objects you want to display in a viewport and the direction from which you want to view them, you can produce different architectural display settings, such as floor plans, reflected plans, elevations, 3D models, or schematic displays.

3. 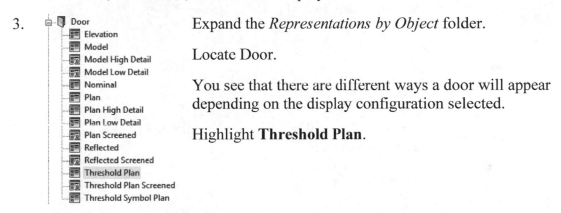 Expand the *Representations by Object* folder.

Locate Door.

You see that there are different ways a door will appear depending on the display configuration selected.

Highlight **Threshold Plan**.

4. You see that the Threshold visibilities are turned off.

5. Highlight the **Plan** configuration.

6.

Layer/Color/Linetype	Other	Version History

Display Component	Visible
Panel	
Frame	
Stop	
Swing	
Direction	
Panel Above Cut Plane	
Frame Above Cut Plane	
Stop Above Cut Plane	
Swing Above Cut Plane	
Panel Below Cut Plane	
Frame Below Cut Plane	
Stop Below Cut Plane	
Swing Below Cut Plane	

You see that some door components are turned on and others are turned off.

7.

Display Theme
Door
  Elevation
  Model
  Model High Detail
  Model Low Detail

Highlight the Model configuration.

8.

Layer/Color/Linetype	Muntins	Other	Version

Display Component	Visible
Panel	
Frame	
Stop	
Swing	
Glass	

You see that some door components are turned on and others are turned off.

9.

ex1-8.dwg
  Configurations
  Sets
    Model
    Model High Detail
    Model Low Detail
    Model Presentation
    Model Structural
    Plan
    Plan Diagnostic
    Plan High Detail

Go to the Sets folder. The Set highlighted in bold is the active Display Representation.

Highlight **Plan**.

10.

General	Display Representation Control	Display Options	Version History

Select the Display Representation Control tab.

Locate **Door** under Objects.
Note that some display representations are checked and others are unchecked.
A check indicates that the door is visible. Which door components are visible is
controlled under Representations by Object.

The three different folders – Configurations, Sets, and Representations by Object –
are different ways of looking at the same elements. Each folder organizes the
elements in a different way. If you change the display setting in one folder, it
updates in the other two folders.

11.   Expand the **Configurations** folder.

12. Expand **Medium Detail**.
You see the different display sets. Note that Medium Detail does
not hold all the different display sets. You can add or remove
display sets.
Close the Display Manager.

13. Close the drawing without saving.

Exercise 1-9:

Creating a Text Style

Drawing Name: new using QNEW
Estimated Time: 15 minutes

This exercise reinforces the following skills:

- ❑ CUI – Custom User Interface
- ❑ Tab on the ribbon
- ❑ Panel
- ❑ Tab

1. Start a new drawing using the QNEW tool.

2. Select the **Text Style** tool on the Home tab on the ribbon.

    It is located on the Annotation panel under the drop-down.

3. Click the **New** button in the Text Styles dialog box.

4. In the New Text Style dialog box, enter **TEXT1** for the name of the new text style and Click **OK**.

5.
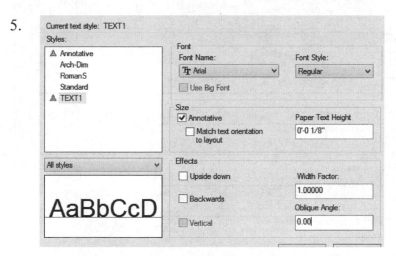

Fill in the remaining information in the Text Style dialog box as shown.

Set the Font Name to **Arial**.
Set the Font Style to **Regular**.
Set the Paper Text Height to **1/8"**.
Set the Width Factor to **1.00**.

6. Click the Apply button first and then the Close button to apply the changes to TEXT1 and then close the dialog box.

7. Save as *fonts.dwg*.

➢ You can use PURGE to eliminate any unused text styles from your drawing.
➢ You can import text styles from one drawing to another using the Design Center.
➢ You can store text styles in your template for easier access.
➢ You can use any Windows font to create AutoCAD Text.

Exercise 1-10:

Project Settings

Drawing Name: new using QNEW
Estimated Time: 5 minutes

This exercise reinforces the following skills:

❑ Project Navigator
❑ Project Path Options

In order for tags on windows, doors, etc. to work properly, you must assign your building model to a project.

1.
Start a new drawing by Clicking the + tab.

2. Right click in the command window and select **Options**.

3. 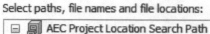 Select the **AEC Project Defaults** tab.

4. Set the AEC Project Location Search Path to the location where you are saving your files.

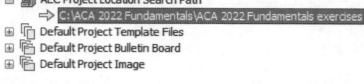

Select paths, file names and file locations:

- AEC Project Location Search Path
  - ⇒ C:\ACA 2022 Fundamentals\ACA 2022 Fundamentals exercises
- Default Project Template Files
- Default Project Bulletin Board
- Default Project Image

Close the dialog.

5. Launch the **Project Navigator** from the Quick Access toolbar.

6. Launch the **Project Browser** using the toolbar on the bottom of the Project Navigator palette.

7. Select the **New Project** tool.

8.

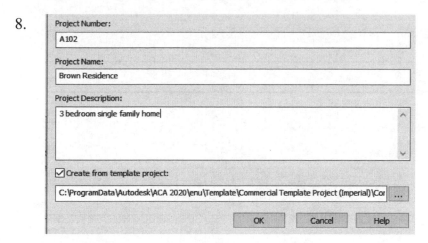

Type **A102** for the Project Number.

Type **Brown Residence** for the Project Name.

Enter a project description.

Click **OK**.

9.   Close the Project Browser.

10. Save as *ex1-10.dwg*.

Notes:

QUIZ 1

True or False

1. Doors, windows, and walls are inserted into the drawing as objects.

2. The Architectural Toolbars are loaded from the ACA Menu Group.

3. To set the template used by the QNEW tool, use Options.

4. If you start a New Drawing using the 'QNew' tool shown above, the Start-Up dialog will appear unless you assign a template.

5. Mass elements are used to create Mass Models.

6. The Layer Manager is used to organize, sort, and group layers.

7. Layer Standards are set using the Layer Manager.

8. You can assign materials to components in wall styles.

Multiple Choice
Select the best answer.

9. If you start a drawing using one of the standard templates, AutoCAD Architecture will automatically create _____ layouts.

    A. A work layout plus Model Space
    B. Four layouts, plus Model Space
    C. Ten layouts, plus Model Space
    D. Eleven layouts, plus Model Space

10. Options are set through:

    A. Options
    B. Desktop
    C. User Settings
    D. Template

11. The Display Manager controls:

    A. How AEC objects are displayed in the graphics window
    B. The number of viewports
    C. The number of layout tabs
    D. Layers

12. Mass Elements are created using the _____ Tool Palette.

    A. Massing
    B. Concept
    C. General Drafting
    D. Documentation

13. Wall Styles are created by:

    A. Highlighting a Wall on the Wall tab of the Tool Palette, right click and select Wall Styles
    B. Type **WallStyle** on the command line
    C. Go to **Format→Style Manager**
    D. All of the above

14. Visual Styles are used to:

    A. Determine which materials are used for rendering
    B. Controls which layers are visible
    C. Determines the display of edges, lighting, and shading in each viewport
    D. Determines the display of AEC elements in the Work layout tab.

15. You can change the way AEC objects are displayed by using:

    A. Edit Object Display
    B. Edit Display Properties
    C. Edit Entity Properties
    D. Edit AEC Properties

ANSWERS:

1) T; 2) T; 3) T; 4) F; 5) T; 6) T; 7) T; 8) T; 9) A; 10) A; 11) A; 12) A; 13) D; 14) C; 15) A

Lesson 2:
Site Plans

Most architectural projects start with a site plan. The site plan indicates the property lines, the house location, a North symbol, any streets surrounding the property, topographical features, location of sewer, gas, and/or electrical lines (assuming they are below ground – above ground connections are not shown), and topographical features.

When laying out the floor plan for the house, many architects take into consideration the path of sun (to optimize natural light), street access (to locate the driveway), and any noise factors. AutoCAD Architecture includes the ability to perform sun studies on your models.

AutoCAD Architecture allows the user to simulate the natural path of the sun based on the longitude and latitude coordinates of the site, so you can test how natural light will affect various house orientations.

A plot plan must include the following features:

- Length and bearing of each property line
- Location, outline, and size of buildings on the site
- Contour of the land
- Elevation of property corners and contour lines
- North symbol
- Trees, shrubs, streams, and other topological items
- Streets, sidewalks, driveways, and patios
- Location of utilities
- Easements and drainages (if any)
- Well, septic, sewage line, and underground cables
- Fences and retaining walls
- Lot number and/or address of the site
- Scale of the drawing

The plot plan is drawn using information provided by the county/city and/or a licensed surveyor.

When drafting with pencil and vellum, the drafter will draw to a scale, such as ⅛″ = 1′, but with AutoCAD Architecture, you draw full-size and then set up your layout to the proper scale. This ensures that all items you draw will fit together properly. This also is important if you collaborate with outside firms. For example, if you want to send your files to a firm that does HVAC, you want their equipment to fit properly in your design. If everyone drafts 1:1 or full-size, then you can ensure there are no interferences or conflicts.

Linetypes

Architectural drafting requires a variety of custom linetypes in order to display specific features. The standard linetypes provided with AutoCAD Architecture are insufficient from an architectural point of view. You may find custom linetypes on Autodesk's website, www.cadalog.com, or any number of websites on the Internet. However, the ability to create linetypes as needed is an excellent skill for an architectural drafter.

It's a good idea to store any custom linetypes in a separate file. The standard file for storing linetypes is acad.lin. If you store any custom linetypes in acad.lin file, you will lose them the next time you upgrade your software.

Exercise 2-1:

Creating Custom Line Types

Drawing Name: New
Estimated Time: 15 minutes

This exercise reinforces the following skills:

- ❑ Creation of linetypes
- ❑ Customization

A video of this lesson is available on my MossDesigns channel on Youtube at https://www.youtube.com/watch?v=gSCyFJm6pfY

> Start a new drawing using **QNEW**.

1. _____   _____   _____ _____

    Draw a property line.
    This property line was created as follows:
        Set ORTHO ON.
        Draw a horizontal line 100 units long.

    Use SNAP FROM to start the next line @30,0 distance from the previous line.
    You can also simply use object tracking to locate the next line.
    The short line is 60 units long.
    Use SNAP FROM to start the next line @30,0 distance from the previous line.
    The second short line is 60 units long.
    Use SNAP FROM to start the next line @30,0 distance from the previous line.
    Draw a second horizontal line 100 units long.

2. 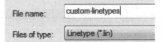 Activate the Express Tools tab on the ribbon.

Select the **Tools** drop-down.

Go to **Make Linetype**.

3.   Browse to the folder where you are storing your work.

File name: custom-linetypes
Files of type: Linetype (*.lin)

Create a file name called *custom-linetypes.lin* and click **Save**.

Place all your custom linetypes in a single drawing file and then use the AutoCAD Design Center to help you locate and load the desired linetype.

4.   When prompted for the linetype name, type property-line.
When prompted for the linetype description, type property-line.
Specify starting point for line definition; select the far left point of the line type.
Specify ending point for line definition; select the far right point of the line type.
When prompted to select the objects, start at the long line on the left and pick the line segments in order.

5.   Type **linetype** to launch the Linetype Manager.

6.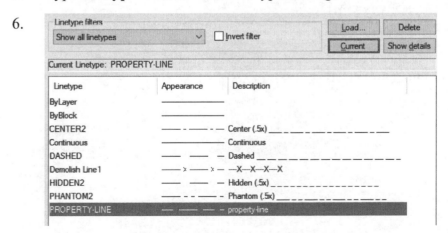

The linetype you created is listed.

Highlight the PROPERTY-LINE linetype and select CURRENT.

Click **OK**.

7.   Draw some lines to see if they look OK. Make sure you make them long enough to see the dashes. If you don't see the dashes, adjust the linetype scale using Properties. Set the scale to 0.0125 or smaller.

8. custom-linetypes   Locate the *custom-linetypes.lin* file you created.

   Open it using NotePad.

9. You see a description of the property-line.

```
custom linetypes - Notepad
File  Edit  Format  View  Help
*PROPERTY-LINE,property line
A,200,-60,120,-60,200,-60,120,-60,120|
```

10. Save as *ex2-1.dwg*.

Exercise 2-2:

Creating New Layers

Drawing Name: New
Estimated Time: 20 minutes

This exercise reinforces the following skills:

- ❑ Design Center
- ❑ Layer Manager
- ❑ Creating New Layers
- ❑ Loading Linetypes

1.   Start a new drawing using QNEW.

   Open ex2-1.dwg.

Start	ex2-1 ✕	Drawing2* ✕

   You should see three drawing tabs:
   Start, ex2-1, and the new drawing

   Activate the **View** ribbon and verify that the File Tabs is shaded.

2.   Launch the Design Center.
     The Design Center is on the Insert ribbon in
     the Content section. It is also located in the
     drop-down under the Content Browser. You
     can also launch using Ctl+2.

3.   Select the **Open Drawings** tab.

     Browse to the e*x2-1.dwg* file.

     Open the Linetypes folder.

     Scroll to the **Property-line** linetype
     definition.

4.   Highlight the PROPERTY-LINE
     linetype.

     Drag and drop into your active
     window or simply drag it onto the
     open drawing listed.

     *This copies the property-line
     linetype into the drawing.*

5.   Close the Design Center.

6.   Activate the **Layer Properties Manager** on the Home
     ribbon.

7. 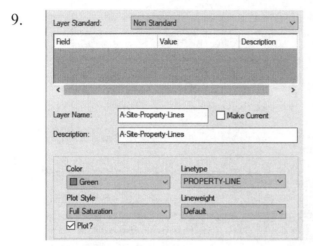 Note that several layers have already been created. The template automatically sets your Layer Standards to AIA.

8. Select the **New Layer from Standard** tool.

9. Under Layer Standard, select **Non Standard**.

Name the layer **A-Site-Property-Lines**.

Set the Color to **Green**.

Select the **Property-Line** linetype.

Set the Lineweight to **Default**.

Enable **Plot**.
Click **Apply**.

10. Create another layer.

Name the layer **A-Contour-Line**.

Set the color to **42**.

Select the linetype pane for the new linetype.

Click **Other**.

11. 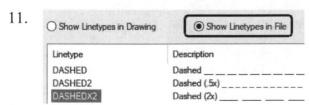 Enable **Show Linetypes in File**.

Highlight **DASHEDX2** and click **OK** to assign it to the selected layer name.

12.

Note that the linetype was assigned properly.

Set the Lineweight to **Default**.

Enable **Plot**.

Click **OK**.

13.

Set the A-Site-Property-Line layer current.

Highlight the layer name then select the green check mark to set current.

You can also double left click to set the layer current.

14. Right click on the header bar and select **Maximize all columns** to see all the properties for each layer.

15. Use the X in the upper corner to close the Layer Manager.

16. Save as *ex2-2.dwg*.

Exercise 2-3:
Creating a Site Plan

Drawing Name: site_plan.dwg
Estimated Time: 30 minutes

This exercise reinforces the following skills:

- ❑ Use of ribbons
- ❑ Documentation Tools
- ❑ Elevation Marks
- ❑ Surveyors' Angles

1.   Open or continue working in *site_plan.dwg*.

2.   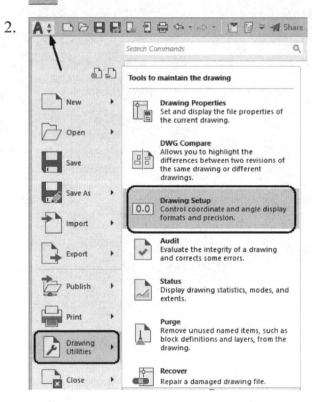 Go to **Drawing Utilities→Drawing Setup**.

   This is located on the Application Menu panel.

3.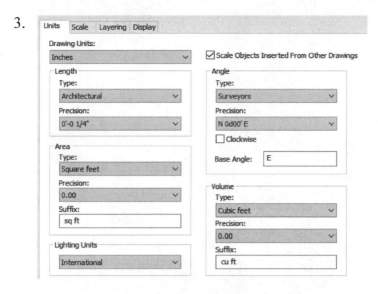

Select the **Units** tab.
Set the Drawing Units to **Inches**.
Set up the Length Type to **Architectural**.
Set the Precision to ¼″.
Set the Angle Type to **Surveyors**.
Set the Precision to **N 0d00′ E**.

4.

Select the **Scale** tab.

Set the Scale to **1/8" = 1'-0"**.

Set the Annotation Plot Size to ¼".

Click **OK**.

5.

When this dialog appears, select the first option. The drawing doesn't have any pre-existing elements, but this option ensures that everything is scaled correctly.

6.

1:1
✓ 1:100
1/64" = 1'-0"
1/32" = 1'-0"
1/16" = 1'-0"
3/32" = 1'-0"
1/8" = 1'-0"
3/16" = 1'-0"
1/4" = 1'-0"
3/8" = 1'-0"
1/2" = 1'-0"
3/4" = 1'-0"
1" = 1'-0"
1 1/2" = 1'-0"
3" = 1'-0"
6" = 1'-0"
1'-0" = 1'-0"
Custom...
Xref scales
Percentages

On the Status bar: verify the scale is set to **1/8" = 1'-0"**.

You can set your units as desired and then enable **Save As Default** ☐ Save As Default .
Then, all future drawings will use your unit settings.

---

7.   Draw the property line shown on the **A-Site-Property-Lines** layer.

Select the Line tool.

Line

8.

Specify first point: 1',5'
Specify next point: @186' 11" < s80de
Specify next point: @75'<n30de
Specify next point: @125'11"<n
Specify next point: @250'<180

This command sequence uses Surveyor's Units.

You can use the TAB key to advance to the surveyor unit box.

186'11"   🔒   S80DE

```
Specify first point: 12,60

Specify next point or [Undo]: @2243<s80de

Specify next point or [Undo]: @900<n30de

Specify next point or [Close/Undo]: @1511<n

Specify next point or [Close/Undo]: @3000<180

Specify next point or [Close/Undo]:
```

Metric data entry using centimeters:

If you double click the mouse wheel, the display will zoom to fit so you can see your figure.

START

Turn ORTHO off before creating the arc.

9.   Draw an arc using **Start, End, Direction** to close the figure.

10.   Select the bottom point as the Start point.
Right click and select the End option.
Select the top point at the End point.
Click inside the figure to set the direction of the arc.

11.   Set the **A-Contour-Line layer** current.

12.   PTYPE   Type **PTYPE** to access the Point Style dialog

13.   Select the Point Style indicated.

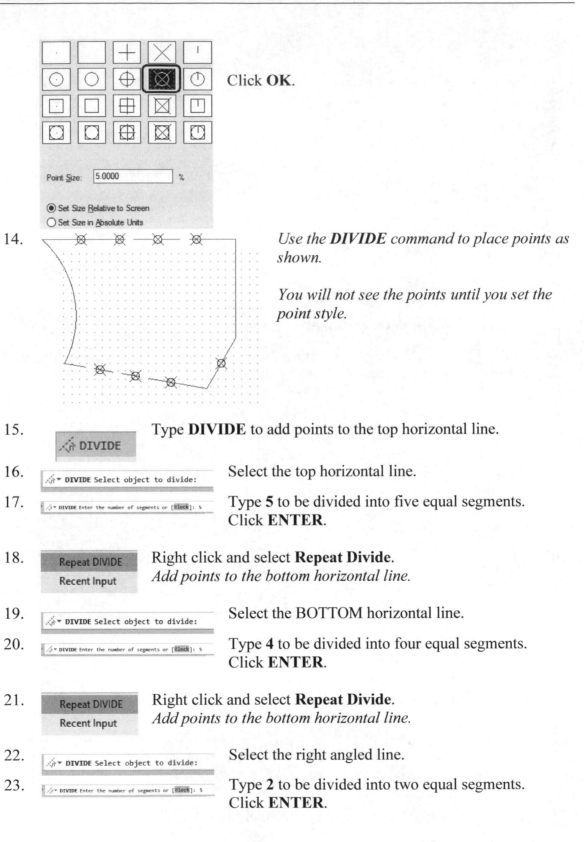

Click **OK**.

14. *Use the **DIVIDE** command to place points as shown.*

You will not see the points until you set the point style.

15. Type **DIVIDE** to add points to the top horizontal line.

16. Select the top horizontal line.

17. Type **5** to be divided into five equal segments. Click **ENTER**.

18. Right click and select **Repeat Divide**.
Add points to the bottom horizontal line.

19. Select the BOTTOM horizontal line.

20. Type **4** to be divided into four equal segments. Click **ENTER**.

21. Right click and select **Repeat Divide**.
Add points to the bottom horizontal line.

22. Select the right angled line.

23. Type **2** to be divided into two equal segments. Click **ENTER**.

24.

Enable the **Node** OSNAP.

25. Draw contour lines using **Pline** and **NODE** Osnaps as shown.

Be sure to place the contour lines on the contour line layer.

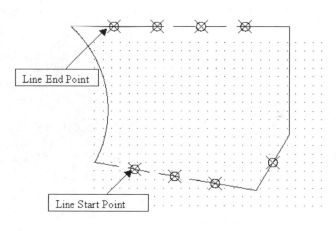

26. Type **qselect** on the *Command* line.

27. 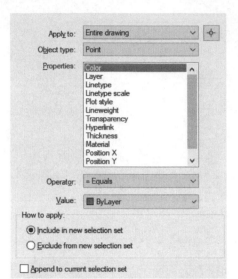 Set the Object Type to **Point**.
Set the Color = Equals **ByLayer**.

Click **OK**.

28. All the points are selected.
Right click and select **Basic Modify Tools→ Delete**.

29. Type UCSICON, OFF to turn off the UCS icon.

 When you start typing in the command line, you will see a list of commands.

Use the up and down arrow keys on your keyboard to select the desired command.

30. Activate the **Design Tools** palette located under the Tools drop-down on the Home ribbon.

31. Right click on the gray bar on the palette to activate the short-cut menu.

Left click on **All Palettes** to enable the other palettes.

32. Activate the Annotation tab on the palette.

 Locate the **Plan Elevation Label**, but it's not the type we need for a site plan.

Instead we'll have to add an elevation label from the Design Center to the Tool Palette.

33. Type **Ctl+2** to launch the Design Center.
Or:
Activate the **Insert** ribbon.
Select the **Design Center** tool under Content.
Or:
Type **DC**.

34. Select the **AEC Content** tab.

35. Browse to

Imperial/Documentation/Elevation Labels/ 2D Section.

[Metric/Documentation/Elevation Labels/2D Section].

36. Locate the Elevation Label (1) file.

Highlight the elevation label.

Drag and drop onto the Tool Palette.

Close the Design Center.

37. Select the Elevation Label on the Tool Palette.

Select the Endpoint shown.

38. Set the Elevation to **0″ [0.00]**.
Set the Prefix to **EL**.
Click **OK**.

39. Zoom in to see the elevation label.

 You can use the **Zoom Object** tool to zoom in quickly.

This is located on the View tab.

The Elevation Label is automatically placed on the G-Anno-Dims layer.

To verify this, just hover over the label and a small dialog will appear displaying information about the label.

40. EL ±0.00"   Place an elevation label on the upper left vertex as shown.

41.   Place labels as shown.

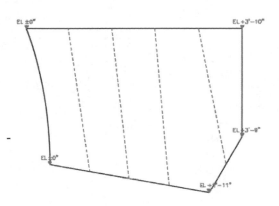

42. To change the size of the labels, select and set the Scale to **36.00** on the Properties dialog.

Scale	
X	36.00000
Y	36.00000
Z	36.00000

43.

Edit Object Display...
Elevation Label Modify...
Edit Multi-View Block Definition...

To modify the value of the elevation label, select the label.

Right click and select **Elevation Label Modify**.

44.

Geometry	
Start X	1'-0"
Start Y	5'-0"
Start Z	0"
End X	185'-0 15/16"
End Y	-27'-5 1/2"
End Z	2'-11"
Delta X	184'-0 15/16"
Delta Y	-32'-5 1/2"

To change the toposurface to a 3D surface, select each line and modify the Z values to match the elevations.

45. *A quick way to modify properties is to use Quick Properties.*

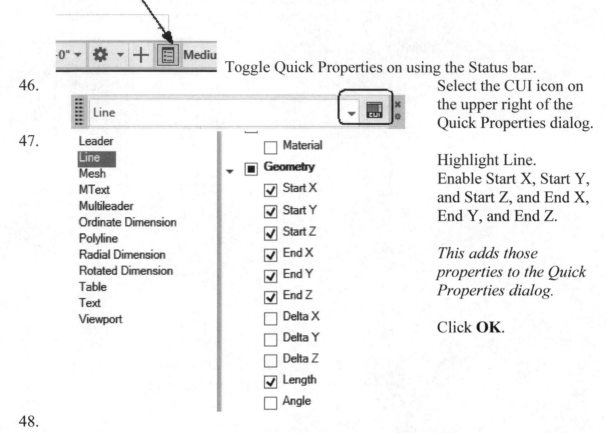

Toggle Quick Properties on using the Status bar.

46.   Select the CUI icon on the upper right of the Quick Properties dialog.

47.

Highlight Line.
Enable Start X, Start Y, and Start Z, and End X, End Y, and End Z.

This adds those properties to the Quick Properties dialog.

Click **OK**.

48.

Then select each line and change the start and end values of Z to match the elevation markers.

49. Use the ViewCube to inspect your toposurface and then return to a top view.

Adjust points as needed to create an enclosed area. Use ID to check the point values of each end point.

You can also type PLAN to return to a 2D view plan view.

50. Open the *fonts.dwg*. This is the file you created in a previous exercise.

51. Type **Ctl+2** to launch the Design Center.

52. Select the Open Drawings tab.

Browse to the Textstyles folder under the fonts.dwg.

53. Drag and drop the **Text1** text style into the ex2-3 drawing.

Close the Design Center.

54. Set **G-Anno-Dims** as the current Layer.

55. Set the Current Text Style to **TEXT1.**

56. Select the **Single Line** text tool from the Home ribbon.

57.

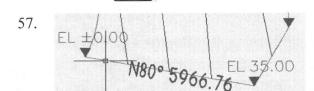

Right click and select **Justify**.
Set the Justification to **Center**.
Select the midpoint of the line as the insertion point.
Set the rotation angle to **–10** degrees.
Use %%d to create the degree symbol.

58. To create the S60… note, use the **TEXT** command.

Use a rotation angle of 60 degrees.

When you are creating the text, it will preview horizontally. However, once you left click or hit ESCAPE to place it, it will automatically rotate to the correct position.

59. Create the **Due South 125′ 11″ [Due South 3840.48]** with a rotation angle of 90 degrees.

Add the text shown on the top horizontal property line.

N 90° 250′ E

60. Add the Chord note shown.
Rotation angle is 90 degrees.

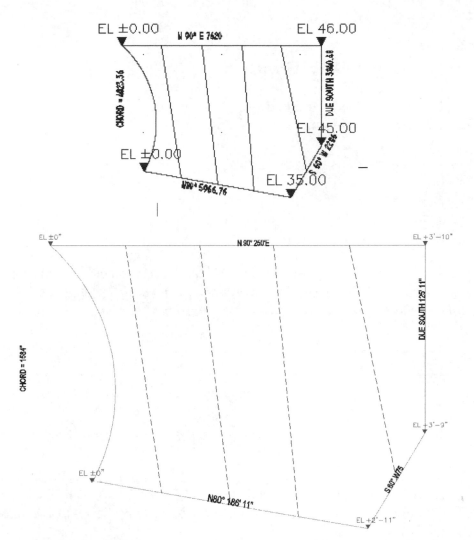

61. Adjust the scale to **1/32″ = 1′-0″** to see the property line labels.

62. Save the file as *ex2-3.dwg*.

Exercise 2-4:

Creating a Layer User Group

Drawing Name: layer_group.dwg
Estimated Time: 15 minutes

This exercise reinforces the following skills:

- ❑ Use of toolbars
- ❑ Layer Manager
- ❑ Layer User Group

A Layer User Group allows you to group your layers, so you can quickly freeze/thaw them, turn them ON/OFF, etc. *We can create a group of layers that are just used for the site plan and then freeze them when we don't need to see them.*

The difference between FREEZING a Layer and turning it OFF is that entities on FROZEN Layers are not included in REGENS. Speed up your processing time by FREEZING layers. You can draw on a layer that is turned OFF. You cannot draw on a layer that is FROZEN.

1. 📂   Open *layer_group.dwg*.

2. 📄   Select the **Layer Properties Manager** tool from the Home tab on the ribbon.

3.
Filters	≪	S..	Name
⊟ 🖫 All		✏	0

Highlight the word **All** in the Filters pane.

Right click and select the **New Group Filter**.

Visibility   >
Lock   >
Viewport   >
Isolate Group   >
Reset Xref Layer Properties   >

New Properties Filter...
New Standards Filter...
New Group Filter
Convert to Group Filter

4. 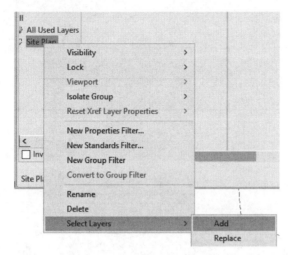 Name the group **Site Plan**.

5. Highlight the Site Plan group.
Right click and select **Select Layers →
Add**.

6. Type **ALL** on the command line.
This selects all the items in the drawing.
Click **ENTER** to finish the selection.
The layers are now listed in the Layer Manager under the Site Plan group.

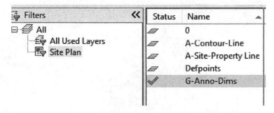

Close the Layer Manager.

7. We can use this group to quickly freeze, turn off, etc. the layers in the Site Plan group.

Save the drawing as *ex2-4.dwg* and close.

Notes:

QUIZ 2

True or False

1. You must load a custom linetype before you can assign it to a layer.
2. The DIVIDE command divides a line or arc segment into smaller elements.
3. The Design Tools palette is used to access blocks and commands.
4. If you design a wall tool on the tool palette for a specific style wall, then whenever you add a wall using that design tool it will place a wall using that wall style.
5. Layer groups control which layers are displayed in the layer drop-down list.

Multiple Choice
Select the best answer.

6. If points are not visible in a view:

   A. Turn on the layer the points are placed on
   B. Bring up the Point Style dialog and set the Size Relative to Screen
   C. Change the Point Style used
   D. All of the above

7. The command to bring up the point style dialog is:

   A. PSTYLE
   B. PMODE
   C. PP
   D. STYLE

8. An easy way to change the units used in a drawing is to:

   A. Change the units on the status bar.
   B. Type UNITS
   C. Use the Drawing Setup dialog.
   D. B or C

9. To turn off the display of the USCICON:

   A. Type USCICON, OFF
   B. Type UCS, OFF
   C. Type UCSICON, 0
   D. Type UCS, 0

Q2-2

ANSWERS:
    1) T; 2) F; 3) T; 4) T; 5) T; 6) D; 7) A; 8) D; 9) A

Lesson 3:
Floor Plans

AutoCAD Architecture comes with 3D content that you use to create your building model and to annotate your views. In ACA 2022, you may have difficulty locating and loading the various content, so this exercise is to help you set up ACA so you can move forward with your design.

The Content Browser lets you store, share, and exchange AutoCAD Architecture content, tools, and tool palettes. The Content Browser runs independently of the software, allowing you to exchange tools and tool palettes with other Autodesk applications.

The Content Browser is a library of tool catalogs containing tools, tool palettes, and tool packages. You can publish catalogs so that multiple users have access to standard tools for projects.

ACA comes with several tool catalogs. When you install ACA, you enable which catalogs you want installed with the software. By default, Imperial, Metric, and Global are enabled. The content is located in the path: C:\ProgramData\Autodesk\ACA 2022\enu\Tool Catalogs.

The floor plan is central to any architectural drawing. In the first exercise, we convert an AutoCAD 2D floor plan to 3D. In the remaining exercises, we work in 3D.

A floor plan is a scaled diagram of a room or building viewed from above. The floor plan may depict an entire building, one floor of a building, or a single room. It may also include measurements, furniture, appliances, or anything else necessary to the purpose of the plan.

Floor plans are useful to help design furniture layout, wiring systems, and much more. They're also a valuable tool for real estate agents and leasing companies in helping sell or rent out a space.

Exercise 3-1:

Going from a 2D to 3D Floor plan

Drawing Name: New
Estimated Time: 45 minutes

This exercise reinforces the following skills:

- ❑   Create Walls
- ❑   Wall Properties
- ❑   Wall Styles
- ❑   Style Manager
- ❑   Insert an AutoCAD drawing
- ❑   Trim, Fillet, Extend Walls

1.   Start a new drawing using QNEW or select the + tab.

2.   Type **UNITS**.

        Set the Units to **Inches**.

        Set the Type to **Architectural.**

        Set the Precision to ¼".

        Click **OK**.

3.   You have changed the units for this drawing, which will be used on all new items. What do you want to do?

        → Rescale modelspace and paperspace objects
            Make all match the new units

        → Rescale only modelspace objects
            Make them match the new units

        → Don't rescale any existing objects

        Select the first option: **Rescale modelspace and paperspace objects.**

4. Activate the **Insert** tab on the ribbon.

Select **Attach**.

5. Locate the *autocad_floor_plan.dwg* file in the exercises. *Set your Files of type to Drawing (*.dwg) to locate the file.* Click **Open**.

File name: autocad_floor_plan

Files of type: Drawing (*.dwg)

6. Uncheck Insertion Point.
Uncheck Scale.
Uncheck Rotation.
This sets everything to the default values.

Click **OK**.

7. Use the ViewCube to switch to a 3D view.

Note that the AutoCAD file is 2D only.

Return to a top view.

8. Select the attached xref.
Right click and select
Bind→Insert.
This converts the xref to an inserted block.

9. Select the block reference and type **EXPLODE** to convert to lines.

You can also use the Explode tool on the Modify panel of the Home tab on the ribbon.

10. Activate the **Home** tab on the ribbon.

Select the **Quick** measure tool from the Utilities panel.

11. Hover the cursor over a wall.

Note that the walls are 1′-11″ thick.

12. Launch the **Design Tools** palette from the Home tab on the ribbon.

13. Activate the **Walls** palette.

14. Right click on the **Stud-4 Rigid-1.5 Air-1 Brick-4** wall style and select **Import Stud-4 Rigid-1.5 Air-1 Brick-4 wall style.**

This makes the wall style available in the active drawing.

15. Right click on the **Stud-4 Rigid-1.5 Air-1 Brick-4** wall style and select **Wall Styles**.

This launches the Style Manager.

16. Architectural Objects
    Wall Styles
    Brick_Block
    Standard
    Stud-4 Rigid-1.5 Air-1 Brick-4

Note that the only wall styles available are Standard, the style you saved in the template, and the style you just imported.

Highlight the **Stud-4 Rigid-1.5 Air-1 Brick-4** wall style.

17.

Name	Priority	Width
Brick Veneer	810	4"
Air Gap	700	1"
Rigid Insulation	600	1 1/2"
Stud	500	4"
GWB	1200	3/4"

General | Components | Materials | En

Activate the **Components** tab.

The components tab lists the materials used in the wall construction.

Total Width: 10 1/2"

Note the components listed in the Style Manager for the wall style. The total wall thickness is 10-1/2".

The total width value is located in the upper right of the dialog. We need a wall style that is 1'–11". We need to add 1'- 1/2" of material to the wall style.

18.

Index	Name	Priority	Width	Edge Offset	Function	Dimension	
1	Brick Veneer	810	4"	2 1/2"	Non-Structural	☑	☐
2	Air Gap	700	1"	1 1/2"	--	☐	☐
3	Rigid Insulation	600	1 1/2"	0"	Non-Structural	☐	☐
4	Stud	500	4"	-4"	Structural	☑	☐
5	GWB	1200	5/8"	-4 5/8"	Non-Structural	☐	☐

Highlight the row that lists the GWB material.

GWB stands for Gypsum Wallboard.

19.

Name	Priority	Width	Edge Offset
Brick Veneer	810	4"	6 1/2"
CMU	810	1'-4"	2 1/2"
Air Gap	700	1"	1 1/2"
Rigid Insulation	600	1 1/2"	0"
Stud	500	4"	-4"
GWB	1200	3/4"	-4"

Change the width of the GWB to **3/4"**.

20. Select the **Add Component** tool.

21.

Index	Name	Priority	Width	Edge Offset
1	Brick Veneer	810	4"	2 1/2"
2	Air Gap	700	1"	1 1/2"
3	Rigid Insulation	600	1 1/2"	0"
4	Stud	500	4"	-4"
5	GWB	1200	3/4"	-3 1/2"
6	GWB	1200	3/4"	-4"

Another 3/4" piece of GWB (gypsum board) is added.

22.

Total Width: 11 1/4"

Note that the thickness of the wall updated to **11 ¼"**.

23.

Index	Name	Priority	Width	Edge Offset	F
1	Brick Veneer	810	4"	2 1/2"	N
2	Air Gap	700	1"	1 1/2"	–
3	Rigid Insulation	600	1 1/2"	0"	N
4	Stud	500	4"	-4"	S
5	GWB	1200	5/8"	-4 5/8"	N
6	GWB	1200	5/8"	-4 5/8"	N

Highlight the Brick Veneer material in the top row.

24. 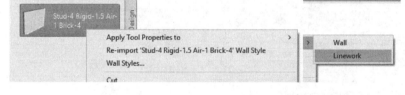 Select the **Add Component** tool.

25.

Name	Priority	Width	Edge Offset
Brick Veneer	810	4"	6 1/2"
CMU	810	1'-4"	2 1/2"
Air Gap	700	1"	1 1/2"
Rigid Insulation	600	1 1/2"	0"
Stud	500	4"	-4"
GWB	1200	3/4"	-4"
GWB	1200	3/4"	-4 3/4"

Change the name of the second row material to **CMU**. Set the width to 1' 4" thick.

To change the values, just place the cursor in that cell and start typing.

26. Verify that your layers are set as shown.
Verify that the total width is 1' 11".

27. Click **OK** to close the Styles Manager dialog.

28.

Stud-4 Rigid-1.5 Air-1 Brick-4	
Apply Tool Properties to	>
Re-import 'Stud-4 Rigid-1.5 Air-1 Brick-4' Wall Style	
Wall Styles...	
Cut	

Wall
Linework

Right click on the **Stud-4 Rigid-1.5 Air-1 Brick-4** wall style and select **Apply Tool Properties to → Linework**.

29.

Select the outside segments of the walls.

Do not select any of the interior walls.

Click ENTER when you are done selecting lines.

30. You will be prompted if you want to erase any of the linework. Enter **NO**.

31.

Zoom into one of the walls that was placed.

Note that it is the correct width. The blue arrow indicates the exterior side of the wall. If the blue arrow is inside the building, click on the blue arrow and it will flip the orientation of the wall.

If necessary, move walls so they are aligned with the floor plan's walls.

32.

Switch to a 3D view.

You should see 3D walls where you selected lines.

33.

To join the walls together, use FILLET with an R value of 0.
Type FILLET, then select the two walls to be joined to form a corner.

34.

In the plan view, the exterior walls should form a closed figure.

Locate the **Stud-4 GWB-0.625-2 Layers Each Side** Wall Style.

Right click and select Wall Styles. *This will launch the Styles Manager.*

35. Highlight the **Stud-4 GWB-0.625-2 Layers Each Side** Wall Style in the Style Manager list.

Select the **Components** tab.

The total width for this wall style is 5 ¼"

36.

Click **OK** to close the Style Manager.

Change the Stud width to **1′ 9 1/2″**.

Adjust the positions of the components so that the wall looks proper.

37. Select the **Stud-4 GWB-0.625-2 Layers Each Side** wall style.

Right click and select **Apply Tool Properties to → Linework**.

38.

Select the inside segments of the walls.

Do not select any of the exterior walls.

Click ENTER when you are done selecting lines.

39. You will be prompted if you want to erase any of the line work. Enter **NO**.

40.

Zoom into one of the walls that was placed. Note that it is the correct width.

The blue arrow indicates the exterior side of the wall. If the blue arrow is inside the building, click on the blue arrow and it will flip the orientation of the wall. Because these are interior walls with gypsum board on both sides, the orientation doesn't matter.

If necessary, move walls so they are aligned with the floor plan's walls.

41.

Use the TRIM, EXTEND, and FILLET tools to edit the interior walls.

42.

Some of your walls may display a warning symbol.

This means that you have walls overlapping each other.

Check to see if you have more than one wall or if you need to trim the walls.

43. Save as *ex3-1.dwg*.

The ex3-1 file can be downloaded from the publisher's website, so you can check your file against mine and see how you did.

Importing a PDF into ACA

Drawing Name: New
Estimated Time: 10 minutes

This exercise reinforces the following skills:

- ❑ Import PDF
- ❑ Create Walls
- ❑ Wall Properties
- ❑ Wall Styles
- ❑ Model and Work space

1.   Go to the Start tab

     Select **New→Aec
     Model(Imperial
     Ctb).dwt**.

     *This starts the new
     drawing using imperial
     units.*

2.

     Activate the **Insert** tab on the ribbon.

     Select the **Import PDF** tool (located in the middle of
     the tab on the ribbon).

3.   Select the *floorplan.pdf* file.

4.   You will see a preview of the pdf file.

Click **Open**.

5.   Uncheck specify insertion point on-screen.

This will insert the pdf to the 0,0 coordinate.

Set the Scale to **1200**.

This will scale the pdf.

Set the rotation to 0.

Enable Vector Geometry.
Enable Solid Fills.
Enable TrueType Text.
This will convert any text to AutoCAD text.
Enable Join line and arc segments.
Enable Convert solid fills to hatches.
Enable Apply lineweight properties.
Enable Use PDF layers.

Click **OK**.

6.

Notice if you hover your mouse over any of the elements imported, they have been converted to ACA elements.

7.

Highlight the **Stud-4 Rigid** wall style on the tool palette.
Right click and select **Apply Tool Properties to Linework.**

8.

Select the outside polyline on the floorplan.
Click ENTER to complete the selection.

When prompted to erase existing lines, select **No**.

9.

Highlight the **Stud 4- GWB** wall style.
Right click and select **Apply Tool Properties to Linework.**

Select the lines used for the interior walls.
Click ENTER to complete the selection.

When prompted to erase existing lines, select **No**.

10.

Use the FILLET, TRIM, and EXTEND tools to place the interior walls.

11. Save as *ex3-2.dwg*.

You can compare your drawing with mine and see how you did.

Exercise 3-3:
Creating Walls

Drawing Name: New
Estimated Time: 10 minutes

This exercise reinforces the following skills:

- ❑ Create Walls
- ❑ Wall Properties
- ❑ Wall Styles
- ❑ Model and Work space

1.   Go to the Start tab.

Select **New→Aec Model(Imperial Ctb).dwt**.

This starts the new drawing using imperial units.

2.   Select the **Wall** tool from the Home tab on the ribbon.

3.   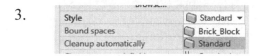 In the Properties dialog, check under the Style drop-down list.

These are the two styles currently available for use loaded in the template.

4. Exit out of the command by clicking ESC.

5.   Launch the Design Tools palette from the Home tab on the ribbon.

6. 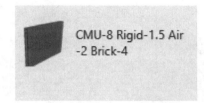 Select the Walls palette.

7.   Select the **CMU-8 Rigid-1.5 Air 2 Brick-4** wall style.

8.   Toggle **ORTHO** ON.

    Start the wall at 0,0.
    Create a rectangle 72 inches [1830 mm] tall and 36 inches [914 mm] wide.

    You can use Close to close the rectangle.

    Place the walls as if you are drawing lines.

9. Go to the **View** tab on the ribbon.

10. Toggle on the Layout tabs.

11. Select the **Work** tab now visible in the lower left corner of the screen.

12. The work tab opens up a layout with two viewports. One viewport is 3D and the other viewport is a top view.

    You see that the walls you placed are really 3-dimensional.

13.   Switch back to the Model space tab.

14.   Select the **Wall** tool from the Home tab on the ribbon.

15.   In the Properties dialog, check under the Style drop-down list.

Note that the CMU wall style is now available under the drop-down list.

16.   Exit out of the command by clicking ESC.

17.   Save your drawing as e*x3-3.dwg*.

> If you draw a wall and the materials composing the wall are on the wrong side, you can reverse the direction of the wall. Simply select the wall, right click and select the Reverse option from the menu.

> To add a wall style to a drawing, you can import it or simply create the wall using the Design Tools.

> Many architects use external drawing references to organize their projects. That way, teams of architects can concentrate just on their portions of a building. External references also use fewer system resources.

> You can convert lines, arcs, circles, or polylines to walls. If you have created a floor plan in AutoCAD and want to convert it to 3D, open the floor plan drawing inside of AutoCAD Architecture. Use the Convert to Walls tool to transform your floor plan into walls.

> To create a freestanding door, click the ENTER key when prompted to pick a wall. You can then use the grips on the door entity to move and place the door wherever you like.

> To move a door along a wall, use Door→Reposition→Along Wall. Use the OSNAP From option to locate a door a specific distance from an adjoining wall.

Exercise 3-4:

Creating a Floor Plan Using an Image

Drawing Name: new.dwg
Estimated Time: 60 minutes

This exercise reinforces the following skills:

❑ Insert Image
❑ Add Wall

1. Go to the Start tab.

    Select **New→Aec Model(Imperial Ctb).dwt**.

    This starts the new drawing using imperial units.

2. Select the **Insert** tab on the ribbon.

    Select the **Attach** tool.

3. Browse to the folder where the exercises are stored.

    Change the Files of type to **All image files**.

4. Select the *floorplan1* file.

    Click **Open**.

5.

Uncheck the insertion point to insert the image at **0, 0, 0**.

Set the Scale to **113.00**.
Set the Angle to **0.0**.

Click **OK**.

6.

To prevent your image from moving around:

Create a new layer called image.
Select the image.
Right click and select Properties.
Assign the image to the image layer.
Lock the image layer.

7.

Open the Design Tools palette.
Select the **Walls** palette.

8.

Turn ORTHO ON.

Locate the **Stud-4 Rigid 1.5 Air-1 Brick-4** wall style and select.

9.

Draw a wall on the far left side of the floor plan, tracing over the wall shown in the image file.

Orient the wall so the exterior side of the wall is on the outside of the building.

10.

Offset the wall 15′ 11-1/8″ to the right.

The additional offset takes into account the wall thickness of 11-1/8".

Flip the wall orientation so the wall exterior is on the outside of the building.

Check the offset distance to ensure the two walls are 15′ apart from inside finish face to inside finish face.

11. Trace a horizontal wall using the **Stud-4 Rigid 1.5 Air-1 Brick-4** wall style.

12.

Offset the horizontal wall 12′ 4.625″.
This is 11′ 5 1/2″ plus 11 1/8″.

Verify that the distance from finish face
to finish face is 11′ 5 ½″ using the Quick
Measure tool.

Select the **Quick Measure** tool from the
Home tab on the ribbon and hover over
one of the bedroom walls.

13. Locate the **Stud-4 GWB-0.625 Each Side** wall style on the
Walls palette.

14. Right click and select **Apply Tool Properties to → Wall**.

15. Select the upper horizontal wall.

Click **ENTER**.

16. The wall style will update.

17.

Place a **Stud-4 Rigid 1.5 Air-1 Brick-4** wall at the top horizontal location of the Master Bedroom.

Verify that the orientation is for the exterior side of the wall outside the building.

18.

Use the FILLET command to create corners between the vertical and horizontal walls.

Type FILLET and select the horizontal wall, then select a vertical wall. Repeat for the other side.

19.

Offset the top horizontal wall 16′ 10.625″.

20. Stud-4 GWB-0.625 Each Side

Locate the **Stud-4 GWB-0.625 Each Side** wall style on the palette.

21. Right click and select **Apply Tool Properties to → Wall**.

22. Select the lower horizontal wall.

Click **ENTER**.

23. Offset the left vertical exterior wall **12′ 4.625″**.

Change the offset wall to the interior **Stud-4 GWB-0.625 Each Side** wall style using the **Apply Tool Properties to → Wall**.

24. Use an offset of 2′ 0″ to create the closet space.

25.

Adjust the position of the walls as needed to ensure they match the floor plan image.

26. 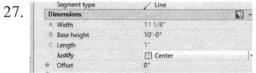 Select the **Stud-4 Rigid 1.5 Air-1 Brick-4** wall tool from the Design Tools palette.

27.

Segment type	Line
Dimensions	
A Width	11 1/8"
B Base height	10'-0"
C Length	1"
Justify	Center
Offset	0"

On the Properties palette, set the Justify option to **Center**.

28. Trace the remaining south walls of the floor plan.

29. Use the flip arrows to orient the exterior side of the walls to the outside of the building.

30. Offset the left garage wall 21′ 3″.

Verify that the dimension from face to face of the interior side of the walls is 19′ 11 ½″.

31. Offset the south garage wall 20′ 8″.

32.

Select the north garage wall.

In the Properties palette:
Change the wall style to **Stud-2.5 GWB-0.625 Each Side**.

33.

Adjust the position of the garage walls so the distance from interior face to interior face north-south is 20′ 8″ and the distance from interior face to interior face west-east is 19′ 11½″.

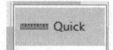 Quick

Use the Quick Measure tool to verify the dimensions.

34.

Offset the south utility room wall up 8′ ¼″.

Verify that the distance from interior face to interior face is 7′ 7″.

35.

Offset the north utility wall 23′ 9.1325″.

Assign the top wall to the **Stud-4 Rigid 1.5 Air-1 Brick-4** wall style.

Verify that the distance from interior face to interior face is 23′ 3½″.

36.

Use the FILLET command to create the northeast corner of the building.

The east wall is located in the Garage area, so you may need to scroll down to select it for the FILLET.

37.

Place the west family room wall.

Verify that the distance from interior face to interior face is 20′ 0″.

38.

Trace over the floor plan to place the **Stud-3.5 Rigid 1.5 Air-1 Brick-4 Wall** walls for the covered porch.

39.

Draw an exterior wall **Stud-3.5 Rigid 1.5 Air-1 Brick-4 Wall** at a 45° angle to designate the wall for the kitchen.

Use the POLAR option to make it easier to place the walls.

40.

Place interior wall segments in the kitchen area using the interior wall style **Stud-2.5 GWB-0.625 Each Side**.

A triangle symbol with an exclamation point indicates that you have a wall interference condition – usually a wall on top of a wall.

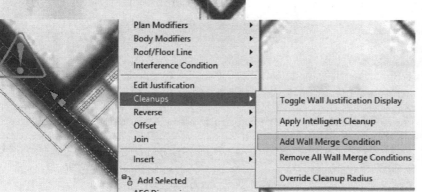

Select the interior wall with the interference condition. Right click and select **Cleanups → Add Wall Merge Condition**.

Select the two exterior walls where it is interfering.

The walls will merge and clean up the intersection area.

41. Zoom into the area near the utility room and notice some of the walls may need to be cleaned up as well.

42. Select one of the interior walls. Right click and select **Cleanups → Add Wall Merge Condition**.

43. Select both walls.

The wall intersection cleans up.

44. Repeat for the south utility wall.

45. Zoom into the Bedroom #2 area.

Use FILLET to eliminate the extra interior walls. Select the walls at the locations indicated to clean up the room.

46.

Offset the south bathroom wall 6' 4.25".

Verify that the distance from interior face to interior face is 5' 11".

47.

Add the interior walls for the lavatory areas.

Use the wall style **Stud-4 GWB-0.625 Each Side**.

48.

Unlock the image layer.

Select the image.

49. On the tab on the ribbon:
    On the Adjust panel.
    You can adjust how much of the image you see so it
    doesn't interfere with your work.

Alternatively, you can freeze the image layer or change
the transparency of the layer.

You can also toggle the Show Image tool
to turn the visibility of the image on or off.

To turn off the image border, type
IMAGEFRAME and set the value to **0**.

50.

You should have a completed floor plan.

Save as *ex3-4.dwg*.

Exercise 3-5:
Adding Doors

Drawing Name: add_doors.dwg
Estimated Time: 45 minutes

This exercise reinforces the following skills:

□ Adding Doors
□ Door Properties

1. Open *add_doors.dwg*.

2. Thaw the image layer so you can see where doors are located if you froze that layer or adjust the image so you can see the door locations.

3. Open the Design Tools palette.

    Select the **Doors** tab on the palette.

4. Highlight the **Bifold - Double** door.
    Right click and select **Properties**.

5.

Expand the **Dimensions** section.
Set the size to
4'-6" x 6'-8".

Set the Opening percent to **50**.

If you left click in the Standard sizes field, a down arrow will appear…select the down arrow and you will get a list of standard sizes. Then, select the size you want.

A 25% opening will show a door swing at a 45-degree angle.
The value of the Opening percentage determines the angle of the arc swing.
A 50% value indicates the door will appear half-open at a 90-degree angle.

6.

Location	
⚹ Relative to grid	--
⚹ Position along wall	Offset/Center
⚹ Automatic offset	6"
⚹ Justification	--
Vertical alignment	--
Head height	--
Threshold height	--

Expand the **Location** section.

Set Position along wall to **Offset/Center**.
This will allow the user to snap to the center position along the wall.

Click **OK** to close the Properties dialog.

7. Place the Bifold - Double doors at the two closets.

The orientation of the door swing is determined by the wall side selected.

In both cases, you want to select the outside face of the wall.
Center the closet door on each wall.

8. Place the **Bifold - Double** door at each of the closets located in Bedroom #2 and Bedroom #3.

9. Place the **Bifold - Double** door at the closets in the Master Bedroom.

10. Bifold - Single   Locate the **Bifold - Single** door on the Doors tab of the Design Tools palette.

Highlight and right click to select **Properties.**

11. 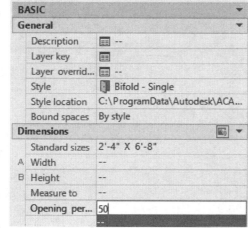 In the Properties palette:

Set the door to use the Standard Size **2′ 4″ x 6′ 8″**.
Set the Opening percent to **50**.
Click **OK** to close the Properties palette.
Place the door in the Linen Closet near the lavatories.

12. Hinged - Single - Exterior   Locate the **Hinged - Single - Exterior** door on the Doors tab of the Design Tools palette.

13. Highlight and right click to select **Properties.**

In the Properties palette,
set the door to use the size
3′ 0″ x 6′ 8″.

Set the Swing angle to **30**.

14. Select the side of the wall that will be used for the door swing and place the entry door.

15. Locate the **Hinged - Single** door on the Doors tab of the Design Tools palette.

16. 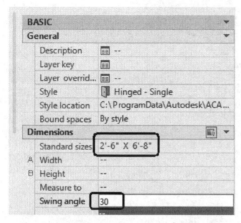 Highlight and right click to select **Properties.**

In the Properties palette,
set the door to use the size
2′ 6″ x 6′ 8″.

Set the Swing angle to **30**.

17. Set the Position along wall to **Offset/Center**.

18. Place the door in Bedroom #2.

19. Place the door in Bedroom #3.

The swing is on the correct side but not the correct direction.

20.

Select the door so it highlights.

The horizontal arrow flips the orientation of the door to the other side of the wall.

The vertical arrow flips the orientation of the door swing.

Left click on the vertical arrow.

The door updates to match the floor plan image.

21.

Place a **Hinged - Single** door in Bath #2.

22.

Place a **Hinged - Single** door in the Utility Room.

23.

Style	Hinged - Single
Style location	C:\ProgramData\Auto...
Bound spaces	By style
Dimensions	
Standard sizes	3'-0" X 6'-8"
A Width	--
B Height	--
Measure to	--
Swing angle	80

Change the size to **3'-0" x 6'-8"**.

Set the swing angle to **80**.

24. Hinged - Single - Exterior

Locate the **Hinged - Single - Exterior** door on the Doors tab of the Design Tools palette.

25.

Highlight and right click to select **Properties.**

In the Properties palette,
set the door to use the Standard Size
2′ 6″ x 6′ 8″.

Set the Swing angle to **30**.

26.

Place the door between the
Utility Room and the Garage.

27.

Place the door on the east wall of
the Utility Room.

28.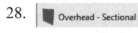

Locate the **Overhead - Sectional** door on the Doors tab of the
Design Tools palette.

29.

Highlight and right click to select **Properties.**

In the Properties palette,
set the door to use the Size
16′ 0″ x 6′ 8″.

To set the size, select the Custom Size option
in the drop-down list.
Type in the desired width and height. The size
will adjust.

Set the Opening percent to **0**.

30. Place the garage door.

31. 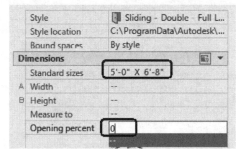 Locate the **Sliding - Double - Full Lite** door on the Doors tab of the Design Tools palette.

32.

Style	Sliding - Double - Full L...
Style location	C:\ProgramData\Autodesk\...
Bound spaces	By style
Dimensions	
Standard sizes	5'-0" X 6'-8"
A Width	--
B Height	--
Measure to	--
Opening percent	0

Highlight and right click to select **Properties.**

In the Properties palette,
set the door to use the Standard Size
5′ 0″ x 6′ 8″.

Set the Opening percent to **0**.

33. Place the door in the family room.

34.

Place a second **Sliding - Double - Full Lite** door on the east wall of the Master Bedroom.

35.

Set the door to use the size **10′ 0″ x 6′ 8″**.
Set the Opening Percent to **0**.

36.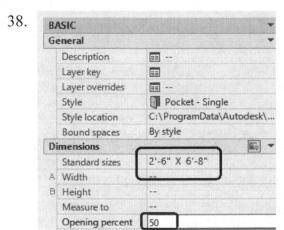

Center the door on the north wall of the Living Room.

37.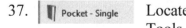

Locate the **Pocket - Single** door on the Doors tab of the Design Tools palette.

38.

BASIC		▾
General		▾
Description	📇 --	
Layer key	📇	
Layer overrides	📇 --	
Style	🚪 Pocket - Single	
Style location	C:\ProgramData\Autodesk\...	
Bound spaces	By style	
Dimensions		📇 ▾
Standard sizes	2'-6" X 6'-8"	▾
A Width	--	
B Height	--	
Measure to	--	
Opening percent	50	

Highlight and right click to select **Properties.**

In the Properties palette set the door to use the size: **2′ 6″ x 6′ 8″**.

Set the Opening percent to **50**.

39. Place the door in the lower right corner of the Master Bedroom.

40. In the Properties palette,
set the door to use the Standard Size **2′ 4″ x 6′ 8″**.

Set the Opening percent to **50**.

41. Center the pocket door on the lower horizontal wall between the Master Bedroom closets.

42. Image layer is frozen.

This is the floor plan so far.

43. Save as *ex3-5.dwg*.

Switch to an isometric view and you will see that your model is 3D.

Look at the model using different visual styles. Which style do you like best? The model shown uses a Hidden visual style with a white background.

This is a Realistic style.

Exercise 3-6:
Create an Arched Opening Tool

Drawing Name: arched_opening.dwg
Estimated Time: 10 minutes

This exercise reinforces the following skills:

- Copying Tools
- Tool Properties

1.   Open *arched_opening.dwg.*

2.   Locate the **Cased Opening** tool on the Doors palette.

3.   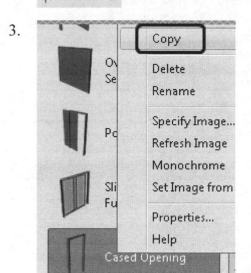   Right click and select **Copy**.

4.   Select the **Doors** tab.
Right click and select **Paste**.

5.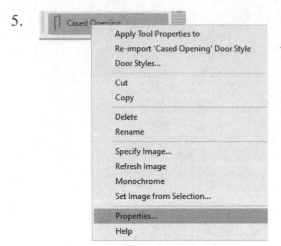

The copied tool is located at the bottom of the palette.

Highlight the copied tool.
Right click and select **Properties**.

6.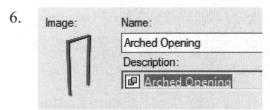

Change the Name to **Arched Opening**.
Change the Description to **Arched Opening**.
Click **OK**.

7.

Expand the General section.
Set the Description to **Creates an Arched Opening**.
Click **OK**.

8.

Set the Layer key to **OPENING**.
Set the Style to **Cased Opening-Half round**.

Click **OK**.

The tool is defined in the palette.

Move the tool up the palette to a new position.

9. Save as *ex3-6.dwg*.

Openings

Openings can be any size and elevation. They can be applied to a wall or be freestanding. The Add Opening Properties allow the user to either select a Pre-defined shape for the opening or use a custom shape.

Exercise 3-7:
Adding an Opening

Drawing Name: opening.dwg
Estimated Time: 15 minutes

This exercise reinforces the following skills:

 ❑ Adding Openings
 ❑ Opening Properties
 ❑ Copying Tools
 ❑ Set Image from Selection

An opening will be added to the upper wall between the Master Bedroom closets.

1. Open *opening.dwg*.

2.   Select the **Arched Opening** tool.

3.

Style	Cased Opening - Halfround
Bound spaces	By style (Yes)
Dimensions	
Standard sizes	2'-6" X 6'-8"
A Width	2'-6"
B Height	6'-8"
Measure to	Inside of frame
Opening percent	50

In the Properties palette, set the door to use the size **2' 6" x 6' 8"**.

4.

Location	
❋ Relative to grid	No
❋ Position along wall	Offset/Center
❋ Automatic offset	6"
❋ Justification	Center
❋ Multiple insert	No
Vertical alignment	Threshold

Expand the Location section in the Properties palette.
Set the Position along wall to **Offset/Center**.
Set the Automatic offset to **6" [300.00]**.

5. Place the arched opening in the wall between the closets in the Master Bedroom. Center it on the wall.

6.

Dimensions	
Standard sizes	3'-0" X 6'-8"
A Width	3'-0"
B Height	6'-8"
Measure to	Inside of frame
Opening percent	50

In the Properties palette, set the door to use the size **3′ 0″ x 6′ 8″**.

7. Place the Arched Opening on the left side of the Foyer above the Entry.

8. Use the View tools on the View tab on the ribbon **View → NE Isometric** and **3D orbit** to view the arched opening.

9. On the View tab on the ribbon,

Switch to a **Shades of Gray** display.

If your walls are reversed, you can change the orientation in the plan/top view.

10.   Set the **Materials/Textures On**.

11.   Set to **Full Shadows**.

Note how the display changes.

When materials, textures, and shadows are enabled, more memory resources are used.

12.   Locate the Arched Opening placed in the Master Bedroom.

Hold down the SHIFT button on the keyboard and hold down the scroll wheel on the mouse to rotate/orbit the 3D model.

13.   Select the **Arched Opening** icon on the tool palette. Right click and select **Set Image from Selection...** Pick the arched opening you created. Click **Enter**.

A dialog box allows you to choose which object to use for the image selection.

If you have Selection Cycling enabled, you will see a selection dialog box.

Select **Opening**.

Click **Enter**.

You can select more than one object for your image selection.

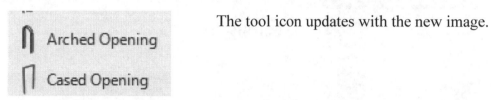 The tool icon updates with the new image.

14. Select the Work tab to view your model.

15.

16. Save the file as *ex3-7.dwg*.

Exercise 3-8:
Add Window Assemblies

Drawing Name: windows.dwg
Estimated Time: 30 minutes

This exercise reinforces the following skills:

- ❑ Add Windows

1. Open *windows.dwg.*

    Activate the Model tab.
    Switch to a Top View.

2. Set the View style to **2D Wireframe**.

    Remember you can change the view settings in the upper left corner of the display window.

3. Activate the **Design Tools** from the Home tab on the ribbon, if they are not launched.

4. 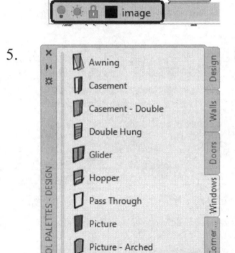 Thaw the image layer, so you can see the location of the windows.

5. Select the Windows tab of the Tool palette.

6. Select the **Picture** window.

7. Expand the Dimensions section.
Set the size to **6′-0″ x 5′-0″**.

Dimensions	
Standard sizes	6'-0" X 5'-0"
A Width	6'-0"
B Height	5'-0"
Measure to	Outside of frame
Opening percent	0

8.

Location		
✿	Relative to grid	No
✿	Position along wall	Offset/Center
✿	Automatic offset	6"
✿	Justification	Center
✿	Multiple insert	No
	Vertical alignment	Head
	Head height	6'-8"
	Sill height	1'-8"
	Rotation	0.00

Expand the Location section.
Set the Position to **Offset/Center**.
Set the Automatic Offset to **6″**.

9.

Select the midpoint of the north Master Bedroom wall.

10.

Dimensions		
	Standard sizes	9'-0" X 4'-0" (Custom Size)
A	Width	9'-0"
B	Height	4'-0"
	Measure to	Outside of frame
	Opening percent	0

On the Properties palette, expand the Dimensions section.

Change the Width to **9′-0″**.
Change the Height to **4′-0″**.

11.

Place the window at the midpoint of the south wall in the Dining Area.

12.

Dimensions		
	Standard sizes	12'-10" X 4'-0" (Custom Size)
A	Width	12'-10"
B	Height	4'-0"
	Measure to	Outside of frame
	Opening percent	0

On the Properties palette, expand the Dimensions section.

Change the Width to **12′-10″**.
Change the Height to **4′-0″**.

13.

Place the window at the midpoint of the north wall for the Family Room.

14.

Casement - Double

Select the **Casement - Double** window on the Windows palette.

15.

Dimensions	
Standard sizes	4'-0" X 4'-0"
A Width	4'-0"
B Height	4'-0"
Measure to	Outside of frame
Swing angle	0

On the Properties palette, expand the Dimensions section.

Set the Standard size to **4'-0" x 4'-0"**.

16.

Place the window in the west wall of Bedroom #2.

17.

Place the window in the west wall of Bedroom #3.

18. [Casement] Select the **Casement** window.

19.

Dimensions	
Standard sizes	2'-0" X 4'-0" (Custom Size)
A Width	2'-0"
B Height	4'-0"
Measure to	Outside of frame
Swing angle	0

On the Properties palette,
expand the Dimensions section.

Change the Width to **2'-0"** .
Change the Height to **4'-0"**.

20.

Place two windows on
the west wall of the
bathrooms.

21.

Place two windows on the east wall of the Family
Room.

22.

Dimensions	
Standard sizes	3'-0" X 4'-0" (Custom Size)
A Width	3'-0"
B Height	4'-0"
Measure to	Outside of frame
Swing angle	0

On the Properties palette,
expand the Dimensions section.

Change the Width to **3'-0"** .
Change the Height to **4'-0"**.

23.

Place the window in the
south wall of the
Garage.

24. Save as *ex3-8.dwg*.

Grids

Grids are used in floor plans to help architects and designers locate AEC elements, such as columns, walls, windows, and doors. The grid is one of the oldest architectural design tools – dating back to the Greeks. It is a useful tool for controlling the position of building elements. Grids may fill the entire design work area or just a small area.

In laying out wood framed buildings, a 16" or 24" grid is useful because that system relies on a stud spacing of 16" or 24".

In large projects, the layout design of different building sub-systems and services are usually assigned to different teams. By setting up an initial set of rules on how the grid is to be laid out, designers can proceed independently and use the grid to ensure that the elements will interact properly.

ACA comes with several grid tools.

The Enhanced Custom Grid allows you to place an entire grid using a dialog box to designate the bay spacing.

The Custom Grid Convert tool allows you to convert lines and arcs to grid lines. After the grid lines are placed, you have to manually edit the labels for each bubble.

The Column Grid tool allows you to place a rectangular grid with equal spacing between the grid lines.

Use the Enhanced Custom Grid tool if you want to use different spacing between grid lines or if you want to place radial grid lines.

Exercise 3-9:
Place a Grid

Drawing Name: grid.dwg
Estimated Time: 5 minutes

This exercise reinforces the following skills:

❑   Place a grid

1.   Open *grid.dwg.*

Activate the Model tab.
Switch to a Top View.

2.   Click on **Enhanced Custom Grid** on the Home tab.

3.   Click **5100**.

The first two grids are defined.

There is a preview window which shows the grids spaced 5100 mm apart.

4.   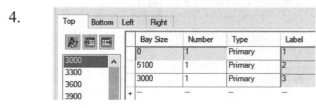   Click 3000.

A third grid is placed.

5.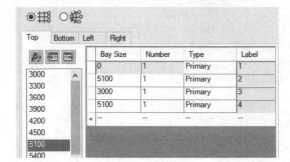

Click **5100**.

A fourth grid is placed.

6.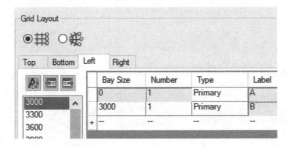

Switch to the Left tab.

Click **3000**.

The first two grids are defined.

There is a preview window which shows the grids spaced 3000 mm apart horizontally.

Click **3000.**

7.

A third grid is placed.

Notice that because the spacing is set the same, it is listed with the previous grid.

Click **OK** to close the dialog. Type **0,0** for the insertion point.

8. CUSTOMCOLUMNGRID Specify insertion point or [Rotate]: 0,0

9. CUSTOMCOLUMNGRID Specify rotation angle <0.0>: |

Click **ENTER** to accept the default rotation of 0 degrees.

10.

Click ENTER to exit the command.

Double click the wheel of the mouse to Zoom Extents.

The grid is placed.

Save as *ex3-9.dwg*.

Exercise 3-10:
Convert to Grid

Drawing Name: convert_grid.dwg
Estimated Time: 5 minutes

This exercise reinforces the following skills:

❑   Convert an arc to a grid

1.

[−][Top][2D Wireframe]

Open *convert_grid.dwg*.

Activate the Model tab.
Switch to a Top View.

We are going to convert the arc to a grid line.

The Enhanced Custom Grid tool also allows you to place and create radial grids.

2.

Click **Custom Grid Convert** on the Home tab.

3.

Click on the arc to select.

Click **ENTER** to complete the selection.

4.

Click **ENTER** to accept the default value for the label extensions.

5.

▼ **CUSTOMCOLUMNGRIDADD** Erase selected linework? [Yes No] <No>:

Click **Yes** to erase the existing linework.

6.

The grid is placed but notice that the labels have not been defined.

Click **ESC** to release the selection.

7. Select one of the grid bubbles.

8.

In the Properties palette, select **Attributes**.

9.

Change the Value to **D**.
Change the Display to **D**.

Click **OK**.

Click **ESC** to release the selection.

10.

Note that one label updated, but not the other.

Repeat to update the other bubble to also display **D**.

11.

Save as *ex3-10.dwg*.

Exercise 3-11:
Place a Curtain Wall

Drawing Name: curtain_wall.dwg
Estimated Time: 5 minutes

This exercise reinforces the following skills:

❑   Place a curtain wall

1.   Open *curtain_wall.dwg.*

Activate the Model tab.

[–][Top][2D Wireframe]   Switch to a Top View.

2.   Select the **Curtain Wall** tool on the Home tab.

3.   Set the Segment type to **Arc**.

Set the Base height to **12000**.

4.   Select the intersection of A1 as the start point.

5.   Select the Midpoint between Grids 2 and 3 as the midpoint.

6. Select the intersection of A4 as the end point.

Click **ENTER** to complete the wall.

7.

[−][SW Isometric][2D Wireframe]

Switch to a SW Isometric view to see the curtain wall.

Save as *ex3-11.dwg*.

QUIZ 3

True or False

1. When you insert a PDF into a drawing, it cannot be converted to AutoCAD elements, like lines or text.

2. When you insert an image, it cannot be converted to AutoCAD elements, like lines or text.

3. The direction you place walls – clockwise or counter-clockwise – determines which side of the wall is oriented as exterior.

4. Curtain walls can only be linear, not arcs, in AutoCAD Architecture.

5. Grids can only be lines, not arcs, in AutoCAD Architecture.

6. To re-orient a door, use the Rotate command.

7. You can set cut planes for individual objects (such as windows), an object style (such as walls) or as the system default.

Multiple Choice

8. To change the hatch display of wall components in a wall style:

    A.   Modify the wall style
    B.   Change the visual style
    C.   Change the display style
    D.   Switch to a plan\top view

9. This tool on the status bar:

    A.   Sets the elevation of the active level
    B.   Controls the default cut plane of the view and the display range
    C.   Sets the distance between levels
    D.   Sets the elevation of the active plane

10. To assign a material to a door:

    A.   Modify the door component by editing the door style
    B.   Drag and drop the material from the Material Browser onto a door
    C.   Use the Display Manager
    D.   Define a new Visual Style

ANSWERS:

1) F; 2) T; 3) T; 4) F; 5) F; 6) F; 7) T; 8) A; 9) B; 10) A

Lesson 4:
Space Planning

A residential structure is divided into three basic areas:

- ❏ Bedrooms: Used for sleeping and privacy
- ❏ Common Areas: Used for gathering and entertainment, such as family rooms and living rooms, and dining area
- ❏ Service Areas: Used to perform functions, such as the kitchen, laundry room, garage, and storage areas

When drawing your floor plan, you need to verify that enough space is provided to allow placement of items, such as beds, tables, entertainment equipment, cars, stoves, bathtubs, lavatories, etc.

AutoCAD Architecture comes with Design Content to allow designers to place furniture to test their space.

Exercise 4-1:
Creating AEC Content

Drawing Name: New
Estimated Time: 20 minutes

This lesson reinforces the following skills:

- ◻ Design Center
- ◻ AEC Content
- ◻ Customization

1.   Start a new drawing using the *Aec Model (Imperial.Ctb)* template.

2.

Activate the Insert tab on the ribbon.

Select **Attach**.

3.

Browse for *residence.dwg* and Click **Open**.

4.

Accept the defaults.

Uncheck **Specify On-screen** for the insertion point.

Click **OK**.

5.

Launch the XREF Manager by selecting the small arrow in the Reference drop-down.

6.   The palette lists the file references now loaded in the drawing.
Notice that the floorplan image file is listed as a reference.

7. Zoom Extents.

You can do this by typing Z,E on the command line or using the tool on the View tab on the ribbon or double clicking the mouse wheel.

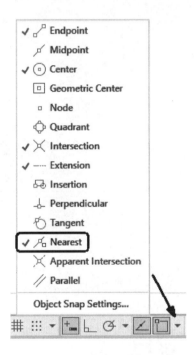

Enable the Nearest OSNAP to make it easier to place furniture.

8. Launch the Design Center from the Insert tab on the ribbon or Click Ctrl+2 or type **DC**.

9. Select the **AEC Content** tab.

10. Browse to *AutoCAD Architecture/Imperial/Design/ Furnishing/Furniture/Bed*.

11. 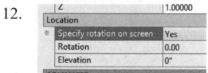 Select the *Double.dwg* file.
Right click and select **Insert**.

12. Set Specify rotation to **Yes** in the Properties dialog.

13. Place the bed in Bedroom #2.

Right click and select ENTER to exit the command.

14. Locate the *Twin.dwg*.

15.   Place the *Twin.dwg* in Bedroom#3.

Right click and select ENTER to exit the command.

16.   Browse to the *Bedroom* folder in the *Metric/Design/Domestic Furniture* folder.

17.   Locate the *3D 6 Drawer Chest*.

3D 6 Drawer
Chest

18.   — Place a *3D 6 Drawer Chest* in the Bedroom #2. Right click and select ENTER to exit the command.

19.

3D 3 Drawer
Chest

Add a 3D 3 Drawer Chest to Bedroom #3.

20. Browse to the *Desk* folder under *AutoCAD Architecture/Imperial/Design/Furnishing/Furniture/*.

21. Locate the *36x18 Left.dwg* file under the *Desk* folder.
Place into Bedroom #2.

36x18 Left

22. Locate the *6 Shelves.dwg* bookcase in the *Bookcase* folder.

23. Place in Bedroom #3.

6 Shelves

24.

Switch to a 3D view and use 3D Orbit to view the furniture placement.

25.   Save as *ex4-1.dwg*.

The Space Planning process is not just to ensure that the rooms can hold the necessary equipment but also requires the drafter to think about plumbing, wiring, and HVAC requirements based on where and how items are placed.

As an additional exercise, place towel bars, soap dishes and other items in the bathrooms.

Exercise 4-2:
Furnishing the Common Areas

Drawing Name: ex4-1.dwg
Estimated Time: 15 minutes

Common areas are the Living Room, Dining Room, and Family Room.

This lesson reinforces the following skills:

- ☐ Insert
- ☐ ADC

1.   Open *ex4-1.dwg.*

2.   Change to a PLAN view by typing **PLAN** and **ENTER**..

3.

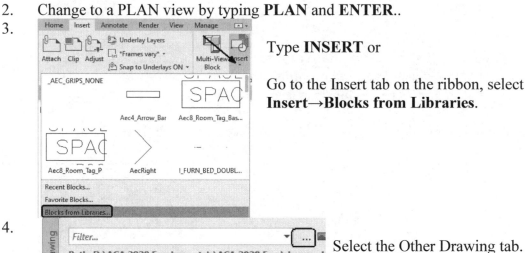

Type **INSERT** or

Go to the Insert tab on the ribbon, select
Insert→Blocks from Libraries.

4.   Select the Other Drawing tab.

Select the browse… button.

5. Select *dining group* from the exercise files.
Click **Open**.

6. Left click to add the **Dining Set** to the dining room area by the kitchen.

7. Select the Other Drawing tab.

Select the down arrow and click **Browse Block Libraries.**

8. Select *entertainment center* from the exercise files.
Click **Open**.

9. 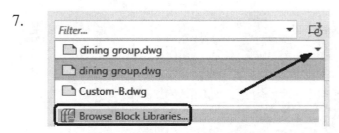 Under Options:
Enable **Insertion Point.**
Enable **Rotation.**

10. Highlight the preview of the entertainment center in the upper left of the top pane.

Notice that the bottom pane grays out.

11. Place in the family room.

12. Add a sofa and coffee table to the family room using the Design Center.

Save the file as *ex4-2.dwg*.

Tips & Tricks

If the drawing preview in the Design Center is displayed as 2D, then it is a 2D drawing.

Exercise 4-3:

Adding to the Service Areas

Drawing Name: ex4-2.dwg
Estimated Time: 30 minutes

1.   Open *ex4-2.dwg*.
                   Select the Model tab.
                   Switch to a top view.

2.   Launch the Design Center.

3.   Select the AEC Content tab.
                   Browse to the *AutoCAD Architecture/Imperial/Design/Site/Basic*
                   Site/Vehicles folder.

4.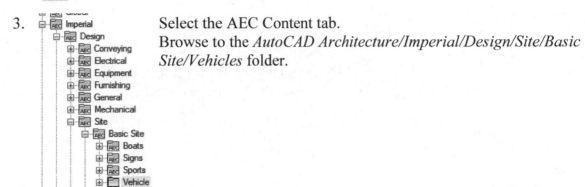

Drag and drop the *Sub-Compact* car into the garage.

All that remains are the kitchen, bathroom, and laundry areas.

5.   Activate the Insert tab on the ribbon.

                   Select **Insert→Blocks from Libraries**.

6.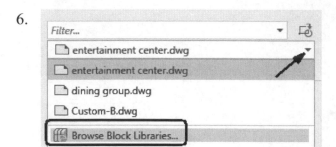

Select the drop down arrow and **Browse Block Libraries.**

7.

Locate the *cocina 3d.dwg* in the exercise files. Click **Open**.

Cocina means kitchen in Spanish.

8.

In the lower pane:
Enable **Insertion Point.**
Set the **Rotation** to **45.**

9.

Left click on the drawing in the upper pane.

10.

Place the kitchen above the model in the display window.

Change the view to SW Isometric.

11.

Enable **Polar.**

12.

Type **SC** for scale.
Select the kitchen block.
Click ENTER to complete the selection.

When prompted for the base point, select the insertion point indicated.

13.

Right click and select **Reference**.

14.

Select the basepoint and the lower right corner as the reference length.

15.

Right click and select Points when prompted for the new length.

Select the corner points indicated for the new length.

16.

Use the MOVE tool to move the kitchen block into the kitchen area.

17.

Switch to a **SE isometric** 3D view.
Change the visual display to **Realistic.**

18.

Inspect the kitchen.

19. [−][Top][Hidden]

Switch to a **Top Hidden** view.

20.

On the Design Center:

Locate the *Residential* folder uner *Design/Equipment*.

21.

Place a washer and dryer in the laundry room.

Place a water heater in the garage.

22. The completed floor plan should look similar to this.

Your floor plan may look differently depending on which furnishings you used.

23. Save the file as *ex 4-3.dwg*.

Exercise 4-4:

Adding Components to the Bathrooms

Drawing Name: ex4-3.dwg
Estimated Time: 30 minutes

1.   Open *ex4-3.dwg*.
Select the Model tab.
Switch to a top view.

2.   Zoom into the bathroom area.

3.   Thaw the image layer.

    ex3-8|G-Anno-Stnd-Nplt
    ex3-8|G-Anno-Stnd-Scrn
    ex3-8|image
    G-Anno-Nplt

Note the location of the sinks, toilets, tub, and shower.

4.   Launch the Design Center.

5.
Global
    Design
        Bathroom
            Basin
            Bath
            Bidet
            Drinking Fountain
            Floor Sink
            Grab Rail
            Layouts
            Shower
            Toilet
         Urinal

Select the AEC Content tab on the Design Center palette.
Browse to the *AutoCAD Architecture/Global//Design/Bathroom/Toilet* folder.

3D Toilet - Flush Valve

Place a toilet in the two bathrooms.

6.
3D Toilet Flush V...
Insert...
Open
Edit...
Delete
Copy

Highlight the **3D Toilet – Flush Valve**.

Right click and select **Insert**.

7.

Master Bath
5'-1" X 15'-0"

Un. Cl.

Bath #2
5'-11" X 11'-5 1/2"

Left click to place the toilet.
Use the cursor to rotate the toilet into the correct orientation.
Left click to complete placement.

Move the cursor to the second toilet location.
Left click to place the toilet.
Use the cursor to rotate the toilet into the correct orientation.
Left click to complete placement.
Click **ESC** to exit the Insert command.

8.
ex3-8|G-Anno-Stnd-Scrn
ex3-8|image
G-Anno-Nplt

Freeze the image layer.

This will make it easier to place the remaining items.

The bathrooms should currently show two toilets.

9.

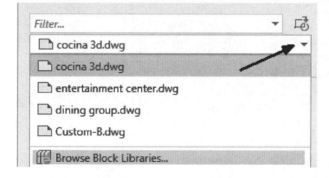

Enable ORTHO, OBJECT TRACKING, and OSNAPS to place the blocks.

10.

Activate the Insert tab on the ribbon.

Select **Insert→Blocks from Libraries**.

Blocks for the tub, shower, and vanities have been provided in the exercise files.

11.

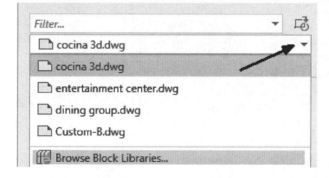

Select **Browse Block Libraries** on the Blocks palette.

12.

Select *Double_Vanity.dwg* from the exercise files.

Click **Open.**

13.

Under Options:

Enable **Insertion Point**.
Enable **Rotation**.

14.

Highlight the block.
Right click and select **Insert**.

15.

Place the double vanity between the two short walls in the master bath.

16.

Select **Browse Block Libraries** on the Blocks palette.

17.

Select *Vanity.dwg* from the exercise files.

Click **Open.**

18.

Under Options:

Enable **Insertion Point**.
Enable **Rotation**.

19. Highlight the block.
    Right click and select **Insert**.

20. Place the vanity in the bathroom.

21. Select **Browse Block Libraries** on the Blocks palette.

22. Select *Large_Tub.dwg* from the exercise files.

    Click **Open.**

23. Under Insertion Options:

    Enable **Insertion Point**.
    Enable **Rotation**.

24. Highlight the block.
    Right click and select **Insert**.

25.

Place the tub in the bathroom.

26.

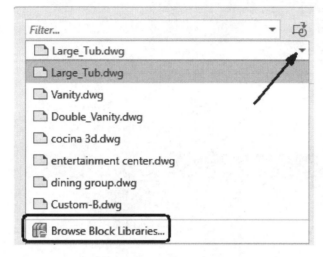

Select **Browse Block Libraries** on the Blocks palette.

27.

Select *shower.dwg* from the exercise files.

Click **Open.**

28.

Under Insertion Options:

Enable **Insertion Point**.
Enable **Rotation**.

29.

Highlight the block.
Right click and select **Insert**.

30. Place the shower in the master bathroom.

31.   Save as *ex4-4.dwg*.

Extra:

Add towel bars, plants, mirrors, and other accessories to the floor plan using blocks from the design center or downloaded from the internet.

QUIZ 4

True or False

1. Custom content can be located in any subdirectory and still function properly.

2. The sole purpose of the Space Planning process is to arrange furniture in a floor plan.

3. The Design Center only has 3D objects stored in the Content area because ADT is strictly a 3D software.

4. Appliances are automatically placed on the APPLIANCE layer.

5. When you place a wall cabinet, it is automatically placed at the specified height.

6. You can create tools on a tool palette by dragging and dropping the objects from the Design Center onto the palette.

Multiple Choice

7. A residential structure is divided into:

    A. Four basic areas
    B. Three basic areas
    C. Two basic areas
    D. One basic area

8. Kitchen cabinets are located in the _____ subfolder.

    A. Casework
    B. Cabinets
    C. Bookcases
    D. Furniture

9. Select the area type that is NOT part of a private residence:

    A. Bedrooms
    B. Common Areas
    C. Service Areas
    D. Public Areas

10. To set the layer properties of a tool on a tool palette:

    A. Use the Layer Manager
    B. Select the tool, right click and select Properties
    C. Launch the Properties dialog
    D. All of the above

11. Vehicles placed from the Design Center are automatically placed on this layer:

    A. A-Site-Vhcl
    B. A-Vhcl
    C. C-Site Vhcl
    D. None of the above

12. The **Roof** tool is located on this tool palette:

    A. DESIGN
    B. GENERAL DRAFTING
    C. MASSING
    D. TOOLS

ANSWERS:

1) T; 2) F; 3) F; 4) F; 5) T; 6) T; 7) B; 8) A; 9) D; 10) B; 11) C; 12) A

Lesson 5:
Roofs

Roofs can be created with single or double slopes, with or without gable ends, and with or without overhangs. Once you input all your roof settings, you simply pick the points around the perimeter of the building to define your roof outline. If you make an error, you can easily modify or redefine your roof.

You need to pick three points before the roof will begin to preview in your graphics window. There is no limit to the number of points to select to define the perimeter.

To create a gable roof, uncheck the gable box in the Roof dialog. Pick the two end points for the sloped portion of the roof. Turn on the Gable box. Pick the end point for the gable side. Turn off the Gable box. Pick the end point for the sloped side. Turn the Gable box on. Pick the viewport and then Click ENTER. A Gable cannot be defined with more than three consecutive edges.

Roofs can be created using two methods: ROOFADD places a roof based on points selected or ROOFCONVERT which converts a closed polyline or closed walls to develop a roof.

- ➢ If you opt to use ROOFCONVERT and use existing closed walls, be sure that the walls are intersecting properly. If your walls are not properly cleaned up with each other, the roof conversion is unpredictable.
- ➢ The Plate Height of a roof should be set equal to the Wall Height.
- ➢ You can create a gable on a roof by gripping any ridgeline point and stretching it past the roof edge. You cannot make a gable into a hip using grips.

Shape – Select the Shape option on the command line by typing 'S.'	Single Slope – Extends a roof plane at an angle from the Plate Height.	 end elevation view
	Double Slope – Includes a single slope and adds another slope, which begins at the intersection of the first slope and the height specified for the first slope.	 end elevation view
Gable – Select the Gable option on the command line by typing 'G.'	If this is enabled, turns off the slope of the roof place. To create a gable edge, select Gable prior to identifying the first corner of the gable end. Turn off gable to continue to create the roof.	 gable roof end
Plate Height – Set the Plate Height on the command line by typing 'PH.'	Specify the top plate from which the roof plane is projected. The height is relative to the XY plane with a Z coordinate of 0.	
Rise – Set the Rise on the command line by typing 'PR.'	Sets the angle of the roof based on a run value of 12.	A rise value of 5 creates a 5/12 roof, which forms a slope angle of 22.62 degrees.
Slope – Set the Slope on the command line by typing 'PS.'	Angle of the roof rise from the horizontal.	If slope angles are entered, then the rise will automatically be calculated.

Upper Height – Set the Upper Height on the command line by typing 'UH.'	This is only available if a Double Slope roof is being created. This is the height where the second slope will start.	
Rise (upper) – Set the Upper Rise on the command line by typing 'UR.'	This is only available if a Double Slope roof is being created. This is the slope angle for the second slope.	A rise value of 5 creates a 5/12 roof, which forms a slope angle of 22.62 degrees.
Slope (upper) – Set the Upper Slope on the command line by typing 'US.'	This is only available if a Double Slope roof is being created. Defines the slope angle for the second slope.	If an upper rise value is set, this is automatically calculated.
Overhang – To enable on the command line, type 'O.' To set the value of the Overhang, type 'V.'	If enabled, extends the roofline down from the plate height by the value set.	

	The Floating Viewer opens a viewer window displaying a preview of the roof.
	The match button allows you to select an existing roof to match its properties.
	The properties button opens the Roof Properties dialog.
	The Undo button allows you to undo the last roof operation. You can step back as many operations as you like up to the start.
	Opens the Roof Help file.

Exercise 5-1:

Creating a Roof using Existing Walls

Drawing Name: roofs1.dwg
Estimated Time: 10 minutes

This exercise reinforces the following skills:

- ❑   Roof
- ❑   Roof Properties
- ❑   Visual Styles

1.   Open *roofs1.dwg*.

2.

    Select the Work icon. Activate the right viewport that shows the top or plan view.

3.   Select the **Roof** tool from the Home tab on the ribbon.

4.

Expand the Dimensions section.
Set the Thickness to **10″ [254.00 mm]**.
Set the Shape to **Single slope**.
Set the Overhang to **1′-0″ [609.6 mm]**.

Dimensions	
Thickness	254.00
Edge cut	Square
Shape	Single slope
Overhang	609.60
	Edges/Faces

5.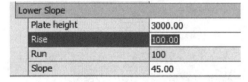

Expand the Lower Slope section.
Set the Plate height to **10′-0″ [3000 mm]**.

The plate height determines the level where the roof rests.

6.

Set the Rise to **1′-0″ [100 mm]**.

Lower Slope	
Plate height	3000.00
Rise	100.00
Run	100
Slope	45.00

7.

Pick the corners indicated to place the roof.

Click **Enter**.

8. Activate the left 3D viewport.

9. Activate the View tab on the ribbon.

Select the **Shades of Gray** under Visual Styles.

10. Save as *ex5-1.dwg*.

In order to edit a roof, you have to convert it to Roof Slabs.

Roof Slabs

A roof slab is a single face of a roof. Roof slab elements differ from roof elements in that each roof slab is independent of other roof slabs. When you use multiple roof slabs to model a roof, you have more flexibility as you can control the shape and appearance of each slab or section of the roof.

While roof slabs are independent, they can interact. You can use one roof slab as a trim or extend boundary. You can miter roof slabs together. You can cut holes in roof slabs and add or subtract mass elements.

You can use grips to modify the shapes of roof slabs. You can use basic modify tools, like move or rotate, to reposition roof slabs.

Exercise 5-2:
Roof Slabs

Drawing Name: residence.dwg
Estimated Time: 15 minutes

This exercise reinforces the following skills:

- ❑ Convert to Roof
- ❑ Roof Slab Tools

1. Open *residence.dwg*.

2. Select the **Roof** tool from the Home tab on the ribbon.

3. Select the four corners on the left wing to place a roof.

Click ENTER to complete the command.

4. Repeat and select the four corners on the right wing to place a roof.

5.

Draw a rectangle around the middle section of the floor plan using the rectangle tool.

6.

Select the rectangle.
Right click and select **Properties.**

7.

Change the elevation for the rectangle to 10'-0".

This puts it in-line with the top of the walls.

Material		ByLayer
Geometry		
Current Vertex		1
Vertex X		27'-8 3/8"
Vertex Y		51'-9 5/8"
Start segment width		0"
End segment width		0"
Global width		0"
Elevation		10'-0"

8.   Launch the Design Tools from the Home tab on the ribbon.

9. 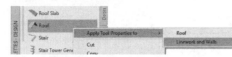 Locate the **Roof** tool on the Design palette by scrolling down.

    Right click and select **Apply Tool Properties to→Linework and Walls.**

10. Select the rectangle.
    Click ENTER to complete the selection.
    When prompted to erase the linework, select **Yes**.
    Click ENTER.
    The middle roof is placed.

    Click ESC to release any selection.

11. Select all three roofs.

    The roofs will highlight.

12. Select **Convert** from the Roof tab on the ribbon.

13. Enable the **Erase layout geometry** checkbox.

    Click **OK**.

14. The roofs will change appearance slightly. They now consist of individual slabs.

15. Save as *ex5-2.dwg*.

Modify Roof Line

Drawing Name: modify_roof.dwg
Estimated Time: 15 minutes

This exercise reinforces the following skills:

- Modify Roof Slabs
- Modify Roof Line

1.   Open *modify_roof.dwg.*

2.   *Erase the two roof slabs indicated.*

Select the slabs, then Click the **Delete** key on the keyboard.

Verify that ORTHO, OTRACK and OSNAP are enabled on the status bar.

3.   Select the left roof slab.

4.

Drag the point/grip at the bottom of the triangle up until it is horizontal to the upper point.

Look for the input that displays the angle at 180°.

5.

Repeat for the right side.

6.

Repeat for the bottom side.

If you are having problems creating a straight edge, draw a horizontal line and snap to the line. Then, erase the line.

7.

Switch to a 3D view to see how the roof has changed.

View Style shown is Hidden, Materials On, Realistic Face Style.

8.

Select the wall indicated.

9. 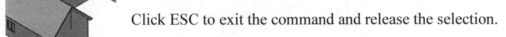 Select **Modify Roof Line** on the ribbon.

10. Type **A** for Autoproject.
    Select the two roof slabs.
    Click ENTER.

11. *The wall will auto-project to the roof.*

    Click ESC to exit the command and release the selection.

12. Rotate the model so you can see the other side of the building.

13. Select the wall indicated.

14. Select **Modify Roof Line** from the tab on the ribbon.

15. Type **A** for Autoproject.
    Select the two roof slabs.
    Click ENTER.

16.   The wall will auto-project to the roof.

    Click ESC to exit the command.

    Release the selection.

17. Save as *ex5-3.dwg*.

Exercise 5-4:
Trimming Roof Slabs

Drawing Name: roof_slabs.dwg
Estimated Time: 30 minutes

This exercise reinforces the following skills:

- ❏ Roof Slabs
- ❏ Trim
- ❏ Grips

1.   Open *roof_slabs.dwg*.

2.

Activate the **View** tab on the ribbon.

Select the **Top** view.

You can also use the control at the top left corner of the display window to change the view orientation.

3.

Delete the roof slabs on the middle roof section.

4.

Draw two rectangles in the middle space, stacked horizontally.

Change the elevation of both rectangles to 10'.

Geometry	
Global width	0"
Elevation	10'-0"

5.

Locate the **Roof Slab** tool on the Design Palette.
Right click and select **Apply Tool Properties to→Linework, Walls and Roof.**
Select both rectangles.
Click **ENTER**.

6.

`ROOFSLABTOOLTOLINEWORK Erase layout geometry? [Yes No] <No>: y`

When prompted to erase layout geometry, type **Y** for yes.

7.

`ROOFSLABTOOLTOLINEWORK Creation mode [Direct Projected] <Projected>:`

Click **ENTER** to accept Projected.

8.

`ROOFSLABTOOLTOLINEWORK Specify base height <8'-0">: 10'0"`

Type **10' 0"** to set the base height to 10' 0".

9.

`ROOFSLABTOOLTOLINEWORK Specify slab justification [Top Center Bottom Slopeline] <Bottom>:`

Set the slab justification to **Bottom**.

10.

`ROOFSLABTOOLTOLINEWORK Select the pivot edge for the Slab:`

When prompted for the pivot edge of the slab, select the outside edge of each slab.

Click ESC to release the selection.

11.

Slope	
Rise	-3 7/32"
Run	1'-0"
Slope	345.00
Hold fascia ele...	No
Pivot Point X	-38'-5 1/4"
Pivot Point Y	15'-0"
Pivot Point Z	-50'-3 7/32"

Location	
Elevation	15'-0"
	Additional information

Select the top roof slab and set the Slope to **345**.

Set the Elevation to **15'**.

Click ESC to release the selection.

12.

Select the bottom roof slab and set the Slope to **345**.

Set the Elevation to **15'**.

Click ESC to release the selection.

13.

Switch to a **Left 2D Wireframe** view.

You can see how the slabs are positioned.

Adjust their position if necessary.

14.

[−][SW Isometric][Hidden]

Switch to a SW Isometric Hidden view.

15.

Select a roof slab.

16.

Select **Trim** on the ribbon.

17.

Select the other roof slab to use as the trimming object.

Then select the edge of the roof to be trimmed.

The roof slab adjusts.

18.

Activate the NE Isometric view.

19.

Select the untrimmed roof slab.

20.

Select **Trim** on the tab on the ribbon.

21.

Select the other roof slab to use as the trimming object.

Then select the edge of the roof to be trimmed.

The roof slab adjusts.

22.

Select one of the middle roof slabs.

Select **Extend** from the tab on the ribbon.

When prompted for object to extend to: select one of the adjoining roof slabs.

23.

When prompted to select an edge to lengthen, select the upper edge of the roof slab closest to the adjoining roof slab used as the boundary.

24.

When prompted to select a second edge, select the lower edge of the roof slab to be extended.

25.

Repeat the EXTEND for the other side of the roof slab.

26.

Use the EXTEND tool to clean up the roof slab on the other side.

If you struggle getting one side of the roof correct, delete that roof slab. Switch to a TOP view and mirror the roof slab that looks correct.

27.

Save as *ex5-4.dwg*.

Exercise 5-5:
Add a Hole to a Roof

Drawing Name: add_hole.dwg
Estimated Time: 10 minutes

This exercise reinforces the following skills:

❑   Roof Slabs
❑   Add Hole

1.   Open *add_hole.dwg*.

2.   [−][Top][Hidden]   Switch to a **Top** view.

3.

Verify that only Endpoint and Midpoint should be enabled on the OSNAP settings.

4.

Draw a rectangle **10' 0"** below the top edge of the far right roof slab.

The rectangle should be 5' 0" wide and 7' 0" high.

Do not add dimensions…those are for reference only.

If you use lines to place, use the PE polyline edit command to create a closed polyline.

5.

Turn ORTHO **ON**.
Start the Rectangle command.
Right click and select TEMPORARY TRACK POINT.

6.

Left pick to select the upper right corner of the roof. *Look for the small green X to indicate tracking is enabled.*

Drag the mouse straight down and type 10' to start the rectangle 10' below the tracking point.

7.

Type **@-5',-7'** to complete the rectangle.

This means you are moving five feet to the left and seven feet down to complete the rectangle.

8.

Select the far right roof slab.

9.

Select **Hole→Add** from the tab on the ribbon.

Trim Extend Miter Cut Vertex

Modify

☐ Hole ▾

■ Add

☐ Remo

10. Select the rectangle.
Click **ENTER**.
Type **Y** to erase the layout geometry.

▸ **ROOFSLABADDHOLE** Select closed polylines or connected solid objects to define holes:

11.

Switch to an isometric view and orbit around to see the hole that was created.

12. Save as *ex5-5.dwg*.

Exercise 5-6:

Add a Gabled Roof

Drawing Name: gable.dwg
Estimated Time: 20 minutes

This exercise reinforces the following skills:

- ❑ Roof
- ❑ Modify Wall

1.   Open *gable.dwg*.

2.   [−][Top][Hidden]   Switch to a **Top** view.

3.   Roof   Select the **Roof** tool from the Design palette.

4.

Edge cut	Square
Next Edge	
Shape	Single slope
Overhang	1'-0"

We change the style of roof for each side to create a gable roof.

Set the Shape to **Single slope**.

5.   Select Points **A** and **D**.

6.

Edge cut	Square
Next Edge	
Shape	Single slope
Overhang	1'-0"

Set the Shape to **Single slope**.
Select Points **D** and **C**.

7.

In the Properties pane,
set the Shape to **Gable**.

8.

Select the two vertex points of the rectangle on the
right side.

Select Point B and then Point C.

9.

Set the Shape to **Single slope.**

10.

Select Point D and then Point C.

The gable roof is created.

Click **ENTER**.

11.   [−][Right][Hidden]   Switch to a Right view.

12.

You see the gable that was created.

Select the gable.

13.

Set the Plate Height to **17' 0"** on the Properties palette.

This will raise the gable.

14.

You can orbit the view slightly to check the gable position.

15.

Select the lower wall below the gable.

16. Select **Modify Roof Line** on the ribbon.

17. Select **Auto project**.

Select the gabled roof. Click ENTER.

The wall will adjust.

18. Save as *ex5-6.dwg*.

Exercise 5-7:

Modify a Hole in a Roof Slab

Drawing Name: hole_modify.dwg
Estimated Time: 10 minutes

This exercise reinforces the following skills:

- ❑ Roof Slabs

1. Open hole_modify.dwg.

2. [−][Top][2D Wireframe]   Switch to a **Top 2D Wireframe** view.

3. *We need to adjust the opening in the roof slab to accommodate the modified wall.*

Select the roof slab.

4. Select the middle top grip arrow of the opening.

5.   Move the edge up to align with the end of the wall.

6.   Repeat on the bottom edge of the opening.

Select the slab.
Select the middle bottom grip arrow.
Move the edge down to align with the end of the wall.

7.   Verify that the opening aligns with the wall ends.

8.   [−][NE Isometric][Hidden]

Switch to a NE Isometric Hidden view.

Note how the opening has updated.

9.   Save as *ex5-7.dwg.*

Exercise 5-8:

Add Walls to a Gabled Roof

Drawing Name: gable_walls.dwg
Estimated Time: 20 minutes

This exercise reinforces the following skills:

- Walls
- Wall Properties
- Global Cut Plane Display

1. Open *gable_walls.dwg*.

2. [−][Top][2D Wireframe]   Switch to a **Top 2D Wireframe** view.

3. Home   Insert

   Wall

   Wall

   Select the **Wall** tool from the Home tab on the ribbon.

4. Browse...

   Style   Stud-4 Rigid-1.5 Air-1 Brick-4

   Bound s... By style (Yes)

   In the Properties pane:
   Set the Style to **Stud-4 Rigid-1.5 Air- 1 Brick 4.**

5. Place two short walls to act as the sides of the gable.

   The top wall should be left justified.
   The bottom wall should be right justified.

Dimensions		
A	Width	11 1/8"
B	Base height	10'-0"
C	Length	2'-11 3/8"
	Justify	☐ Right

   Verify that the exterior sides of the walls are located correctly.

6.

Select the two short walls.

Change their elevations to **10'** using the Properties pane.

When the elevation changes, they will disappear from the view.

7.

To see the walls in the Plan view, you need to change the global cut plane.

On the Status bar:
Select the Cut Plane icon.
In the dialog, set the Cut Height to **14'0**.
Click **OK**.

8.

Position the short walls so they are *completely* inside the gabled roof boundaries. Otherwise, we can't use the roof to trim up the walls.

Use FILLET to clean up the corners between the short walls and the exterior wall.

9.

Select the **Layer Properties** dialog from the Home tab on the ribbon.

10. Create a layer called **HIDE IN VIEW**.

We will use this layer to temporarily hide elements to allow easier editing.

11. Switch to a **NW Isometric Hidden** view.

12.

Select the north roof slab next to the gable and the far side roof slab and assign to the **HIDE IN VIEW** layer.

13. Set the **HIDE IN VIEW** layer to frozen.

14. Select a short wall.
From the tab on the ribbon:
Select **Modify Roof Line**.
Select **Auto-Project** as the option.
Select the gabled roof.

Click **ENTER**.

Repeat for the other short wall.

If the walls don't trim properly check to see that they are entirely below the gabled roof boundary.

15.

If you orbit the model you see the wall goes below the roof.

To orbit, hold down the SHIFT key and the wheel on the mouse at the same time.

16.

Select one of the short walls.

From the tab on the ribbon:
Select **Modify Floor Line**.
Select **Auto-Project** as the option.
Select the sloped roof slab that intersects the wall.

Click **ENTER**.

Repeat for the other short wall.

17.

Switch to a BACK view so you can see how the walls adjusted.

If one of the short walls did not adjust properly, Switch to a TOP view, delete the unresponsive wall and mirror the other wall over.

18.

Thaw the **HIDE IN VIEW** layer.

19.

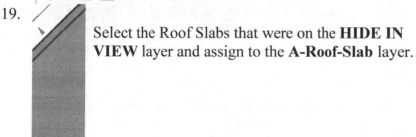

Select the Roof Slabs that were on the **HIDE IN VIEW** layer and assign to the **A-Roof-Slab** layer.

20. Save as *ex5-8.rvt*.

Exercise 5-9:

Roof Slab Styles

Drawing Name: slab_style2.dwg
Estimated Time: 20 minutes

This exercise reinforces the following skills:

- ❑ Roof Slab Styles
- ❑ Design Palette
- ❑ Materials
- ❑ Style Manager

1.   Open *slab_style2.dwg.*

2.   [–][SW Isometric][Hidden]   Switch to an **SW Isometric Hidden** view.

3.   Launch the Design Tools.

4. 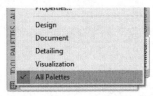   Right click on the title bar of the Design Tools and enable **All Palettes**.

5.   Right click on the tabs of the Design Tools and enable **Materials**.

6.   Right click on the **Thermal & Moisture.Shingles.Asphalt Shingles.3-Tab.Black.**

7.

Select **Apply Tool Properties to Object.**

Select one of the roof slabs.

Click **ENTER.**

The roof slab updates with the new material definition.

The material definition has now been added to the drawing so it can be used in the Style Manager.

8.

Activate the Manage tab on the ribbon.

Select the **Style Manager.**

9.

Locate the Roof Slab Styles under Architectural Objects.

Note that there is only one slab style available in the drawing.

10.

Right click on the Roof Slab Style and select **New.**

11.

Rename the style **Asphalt Shingles.**

12.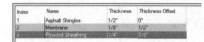

Define three components:
- Asphalt Shingles with a thickness of ½" and Thickness Offset of 0.
- Membrane with a Thickness of 1/8" and Thickness offset of ½".
- Plywood Sheathing with a thickness of ¼" and Thickness offset of 5/8".

13.

Use the preview to check the placement of each component.

14.

Create new material definitions for the three new component types:

- Asphalt Shingles
- Membrane
- Plywood Sheathing

15.

Highlight the Asphalt Shingles component.
Select **Edit Material Definition**.

16.

Select the General Medium Detail style override.

Set the Hatch to use **AR-RSHKE**.

17.

Set the Angles to **0**.

Click **OK**.

18.

Select the **Other** tab.
Under Surface Rendering,
set the Render Material to the Asphalt Material that was placed in the file earlier.

Click **OK**.
Close the Style Manager.

19. Save as *ex5-9.dwg.*

Exercise 5-10:

Applying a Roof Slab Style

Drawing Name: roof_slab2.dwg
Estimated Time: 10 minutes

This exercise reinforces the following skills:

- ❑ Roof Slab Styles
- ❑ Select Similar
- ❑ Properties
- ❑ Design Palette

1. Open *roof_slab2.dwg*.

2. [−][SW Isometric][Hidden]   Switch to an **SW Isometric Hidden** view.

3. 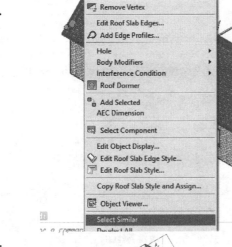   Select a roof slab.
Right click and select **Select Similar**.

4.   *Notice several of the roof slabs are selected, but not all of them.*

   The ones that weren't selected are still on the HIDE IN VIEW layer. If you skipped this step in the previous exercise, assign the roof slabs back to the A-ROOF-SLAB layer.

5.   Right click and select **AECSELECTSIMILAR**.

6.

All the roof slabs are selected, but not the gabled roof. That is because it is a roof object and not a roof slab object.

Right click and select **Properties**.

7.

On the Properties palette,
set the Style to **Asphalt Shingles**.

Click **ESC** to release the selection.

8.

Select the gabled roof.

Select **Convert** on the tab on the ribbon to convert to roof slabs.

9.

Select **Asphalt Shingles** from the drop-down list.
Enable **Erase Layout Geometry**.
Click **OK**.
Click **ESC** to release the selection.

Only one of the roof slabs shows the asphalt shingle material. This is because the materials display is separate from the style definition.

10.

Right click on the **Thermal & Moisture.Shingles.Asphalt Shingles.3-Tab.Black.**

Select **Apply Tool Properties to Object.**
Select one of the roof slabs and Click **ENTER.**

11.

Save as *ex5-10.dwg.*

More materials are available in the Content Browser that can be used to change the appearance of your model.

QUIZ 5

True or False

1. Roof slabs are a single face of a roof, not an entire roof.

2. The thickness of a roof slab can be modified for an individual element without affecting the roof slab style.

3. If you change the slope of a roof slab, it rotates around the slope pivot point.

4. Once you place a roof or roof slab, it cannot be modified.

5. You can use the TRIM and EXTEND tools to modify roof slabs.

Multiple Choice

6. Materials are displayed when the view setting is: (select all that apply)

   A. wireframe
   B. Shaded
   C. Hidden
   D. Rendered

7. Roof slab styles control the following properties: (select all that apply)

   A. Slab Thickness
   B. Slab Elevation
   C. Physical components (concrete, metal, membrane)
   D. Materials

8. Identify the tool shown.

   A. Add Roof
   B. Add Roof Slab
   C. Add Gable
   D. Modify Roof

9. To change the elevation of a slab:

   A. Modify the slab style.
   B. Use Properties to change the Elevation.
   C. Set layer properties.
   D. All of the above.

10. Roof slabs can be created: (select all that apply)

    A. Independently (from scratch)
    B. From Existing Roofs
    C. From Walls
    D. From Polylines

ANSWERS:

1) T; 2) T; 3) T; 4) F; 5) T; 6) A, B, D; 7) A, C, D; 8) B; 9) B; 10) A, B, C

Lesson 6:
Structural Members

Architectural documentation for residential construction will always include plans (top views) of each floor of a building, showing features and structural information of the floor platform itself. Walls are located on the plan but not shown in structural detail.

Wall sections and details are used to show:

- the elements within walls (exterior siding, sheathing, block, brick or wood studs, insulation, air cavities, interior sheathing, trim)
- how walls relate to floors, ceilings, roofs, and eaves
- openings within the walls (doors/windows with their associated sills and headers)
- how walls relate to openings in floors (stairs).

Stick-framed (stud) walls usually have their framing patterns determined by the carpenters on site. Once window and door openings are located on the plan and stud spacing is specified by the designer (or the local building code), the specific arrangement of vertical members is usually left to the fabricators and not drafted, except where specific structural details require explanation.

The structural members in framed floors that have to hold themselves and/or other walls and floors up are usually drafted as framing plans. Designers must specify the size and spacing of joists or trusses, beams and columns. Plans show the orientation and relation of members, locate openings through the floor and show support information for openings and other specific conditions.

In the next exercises, we shall create a floor framing plan. Since the ground floor of our one-story lesson house has already been defined as a concrete slab, we'll assume that the ground level slopes down at the rear of the house and create a wood deck at the sliding door to the family room. The deck will need a railing for safety.

Autodesk AutoCAD Architecture includes a Structural Member Catalog that allows you to easily access industry-standard structural shapes. To create most standard column, brace, and beam styles, you can access the Structural Member Catalog, select a structural member shape, and create a style that contains the shape that you selected. The shape, similar to an AEC profile, is a 2D cross-section of a structural member. When you create a structural member with a style that you created from the Structural Member Catalog, you define the path to extrude the shape along.

You can create your own structural shapes that you can add to existing structural members or use to create new structural members. The design rules in a structural member style allow you to add these custom shapes to a structural member, as well as create custom structural members from more than one shape.

All the columns, braces, and beams that you create are sub-types of a single Structural Member object type. The styles that you create for columns, braces, and beams have the same Structural Member Styles style type as well. When you change the display or style of a structural member, use the Structural Member object in the Display Manager and the Structural Member Styles style type in the Style Manager.

If you are operating with the AIA layering system as your current layer standard, when you create members or convert AutoCAD entities to structural members using the menu picks or toolbars, AutoCAD Architecture assigns the new members to layers: A-Cols, A-Cols-Brce or A-Beam, respectively. If Generic AutoCAD Architecture is your standard, the layers used are A_Columns, A_Beams and A_Braces. If your layer standard is Current Layer, new entities come in on the current layer, as in plain vanilla AutoCAD.

The Structural Member Catalog includes specifications for standard structural shapes. You can choose shapes from the Structural Member Catalog and generate styles for structural members that you create in your drawings.

> A style that contains the catalog shape that you selected is created. You can view the style in the Style Manager, create a new structural member from the style, or apply the style to an existing member.

> When you add a structural member to your drawing, the shape inside the style that you created defines the shape of the member. You define the length, justification, roll or rise, and start and end offsets of the structural member when you draw it.

You cannot use the following special characters in your style names:

- less-than and greater-than symbols (< >)
- forward slashes and backslashes (/ \)
- quotation marks (")
- colons (:)
- semicolons (;)
- question marks (?)
- commas (,)
- asterisks (*)
- vertical bars (|)
- equal signs (=)
- backquotes (`)

The left pane of the Structural Member Catalog contains a hierarchical tree view. Several industry standard catalogs are organized in the tree, first by imperial or metric units, and then by material.

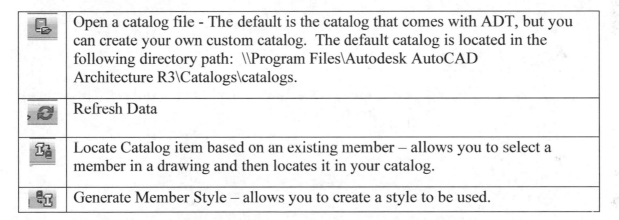

	Open a catalog file - The default is the catalog that comes with ADT, but you can create your own custom catalog. The default catalog is located in the following directory path: \\Program Files\Autodesk AutoCAD Architecture R3\Catalogs\catalogs.
	Refresh Data
	Locate Catalog item based on an existing member – allows you to select a member in a drawing and then locates it in your catalog.
	Generate Member Style – allows you to create a style to be used.

We will be adding a wood framed deck, 4000 mm x 2750 mm, to the back of the house. For purposes of this exercise we will assume that the ground level is 300 mm below the slab at the back of the house and falls away so that grade level below the edge of the deck away from the house is 2 meters below floor level: - 2 m a.f.f. (above finish floor) in architectural notation. We will place the top of the deck floorboards even with the top of the floor slab.

We will use support and rim joists as in standard wood floor framing, and they will all be at the same level, rather than joists crossing a support beam below. In practice this means the use of metal hangers, which will not be drawn. Once the floor system is drawn we will add support columns at the outside rim joist and braces at the columns.

Exercise 6-1:
Creating Member Styles

Drawing Name: member_styles.dwg
Estimated Time: 5 minutes

This exercise reinforces the following skills:

❑ Creating Member Styles
❑ Use of Structural Members tools

1. Open *member_styles.dwg*.

2. Activate the Manage tab on the ribbon.

   Go to **Style & Display → Structural Member Catalog**.

3. Browse to the **Imperial/Timber/Lumber/Nominal Cut Lumber** folder.

4. In the lower right pane:

    Locate the **2x4** shape designation.

5. 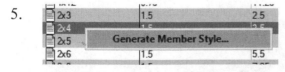 Right click and select **Generate Member Style**.

6. In the Structural Member Style dialog box, the name for your style automatically fills in.

   Click **OK**.

7.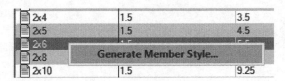

Locate the **2x6** shape designation. Right click and select **Generate Member Style**.

8.

In the Structural Member Style dialog box, the name for your style is displayed.

Click **OK**.

9. Close the dialog.
   Save as *ex6-1.dwg*.

Exercise 6-2:
Creating Member Shapes

Drawing Name: member_shapes.dwg
Estimated Time: 10 minutes

This exercise reinforces the following skills:

❑ Structural Member Wizard

1. Open *member_shapes.dwg*.

2. Activate the **Manage** tab on the ribbon.

   Go to **Style & Display→Structural Member Wizard**.

3.

Select the **Cut Lumber** category under Wood.

Click **Next**.

4.

Set the Section Width to **2″**.

Set the Section Depth to **10″**.

Click **Next**.

5.

Enter the style name as **2x10**.

Click **Finish**.

6.

Activate the **Manage** tab on the ribbon.

Go to **Style & Display → Structural Member Wizard**.

7.

Select the **Cut Lumber** category under Wood.

Click **Next**.

8. Set the Section Width to **4″**.

Set the Section Depth to **4″**.

Click **Next**.

9. Enter the style name as **4x4**.

Click **Finish**.

10. Save as *ex6-2.dwg*.

Exercise 6-3:
Adding Structural Members

Drawing Name: add_columns.dwg
Estimated Time: 25 minutes

This exercise reinforces the following skills:

- ❑ Creating Member Styles
- ❑ Use of Structural Members tools

1. Open *add_columns.dwg*.

2. Activate the **Top** view.

3. Freeze the **A-Roof-Slab** and **A-Roof** layers.

This will make it easier to place the members for the pergola.

4. Thaw the **image** layer.

5. Activate the Design Tools palette if it is not available.

To activate, launch from the Home tab on the ribbon.

6. Activate the **Design** palette.
To do this, right click on the palette and select **Design**.

If you do not see the Design palette, check to see which profile you have active. Set the current profile to AutoCAD Architecture (US Imperial).

AutoCAD Architecture (US Imperial)
AutoCAD Architecture (US Imperial) <default>

We will place two columns at the locations indicated.

7. | Column   Select the **Column** tool on the **Design** tool palette.

8.

Set the Style to **4x4**.

Note all the styles you defined are available.

9.

Set the Justify value to **Middle Center**.
Set the Logical Length to **10′ -0″**.

10.

Place two columns at the locations indicated on the floor plan image.

Click **ENTER** to exit the command.

11.

[−][NW Isometric][Hidden]

Switch to a **NW Isometric Hidden** view.

You should see two columns in the porch area.

12. `[-][Top][Hidden]`   Switch back to a **Top** view.

You can use the Zoom Previous tool to return to the previous view.

13. Beam   Select the **Beam** tool from the Designs Palette.

14.

Style	2x4
Bound spaces	By style (No)
Trim automatically	By style (Yes)
On object	Yes
Member type	Beam
Dimensions	
A Start offset	0"
B End offset	0"
C Logical length	1"
E Roll	0.00
Layout type	Fill
Justify	Bottom Center
Justify cross-section	Maximum
Justify components	Highest priority only

Set the Style to **2x4**.

Set Justify to **Bottom Center**.

15.

Select the center of the column as the start point and perpendicular point at the left wall as the end point.

16.

Place a second beam from the center of the left column to the center of the right column.

17.

Place a third beam starting at the node center of the column and perpendicular to the right wall.

18. Right click and select ENTER to exit the command.

19.

Select all three beams.

20.

Location	
Start point X	*VARIES*
Start point Y	62'-11 25/32"
Start point Z	10'-0"
End point X	*VARIES*
End point Y	62'-11 25/32"
End point Z	10'-0"
Rotation	*VARIES*
Elevation	10'-0"

On the Properties palette:

Set the Start point Z to **10′ 0″**.
Set the End point Z to **10′ 0″**.

Note the Elevation updates to 10′ 0″.

Click ESC to release the selection set.

21. [−][NW Isometric][Hidden]   Activate the **NW Isometric Hidden** view.

22.   Inspect the columns and beams.

23. Save as *ex6-3.dwg*.

Notes:

QUIZ 6

True or False

1. Columns, braces, and beams are created using Structural Members.

2. When you isolate a Layer User Group, you are freezing all the layers in that group.

3. You can isolate a Layer User Group in ALL Viewports, a Single Viewport, or a Selection Set of Viewports.

4. When placing beams, you can switch the justification in the middle of the command.

5. Standard AutoCAD commands, like COPY, MOVE, and ARRAY, cannot be used in ACA.

Multiple Choice

6. Before you can place a beam or column, you must:

    A. Generate a Member Style
    B. Activate the Structural Member Catalog
    C. Select a structural member shape
    D. All of the above

7. Select the character that is OK to use when creating a Structural Member Style Name.

    A. -
    B. ?
    C. =
    D. /

8. Identify the tool shown.

    A. Add Brace
    B. Add Beam
    C. Add Column
    D. Structural Member Catalog

9. Setting a Layer Key

    A. Controls which layer AEC objects will be placed on.
    B. Determines the layer names created.
    C. Sets layer properties.
    D. All of the above.

ANSWERS:

1) T; 2) F; 3) T; 4) T; 5) F; 6) D; 7) A; 8) B; 9) A

Lesson 7:
Floors, Ceilings and Spaces

Slabs are used to model floors and other flat surfaces. You start by defining a slab style which includes the components and materials which are used to construct the floor system.

You can create a floor slab by drawing a polyline and applying the style to the polyline or by selecting the slab tool and then drawing the boundary to be used by the slab.

You can define multi-story buildings using the Project Navigator. In the Navigator, you can specify the number of levels for the building.

Ceiling grids can be used to define drop ceilings.

You can also use spaces to define floors and ceilings. You can use the Space/Zone Manager to apply different styles to floors and ceilings.

There are two reasons why you want to include floors and ceilings in your building model. 1) for your construction documentation and 2) for any renderings.

Exercise 7-1:

Creating Slab Styles

Drawing Name: slab_styles.dwg
Estimated Time: 30 minutes

This exercise reinforces the following skills:

- ❑ Creating Styles
- ❑ Copying Styles
- ❑ Renaming Styles
- ❑ Use of Materials

1. 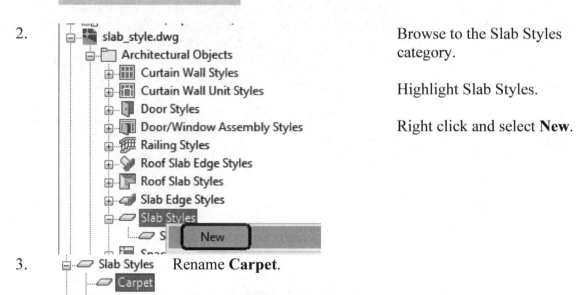   Activate the Manage tab on the ribbon.

    Select **Style Manager**.

2. Browse to the Slab Styles category.

    Highlight Slab Styles.

    Right click and select **New**.

3. Slab Styles   Rename **Carpet**.

4. Create three components:

Index	Name	Thickness	Thickness Offset
1	carpet	1/8"	1/4"
2	plywood	1/4"	0"
3	concrete slab	2"	-2"

    Set the carpet at 1/8" and ¼" Thickness Offset.
    Set the plywood at ¼" and 0" Thickness Offset.
    Set the concrete slab at 2" and -2" Thickness Offset.

5. Use the preview window to verify that the thicknesses and offsets are correct.

6.

Create new materials for each of the components.

I have pre-loaded several materials in the exercise files. Some of the materials use image files that are part of the exercise files.

Component	Material Definition
carpet	carpet
plywood	plywood sheathing
concrete slab	concrete - gray- in-place
Shrink Wrap Body	Standard

7.

Edit the carpet material definition to use the **Berber – Pattern 2** render material.

8.

Edit the plywood material definition to use the **Wood Plywood** render material.

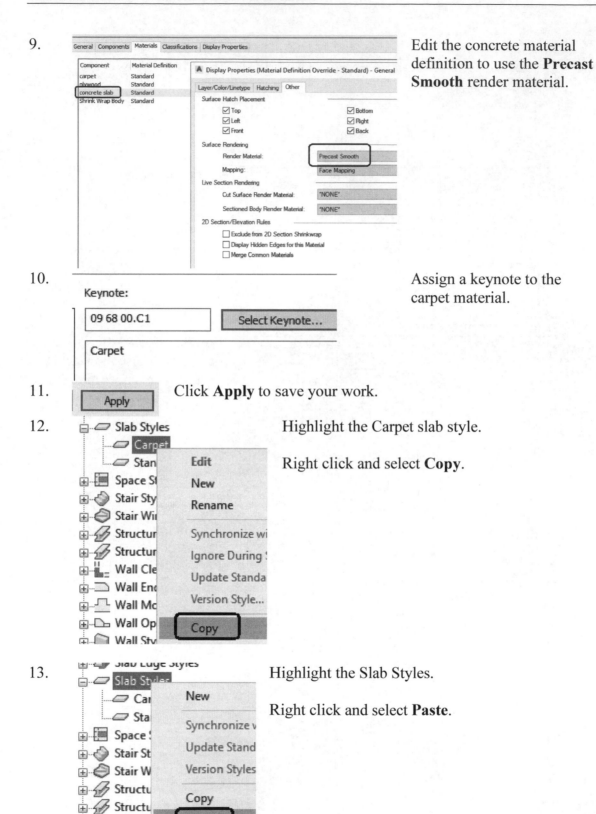

9.   Edit the concrete material definition to use the **Precast Smooth** render material.

10.   Assign a keynote to the carpet material.

11.   Click **Apply** to save your work.

12.   Highlight the Carpet slab style.

Right click and select **Copy**.

13.   Highlight the Slab Styles.

Right click and select **Paste**.

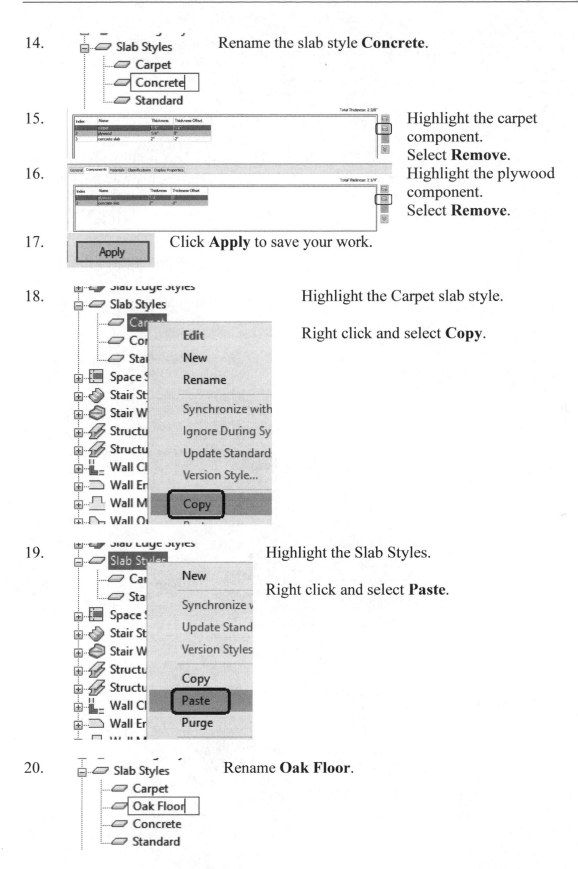

14. Rename the slab style **Concrete**.

15. Highlight the carpet component.
Select **Remove**.

16. Highlight the plywood component.
Select **Remove**.

17. Click **Apply** to save your work.

18. Highlight the Carpet slab style.

Right click and select **Copy**.

19. Highlight the Slab Styles.

Right click and select **Paste**.

20. Rename **Oak Floor**.

21. Change the name of the carpet component to **oak flooring.**

22. Verify that the carpet component is still the top component for the carpet slab style.

23. Verify that the oak flooring component is the top component for the oak floor slab style.

24. Switch to the Materials tab for the oak floor.

    Highlight the oak flooring. Select **Edit Material**. Assign **White Oak** as the Render Material.

25.

26. Click **Apply** to save your work.

27. Highlight the Slab Styles category. Right click and select **New**.

28. Rename **Stucco Ceiling**.

29.

Index	Name	Thickness	Thickness Offset
1	Stucco	1/8"	-1/8"

Make the first component Stucco 1/8" thick with a Thickness Offset of -1/8".

30.

Index	Name	Thickness	Thickness Offset
1	Stucco	1/8"	-1/8"
2	plywood sheathing	1/8"	1/8"

Add a component.
Name it plywood sheathing 1/8" thick with a Thickness Offset of 0".

31.

Index	Name	Thickness	Thickness Offset
1	Stucco	1/8"	-1/8"
2	plywood sheathing	1/8"	0"
3	wood joists	2"	1/8"

Add a component.
Name it wood joists 2" thick with a Thickness Offset of 1/8".

32.

Component	Material Definition
Stucco	stucco
plywood sheathing	plywood sheathing
wood joists	wood joist
Shrink Wrap Body	Standard

Switch to the Materials tab.

Create new materials for the components:

- Stucco
- Plywood sheathing
- Wood joist

33.

Highlight the stucco component.

Set the Render Material to **Plaster – Venetian Smooth**.

34.

Display Co...	Pattern	Scale/...	Angle	Orient...	X Offset
Plan Hatch	user single	3"	45.00	global	0"
Surface Hatch	user single	3"	0.00	object	0"
Section Hatch	user single	3"	45.00	object	0"

Hatch Pattern

Pattern

Type: Predefined

Pattern Name: PLAST

Set the Hatching to **PLAST**.

35.

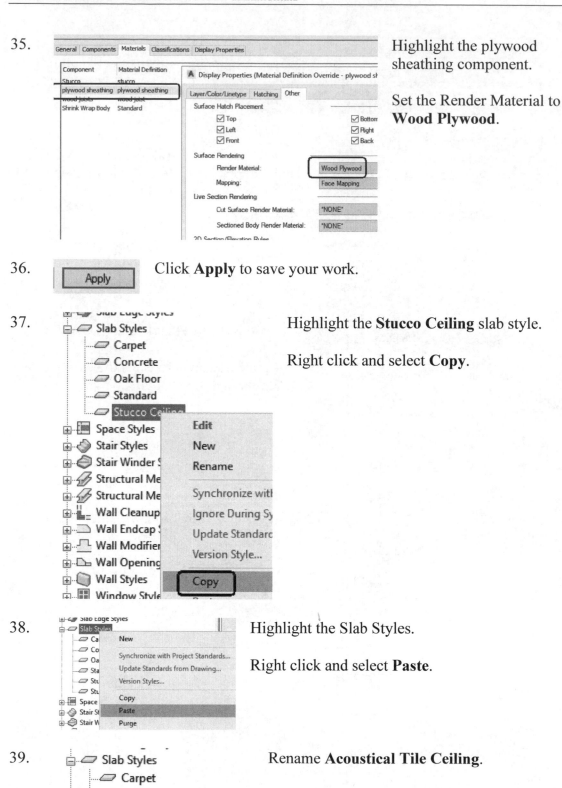

Highlight the plywood sheathing component.

Set the Render Material to **Wood Plywood**.

36. Click **Apply** to save your work.

37. Highlight the **Stucco Ceiling** slab style.

Right click and select **Copy**.

38. Highlight the Slab Styles.

Right click and select **Paste**.

39. Rename **Acoustical Tile Ceiling**.

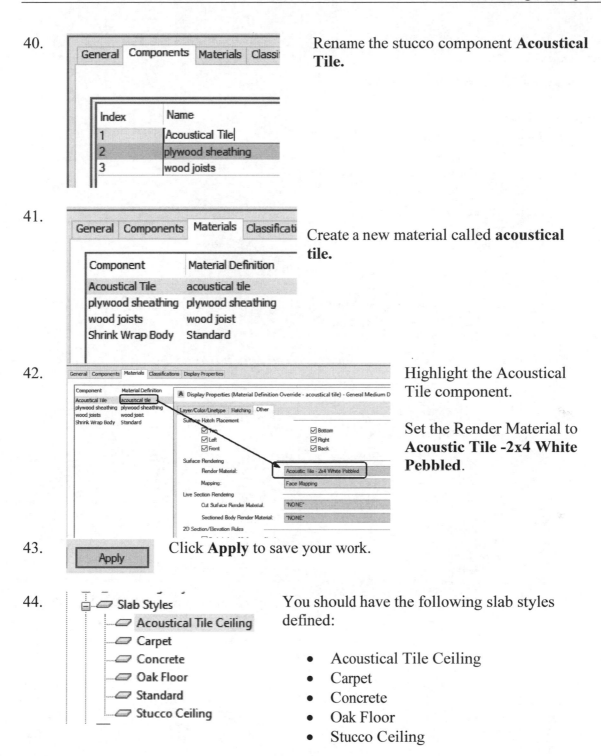

40.   Rename the stucco component **Acoustical Tile.**

41.   Create a new material called **acoustical tile.**

42.   Highlight the Acoustical Tile component.

Set the Render Material to **Acoustic Tile -2x4 White Pebbled**.

43.   Click **Apply** to save your work.

44.   You should have the following slab styles defined:

- Acoustical Tile Ceiling
- Carpet
- Concrete
- Oak Floor
- Stucco Ceiling

Click **OK** to close the dialog.

Exercise 7-2:

Create Slab from Linework

Drawing Name: create_slab1.dwg
Estimated Time: 5 minutes

This exercise reinforces the following skills:

- ❑ Creating Slabs
- ❑ Polylines

1. Switch to a Top View.

   Zoom into the patio area where the columns are located.

   There is a red polyline to be used for the slab outline.

2. Launch the **Design Tools**.

3. Locate the Slab tool.

   Right click and select **Apply Tool Properties to →Linework and Walls.**

4. Select the red polyline.

   Click **ENTER**.

5. Select **Yes**.

   `⧉▾ SLABTOOLTOLINEWORK Erase layout geometry? [Yes No] <No>:`

6. Select **Direct**.

   `⧉▾ SLABTOOLTOLINEWORK Creation mode [Direct Projected] <Projected>:`

7. Set the Justification to **Top**.

   `SLABTOOLTOLINEWORK Specify slab justification [Top Center Bottom Slopeline] <Bottom>:`

8.

Select the midpoint of the top of the boundary as the pivot point for the slab.

The slab will be horizontal, so it doesn't really need a pivot point.

9.

Set the slab style to **Concrete**.

Note that the slope is set to 0.0.

	Browse...
Style	Concrete
Bound spaces	By style (Yes)
Shadow display	Casts and receives shadows
Dimensions	
Thickness	2"
Vertical offset	0"
Horizontal offset	0"
	Edges
Slope	
Rise	0"
Run	1'-0"
Slope	0.00
Hold fascia ele...	No
Pivot Point X	52'-1 31/32"
Pivot Point Y	62'-11 25/32"
Pivot Point Z	10'-0"

10.

Set the Elevation to **0"**.

Location	
Elevation	0"

11.

Switch to an isometric view to inspect your slab floor.

Set the view style to **Realistic.**

Save as *ex7-2.dwg.*

Exercise 7-3:
Create Slab from Boundary

Drawing Name: create_slab2.dwg
Estimated Time: 5 minutes

This exercise reinforces the following skills:

    ❑   Create Slab

1. Zoom into the bedroom located in the lower left of the floor plan.

2. Select the **Slab** tool from the Home tab on the ribbon.

   We will add a carpet slab to this room.

3. Set the Style to **Carpet**.

4. *You are going to trace the boundary for the floor to be placed.*

   Start at the upper left corner of the room.

5.

Trace around the room.

At the last segment, right click and select **Close**.

Click ENTER when the boundary is completed.

6.

If you hover over the boundary, you will see that you placed a slab using the Carpet style.

7.

Switch to an isometric view and inspect the floor you just placed in the bedroom area.

Save as *ex7-3.dwg*.

Exercise 7-4:
Create Ceiling Grid

Drawing Name: ceiling_grid.dwg
Estimated Time: 15 minutes

This exercise reinforces the following skills:

- ❑ Ceiling Grid
- ❑ Properties
- ❑ Set Boundary

1. Set the view to **Top Realistic**.

2. Select **Ceiling Grid**.

3. Select the inside corner of the bedroom.

   Click **ENTER** to accept the default rotation of 0.00.

   Click **ESC** to exit the command.

4. 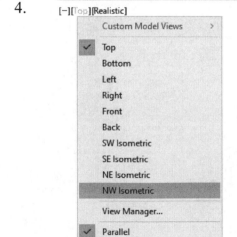 Switch to a **NW Isometric** view.

5.

The ceiling grid was placed at the 0 elevation.

Select the ceiling grid.

6.

Right click and select **Properties.**

Repeat '-VIEW	
Recent Input	
Isolate Objects	
Basic Modify Tools	
Clipboard	
Paste From Content Browser	
AEC Modify Tools	
X Axis	
Y Axis	
Clip	
Resize	
Add Selected	
AEC Dimension	
Select Component	
Edit Object Display...	
Object Viewer...	
Select Similar	
Count	
Deselect All	
Properties	

36'-2 31/32", 4.79675

7.

Change the Elevation to **8' 0"**.

Location	
Rotation	0.00
Elevation	8'-0"

The ceiling grid position will adjust.

8. [–][Top][Realistic]

Switch back to a Top view.

9.

Select the **Rectangle** tool from the Draw panel on the Home tab.

Line

Draw

10.

Place a rectangle in the bedroom.

11.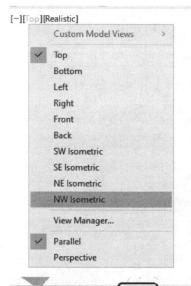

Select the rectangle.

Set the Global Width to ¼"

This just makes it a little easier to see.

Click **ESC** to release the selection.

12.

Switch to a **NW Isometric** view.

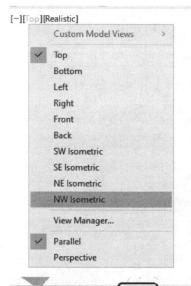

13. Enable **Lineweight**.
Enable **Selection Cycling**.

14. Select the ceiling grid.

15. Select **Set Boundary** from the Clipping panel.

Note: You won't see this tool unless the ceiling grid is selected.

16. Click near the bottom edge of a wall.

The Selection Cycling dialog should list the polyline that is the rectangle.

Click on the Polyline in the list to select.

17.

The ceiling grid boundary is modified to the room.

Click ESC to exit the command.

18.   [−][Top][Realistic]   Switch back to a Top view.

19.

The ceiling grid is visible because Lineweight is enabled.

Save as *ex7-4.dwg*.

Exercise 7-5:

Add Lights to Ceiling Grid

Drawing Name: add_ceiling_light.dwg
Estimated Time: 10 minutes

This exercise reinforces the following skills:

- ❑ Reflected Ceiling Plan Display
- ❑ Viewports
- ❑ Design Center

1. 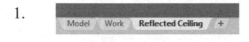   Switch to the Layout tab named **Reflected Ceiling.**

2.   Click inside the viewport to activate Model space.

3. 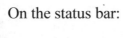   On the status bar:

    Notice that the Display Configuration is set to **Reflected.**

4.   Launch the Design Center.

    Switch to the **AEC Content** tab.

    Browse to *Imperial/Design/Electrical/Lighting/Fluorescent.*

5. Locate the **2x2** lighting.

6. Select and right click.

Select **Insert**.

7. Select the cciling grid when prompted to select the layout node.

Then select the grid intersection to use to place the lighting fixture.

8. Move the cursor over and select another location for the lighting fixture.

9. Place four lighting fixtures.

10. Switch back to the Model tab.

11.

The lighting fixtures are displayed in the ceiling grid.

Save as *ex7-5.dwg*.

Exercise 7-6:
Add a Space

Drawing Name: space.dwg
Estimated Time: 5 minutes

This exercise reinforces the following skills:

❑   Space

1.   Select the **Space** tool from the Build panel on the Home tab.

2.   SPACEADD Start corner or [Name STyle Create type Height]:   Click on **Height**.

3.   SPACEADD Ceiling Height <8'-0">: 8'-2"   Set the Ceiling Height to **8'-2"**.

4.   Draw a rectangle in the top bedroom by selecting the opposing corners.

5.

Switch to an isometric view so you can see the space.

6.   Rotate the view so you can see the underside of the space and the model.

    Save as *ex7-6.dwg*.

Exercise 7-7:
Add a Ceiling and Floor to a Space

Drawing Name: ceiling_space.dwg
Estimated Time: 10 minutes

This exercise reinforces the following skills:

- ❑ Add Slab
- ❑ Slab Styles
- ❑ Properties

1. –][SW Isometric][Hidden]   Switch to a SW Isometric view.

2.   Launch the **Design Tools**.

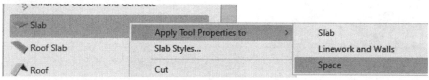

3. Locate the Slab tool.
    Right click and select **Apply Tool Properties to→ Space.**

4. Select the space that is located in the upper bedroom.

Click **ENTER** to complete selection.

5. Enable **Convert Ceiling to Slab**.
Enable **Convert Floor to Slab**.

☑ Convert Ceiling to Slab

☑ Convert Floor to Slab

☑ Apply Interferences to Slab

☐ Erase Layout Geometry

OK   Cancel

Click **OK**.

6. *The two slabs appear.*

Click **ESC** to release the selection.

7. Select the ceiling slab.

8. Set the Style to **Stucco Ceiling**.

Browse	
Style	�.☐ Stucco Ceiling
Bound spaces	By style (Yes)
Shadow display	Casts and receives shadows

Click **ESC** to release the selection.

9.

Orbit the view so you can select the floor slab.

10.

Set the Style to **Oak Floor**.

Click **ESC** to release the selection.

11.

Save as *ex7-7.dwg*.

Exercise 7-8:
Add a Lighting Fixture to a Ceiling

Drawing Name: lighting fixture.dwg
Estimated Time: 5 minutes

This exercise reinforces the following skills:

- Inserting Blocks
- Properties

1. [–][Top][Realistic]   Set the view to **Top Realistic**.

2.

Switch to the Insert tab on the ribbon.

Select **Insert →Blocks from Libraries**.

3.

Select **Browse Block Libraries** from the drop down list.

4.

Locate the *ceiling_fan.dwg* file located in the downloaded exercises.

Click **Open**.

5.

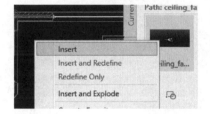

Highlight the file.

Right click and select **Insert**.

6.

Place above the bed in the master bedroom.

7.

Select the fan and set the Position Z to **7'-4"**.

It took me some trial and error to figure out the correct Z value to place the fan.

8.

Switch to an isometric 2D Wireframe view to inspect the placement of the ceiling fan.

Save as *ex7-8.dwg*.

Exercise 7-9:
Creating a Multi-Level Building

Drawing Name: multi-level.dwg
Estimated Time: 15 minutes

This exercise reinforces the following skills:

- ❑ Array
- ❑ Slabs

1.

Set the view to **SW Isometric Realistic**.

[−][SW Isometric][2D Wireframe]

2.

There is already a concrete slab placed on the first level.

Hover your mouse to locate the slab and select.

3.

Right click and select **Basic Modify Tools→Array.**

4. ARRAY Enter array type [Rectangular PAth POlar] <Rectangular>:

Select **Rectangular**.

5.

Set the Columns to **1**.
Set the Rows to **1**.
Set the Levels to **3**.
Set the spacing between Levels to **3000.**

Disable **Associative.**

AEC elements cannot be used in an associative array.

Check the Preview to see the slabs that are placed.

Green check to accept the preview.

6.

Thaw the Linework layer.

7.

If you zoom into the front corner of the building you should be able to locate a polyline that was used to place the floor slab.

We will use this polyline to create a ceiling slab.

8.

Launch the Design Tools.

Locate the Slab tool on the Design tab.

Select **Slab→Apply Tool Properties to →Linework and Walls.**

9.

Select the Polyline.

Hint: Use the Selection Cycling tool to help you select the correct element.

Click ENTER to complete the selection.

When prompted to erase layout geometry, click No.

10. Accept the Bottom default.

11. Select a point to use as the pivot edge.

This is really irrelevant since our ceiling won't have a slope.

12. Set the Style to **Acoustical Tile Ceiling.**

13. Set the Elevation to **2500**.

This allows about 400 mm space between floors and ceilings for HVAC, electrical and plumbing elements.

14. Right click and select **Basic Modify Tools→Array.**

15. Select **Rectangular**.

16.

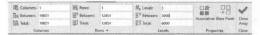

Set the Columns to **1**.
Set the Rows to **1**.
Set the Levels to **3**.
Set the spacing between Levels to **3000.**

Disable **Associative.**

AEC elements cannot be used in an associative array.

Check the Preview to see the slabs that are placed.

Green check to accept the preview.

17.

Save as *ex7-9.dwg*.

Exercise 7-10:
Placing a Stair

Drawing Name: stair.dwg
Estimated Time: 10 minutes

This exercise reinforces the following skills:

- ❑   Stair

1.

Set the view to **Top 2D Wireframe**.

[−][Top][2D Wireframe]

2.

Select the **Stair** tool on the Home tab.

3.

Dimensions	
A Width	1000
B Height	3000
Justify	□ Left
Terminate with	Riser
Flight length	Distance
Calculation rules	⊞ Tread

Set Justify to **Left**.

4.

Select the endpoint of the construction line located between Grids 1 and 2 as the start point.

Draw to the right.

5.

When all the risers are shown, click to end the stair run.

Click ENTER to exit the command.

6.

Switch to a 3D view to inspect your stairs.

Switch to a front view.

7.

If you zoom in, you can see the stairs do not quite meet the floor slab for the second level.

8. Use DIST to measure the distance between the top of the stair and the top of the floor slab.

I got a value for Delta Z of 100 mm.

9. Select the stair.
Right click and select **Properties**.

Adjust the Height to **3100**.

10. Click ESC to release the stair selection.

Verify that the top of the stair meets the top of the floor slab.

11. Save as *ex7-10.dwg*.

Exercise 7-11:
Placing a Railing

Drawing Name: stair_railing.dwg
Estimated Time: 5 minutes

This exercise reinforces the following skills:

❑   railing

1. Set the view to **Top 2D Wireframe**.

[−][Top][2D Wireframe]

2. Select the **Railing** tool.

3. Click **Attach**.

4.

Click **Stair**.

5.

Select the lower side of the stair to place the railing on the lower side.

The upper side is next to the wall.

Click **ENTER** to complete the stair command.

6.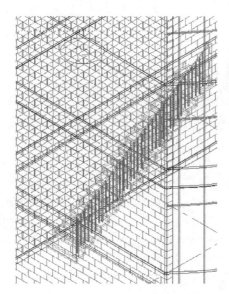

Set the view to **SW Isometric Realistic**.

[−][SW Isometric][2D Wireframe]

Inspect the railing placed on the stair.

7. Save as *ex7-11.dwg*.

Exercise 7-12:
Placing a Stair Tower

Drawing Name: stair_tower.dwg
Estimated Time: 30 minutes

This exercise reinforces the following skills:

- ❑ Array
- ❑ Cut Hole in Slab

1. 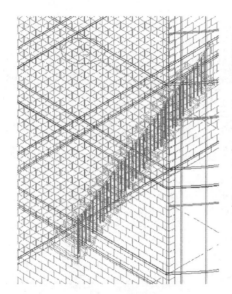 Set the view to **SW Isometric 2D Wireframe**.

   | [−][SW Isometric][2D Wireframe]

   The Stair Tower tool requires that you place the stairs in a separate file and attach it to your floor plan as an external reference using a Construct. I have heard all sorts of issues using this method from the stairs not attaching properly to losing the reference, so this is not my best practice. Sometimes the simplest answer is the best one.

2. 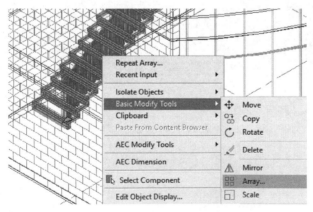 Select the **stairs** and **railing.**

   Right click and select **Basic Modify Tools→Array.**

3.

Select the floor slab and the railing.

Click ENTER to complete the selection.

4.

ARRAY Enter array type [Rectangular PAth POlar] <Rectangular>:

Select **Rectangular**.

5.

Set the Columns to **1**.
Set the Rows to **1**.
Set the Levels to **2**.
Set the spacing between Levels to **3100**.

Disable **Associative.**

AEC elements cannot be used in an associative array.

Check the Preview to see the slabs that are placed.

Green check to accept the preview.

6. [−][Top][2D Wireframe]   Switch to a Top view.

7.

Thaw the Linework layer and set it current.

Unsaved Layer State

Linework

8. Draw a rectangle to indicate the stairwell.

9. [−][SW Isometric][2D Wireframe] Switch back to a **SW Isometric** view.

10. Select the middle ceiling and floor slabs.

These are the slabs that require a hole to define a stairwell.

You can only add a hole to one slab at a time.

11. Select **Hole→Add** from the ribbon.

12. Select the level 1 ceiling slab.

You will be prompted to select a polyline or connected solid.

▾ SLABADDHOLE Select closed polylines

Select the rectangle.
Click ENTER.

13. Click **No**.

▾ SLABADDHOLE Erase layout geometry? [Yes No] <No>:

14.

The hole is added to the level 1 ceiling.

15.

Select the level 2 floor slab.

Select **Hole→Add** from the ribbon.

16.

Select the level 2 floor slab.

You will be prompted to select a polyline or connected solid.

▾ **SLABADDHOLE** Select closed polylines

Select the rectangle.
Click ENTER.

17.

▾ **SLABADDHOLE** Erase layout geometry? [Yes No] <No>:

Click **No**.

18.

You can see the added hole for the stairwell.

19.

Select the level 2 ceiling slab.

Select **Hole→Add** from the ribbon.

20.

You will be prompted to select a polyline or connected solid.

▼ **SLABADDHOLE** Select closed polylines

Select the rectangle.
Click ENTER.

21. ▼ SLABADDHOLE Erase layout geometry? [Yes No] <No>:

Click **No**.

22.

You can see the added hole for the stairwell.

23.

Select the Level 2 floor slab.

24.

Select **Hole→Add** from the ribbon.

25.

You will be prompted to select a polyline or connected solid.

▼ **SLABADDHOLE** Select closed polylines

Select the rectangle.
Click ENTER.

26. ▼ SLABADDHOLE Erase layout geometry? [Yes No] <No>:

Click **No**.

27. You can see the added hole for the stairwell.

28. Save as *ex7-12.dwg*.

Notes:

QUIZ 7

True or False

1. You can create a floor or ceiling slab by converting a space.

2. Once you place a ceiling grid, it can't be modified.

3. When you place a lighting fixture on a ceiling grid, you cannot snap to the grid.

4. Railings are automatically placed on both sides of a selected stair.

5. You can assign materials to different components of a railing.

Multiple Choice

6. Slabs can be used to model: (select all that apply)

    A. Roofs
    B. Floors
    C. Ceilings
    D. Walls

7. Ceiling grids can be created using: (select all that apply)

    A. Linework
    B. Walls
    C. Roof Slabs
    D. Arcs

8. Space Styles: (select all that apply)

    A. Control the hatching displayed
    B. Control the name displayed when spaces are tagged
    C. Cannot be modified
    D. Have materials assigned

9. Railings can have the following: (select all that apply)

    A. Guardrails.
    B. Handrails.
    C. Posts.
    D. Balusters.

10. The first point selected when placing a set of stairs is:

    A. The foot/bottom of the stairs
    B. The head/top of the stairs
    C. The center point of the stairs
    D. Depends on the property settings

ANSWERS:

1) T; 2) F; 3) F; 4) F; 5) T; 6) D; 7) A, B, C; 8) A, B; 9) A, B, C, D; 10) A

Lesson 8:
Rendering & Materials

AutoCAD Architecture divides materials into TWO locations:

- Materials in Active Drawing
- Autodesk Library

You can also create one or more custom libraries for materials you want to use in more than one project. You can only edit materials in the drawing or in the custom library—Autodesk Materials are read-only.

Materials have two asset definitions—Appearance and Information. Materials do not have to be fully defined to be used. Each asset contributes to the definition of a single material.

You can define Appearance independently without assigning/associating it to a material. You can assign the same assets to different materials. Assets can be deleted from a material in a drawing or in a user library, but you cannot remove or delete assets from materials in locked material libraries, such as the Autodesk Materials library or any locked user library. You can delete assets from a user library – BUT be careful because that asset might be used somewhere!

You can only duplicate, replace or delete an asset if it is in the drawing or in a user library. The Autodesk Asset Library is "read-only" and can only be used to check-out or create materials.

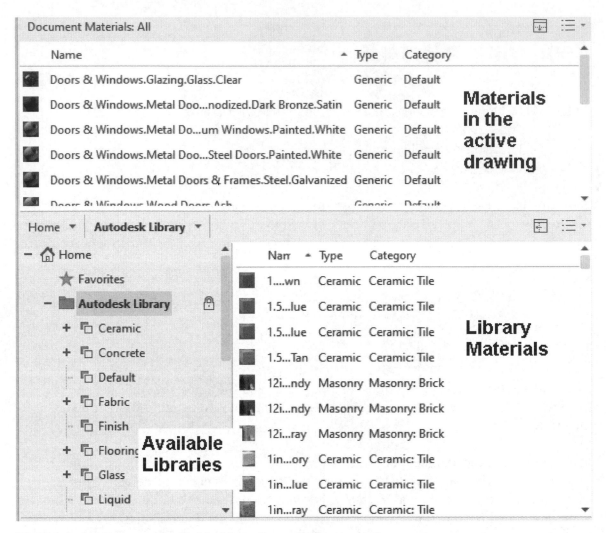

The Material Browser is divided into three distinct panels.
The Document Materials panel lists all the materials available in the drawing.
The Material Libraries list any libraries available.
The Library Materials lists the materials in the material libraries.

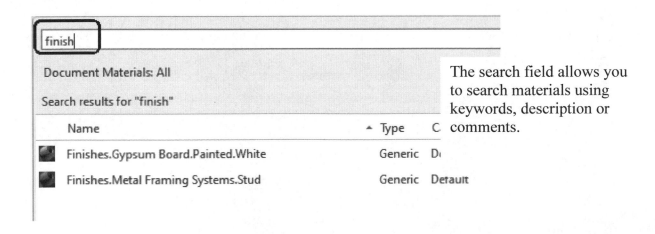

The search field allows you to search materials using keywords, description or comments.

The View control button allows you to control how materials are sorted and displayed in the Material Libraries panel.

Material Editor

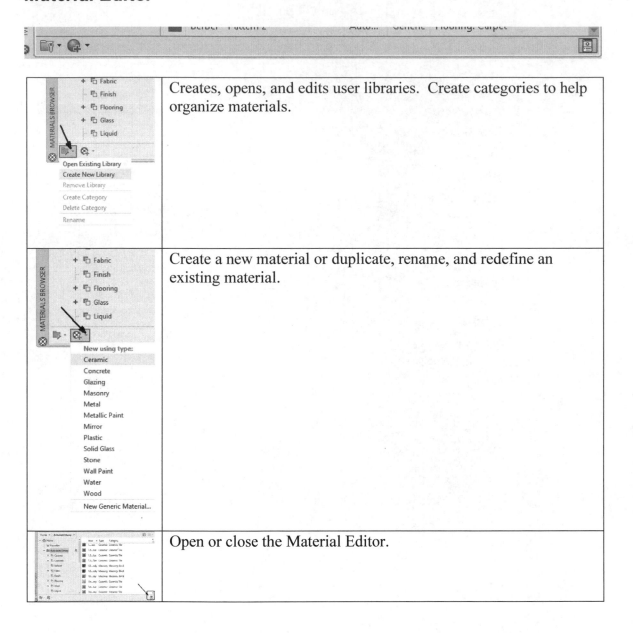

	Creates, opens, and edits user libraries. Create categories to help organize materials.
	Create a new material or duplicate, rename, and redefine an existing material.
	Open or close the Material Editor.

Exercise 8-1:
Modifying the Material Browser Interface

Drawing Name: material_browser.dwg
Estimated Time: 10 minutes

This exercise reinforces the following skills:

❑   Navigating the Material Browser and Material Editor

1.
Activate the **Render** tab on the ribbon.

Select the small arrow in the lower right corner of the materials panel.

This launches the Material Editor.

2.
Launch the Material Browser by selecting the button on the bottom of the Material Editor dialog.

3.

Make the Materials Browser appear as shown.

4.

Change the top pane to use a Text view.

5.

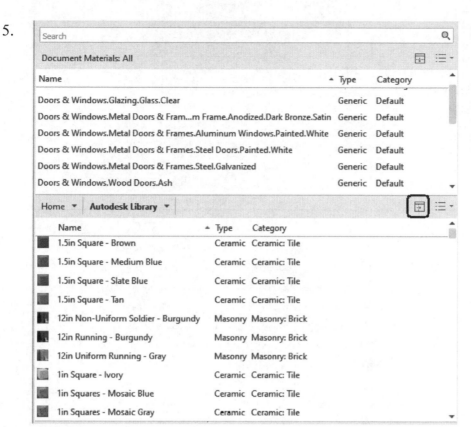

Toggle the Materials Library list OFF by selecting the top button on the Documents pane.

6.

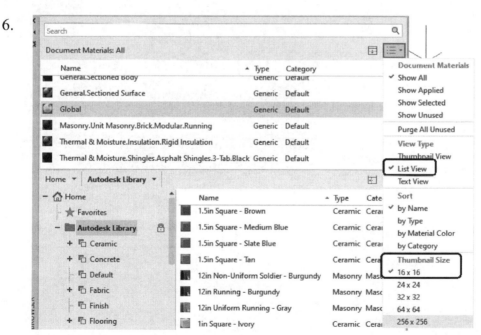

Change the upper pane to a **List View**.
Set the Thumbnail size to **16x16.**

7.

Toggle the Library tree back on.

8.

Document Materials
- ✓ Show All
- Show Applied
- Show Selected
- **Show Unused**
- Purge All Unused

In the Document Materials panel, set the view to **Show Unused**.

Scroll through the list to see what materials are not being used in your drawing.

9.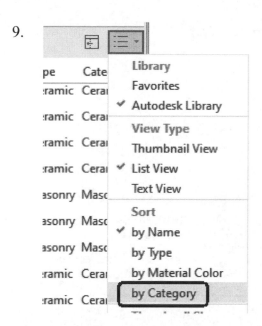

In the Material Library pane, change the view to sort **by Category**.

10. Close the Material dialogs.

11. Save as *ex8-1.dwg*.

The Appearance Tab

Appearance controls how material is displayed in a rendered view, Realistic view, or Ray Trace view.

A zero next to the hand means that only the active/ selected material uses the appearance definition.

Different material types can have different appearance parameters.

The Information Tab

The value in the Description field can be used in Material tags.

Using comments and keywords can be helpful for searches.

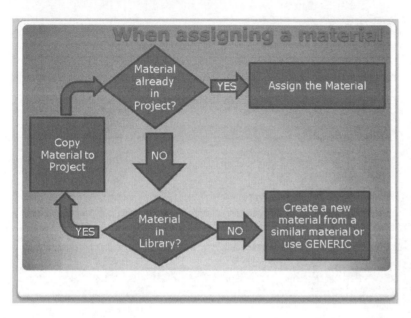

Use this flow chart as a guide to help you decide whether or not you need to create a new material in your project.

Exercise 8-2:

Copy a Material from a Library to a Drawing

Drawing Name: copy_materials.dwg
Estimated Time: 10 minutes

In order to use or assign a material, it must exist in the drawing. You can search for a material and, if one exists in the Autodesk Library, copy it to your active drawing.

This exercise reinforces the following skills:

❑ Copying materials from the Autodesk Materials Library
❑ Modifying materials in the drawing

1. Go to the **Render** tab on the ribbon.

2.   Select the **Materials Browser** tool.

3. 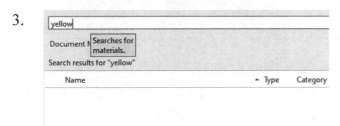   Type **yellow** in the search field.

    There are no yellow materials in the drawing.

4.

    Highlight **Wall Paint** under Autodesk Library.

    There are three yellow wall paints.

    Locate the **Yellow Matte Wall Paint**.

5. 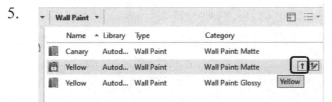   Select the up arrow to copy the material up to the drawing.

The yellow paint material is now listed in the Document Materials.

6. Type **blue** in the search field.

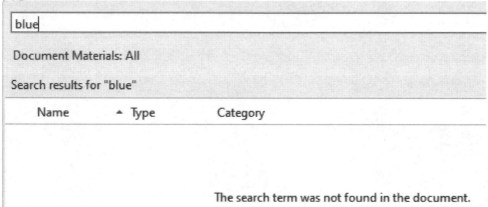

7. There are no blue materials in the drawing, but the Autodesk Library has several different blue materials available.

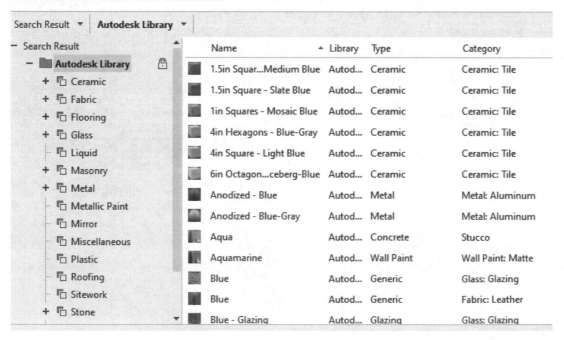

8. Highlight the Wall Paint category in the Library pane.

This confines the search to blue wall paints.

9. 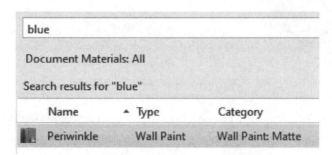 Locate the **Periwinkle Matte** Wall Paint and then copy it over to the drawing.

Notice the lock symbol next to the material name. Materials in the library cannot be modified. However, once you import a material into your document, it can be edited.

The blue wall paint is now available in the drawing.

blue		
Document Materials: All		
Search results for "blue"		
Name ▲	Type	Category
Periwinkle	Wall Paint	Wall Paint: Matte

10. Close the Materials dialog.

11. Save as *ex8-2.dwg*.

You have added material definitions to the active drawing ONLY.

Exercise 8-3:
Adding Color to Walls

Drawing Name: add_color.dwg
Estimated Time: 5 minutes

This exercise reinforces the following skills:

- ❑ Edit External Reference
- ❑ Materials
- ❑ Colors
- ❑ Display Manager
- ❑ Style Manager

1.   Open *add_color.dwg*.

2. Switch to a **SE Isometric** view.

3. Set the layer state to **roof & roof slabs frozen**.

4. Zoom into the kitchen area. We are going to apply a different color to the kitchen wall.

   Select the wall indicated.

5. Right click and select **Edit Wall Style**.

   Notice that there are two GWB components.
   One GWB is for one side of the wall and one is for the other.

6. Rename them **GWB-Yellow** and **GWB-Blue**.

Index	Name	Priority	V
1	GWB-Yellow	1210	5
2	GWB	1200	5
3	Stud	500	4
4	GWB	1200	5
5	GWB-Blue	1210	5

   To rename, just left click in the column and edit the text.

7. Activate the Materials tab.

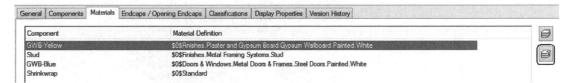

Highlight the **GWB-Yellow** component.
Select the **New** button.

8.

Type **Finishes.Wall Paint.Yellow.**

Click **OK**.

9.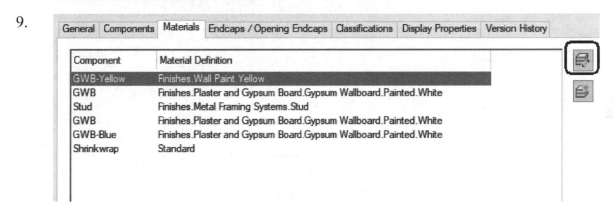

Highlight the **GWB-Yellow** component.
Select the **Edit** button.

10.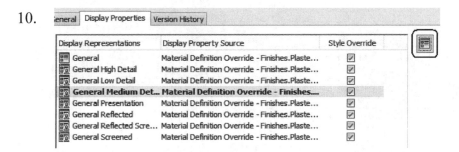

Activate the **Display Properties** tab.
Select the **Edit Display Properties** button.

11.

Activate the **Layer/Color/Linetype** tab.

Highlight **3D Body**.

Left pick on the color square.

12.

Select the color **yellow**.

Click **OK**.

13. Select the **Other** tab.

14. Select **Yellow** in the drop-down list next to Render Material under Surface Rendering.

Note that the materials are in alphabetic order.

15. Click **OK**.

16. Verify that there is a check in the Style Override box.

Click **OK** again.

17.

Highlight the **GWB-Blue** component.
Select the **New** button.

18.

New Name: | Finishes.Wall Paint.Periwinkle
OK   Cancel

Type **Finishes.Wall Paint.Periwinkle**.

Click **OK**.

19.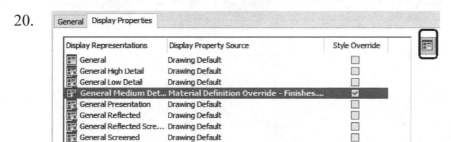

Component	Material Definition
GWB-Yellow	Finishes.Wall Paint.Yellow
GWB	Finishes.Plaster and Gypsum Board.Gypsum Wallboard.Painted.White
Stud	Finishes.Metal Framing Systems.Stud
GWB	Finishes.Plaster and Gypsum Board.Gypsum Wallboard.Painted.White
GWB-Blue	Finishes.Wall Paint.Periwinkle
Shrinkwrap	Standard

Highlight the **GWB-Blue** component.
Select the **Edit** button.

20.

Display Representations	Display Property Source	Style Override
General	Drawing Default	☐
General High Detail	Drawing Default	☐
General Low Detail	Drawing Default	☐
General Medium Det...	Material Definition Override - Finishes....	☑
General Presentation	Drawing Default	☐
General Reflected	Drawing Default	☐
General Reflected Scre...	Drawing Default	☐
General Screened	Drawing Default	☐

Activate the **Display Properties** tab.
Select the **Edit Display Properties** button.

21.

Display Co...	Visible	Layer Key	Layer Overri...	Layer	Color	Linetype	L
Plan Linework				0	BYBLOCK	ByBlock	B
2D Section/Eleva				0	BYBLOCK	ByBlock	B
3D Body				0	BYBLOCK	ByBlock	B
Plan Hatch				0	BYBLOCK	ByBlock	B
Surface Hatch				0	BYBLOCK	ByBlock	B
Section Hatch				0	BYBLOCK	ByBlock	B
Sectioned Boun				0	red	ByBlock	B
Sectioned Body				0	9	ByBlock	B

Activate the **Layer/Color/Linetype** tab.

Highlight **3D Body**.

Left pick on the color square.

22.

ByLayer   ByBlock

Color:
blue

Select the color **blue**.

Click **OK**.

23.

Surface Hatch Placement
☑ Top   ☑ Bottom
☑ Left   ☑ Right
☑ Front   ☑ Back

Surface Rendering
Render Material: Periwinkle
Mapping: Face Mapping

Select the **Other** tab.

Use the drop down list to select the color Periwinkle.

Click **OK**.

24.

Verify that there is a check next to the Style Override.

Click **OK**.

25.

Your components should show two different material definitions for the GWB components.

Click **OK**.

26.

On the View tab on the ribbon, change the display to **Shaded**.

27. Inspect the walls.

Notice that all walls using the wall style have blue on one side and yellow on the other.

In order to apply different colors to different walls, you would have to create a wall style for each color assignment.

28.

To flip the color so walls are yellow/blue, simply use the direction arrows.

29. Save as *ex8-3.dwg*.

Exercise 8-4:

Reference Manager

Drawing Name: ref_manager.dwg
Estimated Time: 5 minutes

This exercise reinforces the following skills:

 ❑ Reference Manager

1. Open *ref_manager.dwg.*

   ref_manager is a host drawing where you placed furniture and used the building model as an external reference.

2. Activate the **Insert** tab on the ribbon.

  Launch the Reference Manager by selecting the small arrow in the right corner of the Reference panel.

3. Highlight the *residence.dwg* file.

  In the bottom pane, locate the Saved Path field.

4.

Highlight the xref drawing.
Use the drop-down to select **Select New Path**.

5.

File name:	new_residence.dwg
Files of type:	Drawing (*.dwg)

Locate and select *new_residence.dwg*.
Click **Open**.

6.

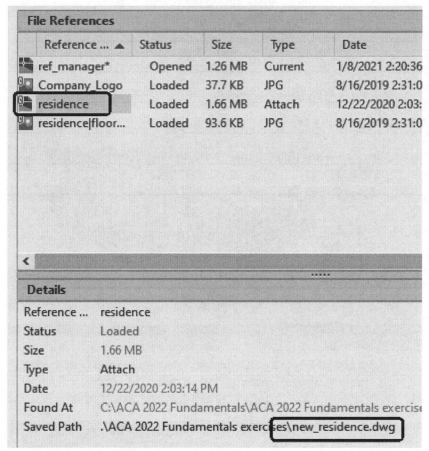

This changes the Saved Path to *new_residence.dwg*.

This updates the external reference and replaces ex3-8 with new_residence.

7.   Select the **Refresh** button.

The file updates. Notice the structural members that were added in the previous lesson. The colors on the interior walls should also display properly in Shaded display mode.

8.   Save the file as *ex8-4.dwg*.

Exercise 8-5:

Camera View

Drawing Name: camera.dwg
Estimated Time: 20 minutes

This exercise reinforces the following skills:

- ❑   Camera
- ❑   Display Settings
- ❑   Navigation Wheel
- ❑   Saved Views
- ❑   Adjust Camera

1.   Open *camera.dwg*.

2. Use the View Cube to orient the floor plan to a Top View with North in correct position. *You can also use the right click menu on the upper left of the display window.*

3. Activate the Render tab on the ribbon.

On the Camera panel,

select **Create Camera**.

4. Place the Camera so it is in the dining area and looking toward the kitchen.

Click ENTER.
Select the camera so it highlights.

5. A Camera Preview window will open.

If you don't see the Camera Preview window, left click on the camera and the window should open.

Set the Visual Style to **Shaded with Edges**.

6.

Camera	
Name	Camera1
Camera X	57'-9 1/32"
Camera Y	47'-6 31/32"
Camera Z	4'-6"
Target X	47'-4 1/4"
Target Y	53'-0 7/16"
Target Z	3'-6"
Lens length (mm)	50.00000
Field of view	39.60

Right click on the camera and select **Properties**.

Change the Camera Z value to **3' 6"**.

Change the Target Z to **3' 6"**.

This points the camera slightly down.

This sets the camera at 3' 6" above floor level.

7.

Note that the Camera Preview window updates.

Close the preview window.

Click ESC to release the camera.

8.

Activate the View tab on the ribbon.

Notice the Camera1 view has been added to the view lists.

Left click to activate the Camera1 view.

9.

Switch to the Render tab on the ribbon.

Click **Adjust**.

10.

You can use the dialog to adjust the view to your liking.

Click **OK**.

11. Switch to the View tab on the ribbon.

Change the Display Style to **Realistic**.

12.

Switch to the Render tab on the ribbon.

Set Materials/Textures **On**.

13.

Set **Full Shadows** on.

14.

Switch to the View tab on the ribbon.

Set **Realistic Face Style** on.

15.

The Camera view should adjust as the different settings are applied.

16.

Activate the View tab on the ribbon.

Select **Full Navigation**.

17.

Use the controls on the navigation wheel to adjust the view.

Try LOOK to look up and down.

Click the small x in the upper right to close when you are satisfied with the view.

18.

Click the bottom arrow on the view list.

Select **View Manager** located at the bottom of the view list.

19.

Select **New**.

View	
Camera X	63'-4 7/16"
Camera Y	46'-3 11/32"
Camera Z	4'-11 29/32"
Target X	50'-0 7/32"
Target Y	53'-4 15/32"
Target Z	2'-4 13/16"
Roll angle	0.00

Current View: Current
Views
Current
Model Views
Layout Views
Preset Views

Set Current
New...
Update Layers
Edit Boundaries...
Delete

20.

Name the view **Kitchen.**

Select the down arrow to expand the dialog.

21.

Set the Visual style to **Realistic**.

Set the background to Solid.

22.

Click in the Color box to set the color.

23.

Set the background color to 255,255,255 which is white.

Click **OK**.

Close all the dialogs other than the View Manager.

24.

The saved view is now listed under Model Views.

Click **OK**.

Save as *ex8-5.dwg*.

Exercise 8-6:
Create Rendering

Drawing Name: rendering.dwg
Estimated Time: 5 minutes

This exercise reinforces the following skills:

- ❑ Render
- ❑ Display Settings
- ❑ Set Location

You need an internet connection in order to perform this exercise.

1.   Open *rendering.dwg*.

2.   Set the Top view active.

3.   Activate the Render tab on the ribbon.

4.   Select **Sky Background and Illumination** from the Render tab on the ribbon.

5.

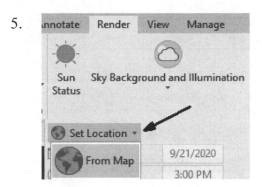

In the drop-down panel under Sky Background and Illumination, select

Set Location→From Map.

6.

Click **Yes** if you have internet access.

7.

Type in an address in the search field where your project is located.

Once it is located on the map, select **Drop Marker here.**

Click **Next**.

8.

Select the coordinate system to be applied to the project.

Highlight **CA-III**, then Click **Next**.

9.

Select the upper left corner of the building as the site location.

Click ENTER to accept the default North location.

10.

Activate the Render tab on the ribbon.

Select the small down arrow at the bottom right of the Sun & Location panel.

11.

Scroll to Sun Angle Calculator.

Set the time to **3:00 PM**.

12.

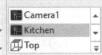

Activate the View tab on the ribbon.

Set the view to **Kitchen**.

13.

Activate the Render tab on the ribbon.

Full Shadows should be set to **ON**.

14. Materials and Textures should be set to **ON**.

15. Set the **Sky Background and Illumination on**.

You should see a slight change in the view.

16. On the Render to Size dropdown, select the **More Output Settings**.

17.

Set the Image Size to **1280x720 px**.
Set the Resolution to **600**.
Click **Save**.

18.

Click on **Render to Size**.

Note the setting you created is enabled.

,

19.

Expand the Render panel in the tab on the ribbon.

Select **Render Window**.

This opens a window where you will see the rendering.

20.
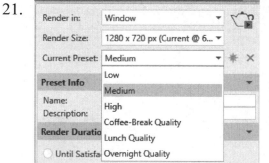
Select the small arrow in the right corner of the Render panel on the ribbon.

21.
Set the Preset Info to **Medium**.

Notice that ACA gives you an idea of how long the rendering will take depending on the preset.

22.
Set the Render Accuracy for the Lights and Materials to **Draft.**

23.

Render in:	Window ▾
Render Size:	1280 x 720 px (Current @ 6... ▾
Current Preset:	Medium ▾ ✳ ✕

Click on the **Render** button.

24.

⚠ Missing assets

C:\Documents and Settings\Administrador\Mis documentos\Autodesk\Textures\image089.jpg
C:\Documents and Settings\Administrador\Mia documentos\Autodesk\Textures\marmol.jpg

☐ Don't show me this again   Continue

If a dialog comes up stating some material images are missing, Click **Continue**.

25. A window will come up where the camera view will be rendered.

If you don't see the window, use the drop-down to open the Render Window.

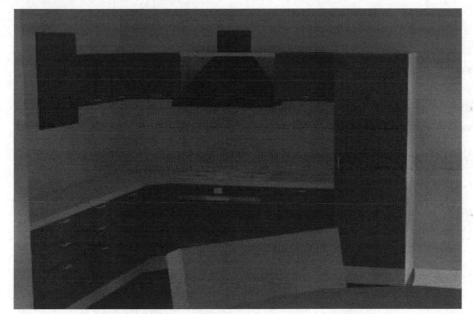

26.

Select the **Save** icon to save the rendered image.

27.

| File name: | kitchen |
| Files of type: | PNG(*.png) |

Save the image file to the exercise folder.

28.

PNG Image Options

Color
- ○ Monochrome
- ○ 8 Bits(256 Grayscale)
- ○ 8 Bits(256 Color)
- ○ 16 Bits(65,536 Grayscale)
- ○ 24 Bits(16.7 Million Colors)
- ● 32 Bits(24 Bits + Alpha)

☐ Progressive

Dots Per Inch: 600

[OK] [Cancel]

Click **OK**.

Close the Render Window.

29. Save as *ex8-6.dwg*.

Exercise 8-7:
Render in Cloud

Drawing Name: cloud_render.dwg
Estimated Time: 5 minutes

This exercise reinforces the following skills:

- ❑ Render in Cloud
- ❑ Design Center
- ❑ Blocks

Autodesk offers a service where you can render your model on their server using an internet connection. You need to register for an account. Educators and students can create a free account. The advantage of using the Cloud for rendering is that you can continue to work while the rendering is being processed. You do need an internet connection for this to work.

1. Open *cloud_render.dwg*.

2.
Activate the View tab on the ribbon.

Switch to a **Top** View.

3.
Set the Display to **2D Wireframe**.

4. Launch the Design Center by typing **ADC**.

5.   Click on the Folders tab.

    Locate the *Men-and-Women-3D.dwg* file which was downloaded from the publisher's website.

    Click on **Blocks.**

6.   Select one of the blocks.

    Right click and select **Insert Block**.

    I selected 02ZFMA02.

7.   Set the Scale to **1.0**.
    Enable **Uniform Scale**.

    Enable **Insertion Point**.

    Enable **Rotation**.

8. Place the block inside the kitchen area.

    Close the Design Center.

9.   Switch to the **Kitchen** view.

10.

You will see the 3D figure inside the kitchen.

Use the Full Navigation Wheel to adjust the view as needed.

In order to render using Autodesk's Cloud Service, you need to sign into an Autodesk account. Registration is free and storage is free to students and educators.

Sign in to your Autodesk account.

You can create an account for free if you are an educator, student or if you are on subscription.

11.

Sign in

Email

name@example.com

NEXT

Enter your log-in information and Click **Sign in**.

12.

Your user name should display once you are signed in.

13. Save the file as *ex8-7.dwg*.

You must save the file before you can render.

14. Activate the Render tab on the ribbon.

Select **Render in Cloud**.

15. Your free preview renderings will appear in your Autodesk Rendering Account online. From there you can view, download, and share, or fine tune render settings to create higher resolution final images, interactive panoramas, and more.

Model View   Render current view

☑ Notify me by e-mail when complete.

Help   Start Rendering   Cancel

Set the Model View to render the current view.

Click the **Start Rendering** model.

16. 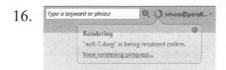 *A small bubble message will appear when the rendering is completed.*

17. *You will also receive an email when the rendering is complete. The email is sent to the address you used to sign into your account.*

18. Select **Render Gallery** on the Render tab on the ribbon to see your renderings.

Render Gallery

19. You can also select View completed rendering from the drop-down menu under your sign in.

You may need to sign into the gallery in order to see your rendering.

Compare the quality of the rendering performed using the Cloud with the rendering done in the previous exercise.

I have found that rendering using the Cloud is faster and produces better quality images. It also allows me to continue working while the rendering is being processed.

Exercise 8-8:
Create an Animation

Drawing Name: animation.dwg
Estimated Time: 5 minutes

This exercise reinforces the following skills:

❑   Walk-Through

It will take the software several minutes to compile the animation. It is a good idea to do this exercise right before a 30-minute break to allow it time to create the animation during the break.

1.   Open *animation.dwg*.

2.   Activate the View tab on the ribbon.

Switch to a **Top** View.

3.   Set the view display to **2D Wireframe**.

4.   Activate the Home tab on the ribbon.

Set the layer named **Walkthrough** Current.

This layer is set so it doesn't plot.

5.   Select the **Polyline** tool located under the Line drop-down list.

6.

Draw a polyline that travels through the floor plan to view different rooms.

7.

Select the polyline.

Right click and select **Properties**.

8.

Set the elevation of the polyline to **5' 3"**.

If you don't raise the line, your camera path is going to be along the floor.

9.   Switch to a **SW Isometric Realistic** view.

10.

Activate the Render tab on the ribbon.

Select **Animation Motion Path**.

11.

Set the Frame Rate to **10**.

Set the Number of frames to **3000**.

Set the Duration to **300**.

Set the Visual Style to **Realistic**.

Set the Format to **AVI**.
This will allow you to play the animation in Windows Media Player.

Set the Resolution to **1024 x 768**.

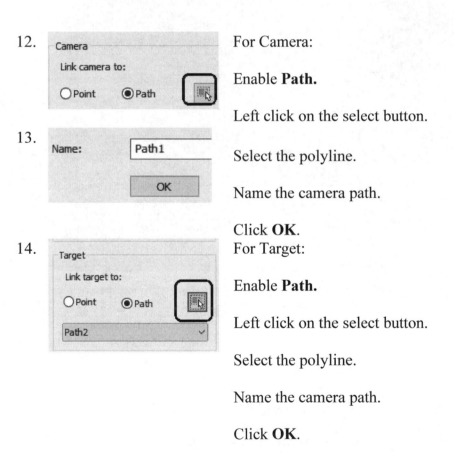

12. For Camera:

Enable **Path.**

Left click on the select button.

13. Select the polyline.

Name the camera path.

Click **OK**.

14. For Target:

Enable **Path.**

Left click on the select button.

Select the polyline.

Name the camera path.

Click **OK**.

15. Click **OK**.

Browse to your classwork folder.

Name the file to create *walkthrough1.avi*.

Click **Save**.

16. You will see the animation preview as it processes.

This will take several minutes.

17. When it is complete, open Windows File Explorer.

Browse to the folder where it is saved.

18. Right click on it and select **Open with Windows Media Player**.

19. Try creating different walkthroughs using different visual styles.
20. Save as *ex8-8.dwg*.

Using the Sun & Sky

Drawing Name: sun_study.dwg
Estimated Time: 15 minutes

This exercise reinforces the following skills:

- ❑ Create a saved view
- ❑ Apply sunlight
- ❑ Add an image as background
- ❑ Adjust background

1.   Open *sun_study.dwg*.

2.   Right click on the ViewCube and select **Parallel**.

How does the view shift?

3.   Right click on the ViewCube and select **Perspective**.

How does the view shift?

4.   Double click the wheel on the mouse to Zoom Extents.

Adjust the view so that the back edge of the slab is horizontal in the view.

Hint: Switch to a Front view then tip the view slightly forward.

5. Switch to the View tab.

Launch the **View Manager**.

6. Click **New**.

Set Current

New...

7. Type **Front Isometric** for the View Name.

View name: Front Isometric

View category: <None>

View type: Still

Boundary

◉ Current display
○ Define window

OK   Cancel

8. Expand the lower pane of the dialog.

Under Background:

Select **Image**.

9. Set image to *sky.JPG*.

File name: sky.JPG

Files of type: JFIF (*.jpg, *.jpeg)

You may need to change the Files of type to JFIF. This file is included in the downloaded exercise files.

Click **Open**.

10.

Click **OK**.

11.

Click **OK**.

Set the Front Isometric as the Current View.

You have now saved the view.

Close the View Manager.

12.

Type **Render** to render the view.

A preview window will open and the view will render.

Close the preview window.

13.

Switch to the Render tab.

Enable **Sky Background and Illumination**.

14.

Enable **Materials/Textures On**.

15. Type **Render** to render the view.

A preview window will open and the view will render.

Close the preview window.

16. Enable **Full Shadows**.

17. Click the small arrow in the lower right corner of the Sun & Location panel.

18. 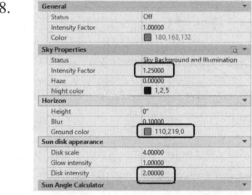 Set the Intensity Factor to **1.25**.
Set the Ground color to **110,219,0**.
(This is a light green.)
Set the Disk Intensity to **2.**

Close the dialog.

19. Type **Render** to render the view.

A preview window will open and the view will render.

Close the preview window.

20. Save as *ex8-9.dwg*.

Exercise 8-10:
Applying Materials

Drawing Name: materials.dwg
Estimated Time: 45 minutes

This exercise reinforces the following skills:

- ❑ Navigate the Materials Browser
- ❑ Apply materials to model components
- ❑ Edit Styles
- ❑ Change environment
- ❑ View Manager
- ❑ Render

1.   Open *materials.dwg*.

2.   **[−][SW Isometric][Realistic]**   Set the display to **Realistic**.

   If you don't set the display to Realistic, you won't see the material changes.

3.   Switch to the Render tab on the ribbon.

   Click on **Materials Browser**.

4.   Locate **Beechwood – Honey** and load into the drawing.

   This is for the flooring.

5.   Locate **Glass Clear - Light** and load into the drawing.

   This is for the window glazing.

6.   Locate **Wall Texture - Salmon** and load into the drawing.

   This is for the walls.

7.

Wall Paint ▾			
Name ▲	Library	Type	Category
Sand	Autodesk Library	Wall Paint	Wall Paint: Glossy

Locate **Sand Wall Paint** and load into the drawing.

This is for the wall and window trim.

8.

Document Materials
✓ Show All
Show Applied
Show Selected
Show Unused
Purge All Unused
~~View Type~~
✓ Thumbnail View
List View
Text View
Sort
✓ by Name

Change the Material Browser View to use a Thumbnail View.

Now you can see swatches of all the materials available in your drawing.

Close the Materials Browser.

9.

Edit Style ▾

Select a wall.

On the ribbon:
Select **Edit Style**.

10.

| General | Components | Materials | Endcaps / Opening Endcaps | Classifications | Display Properties |

Component	Material Definition
Unnamed	Standard
Shrinkwrap	Standard

Highlight the top component for the wall.
Click on the **Edit Material** button.

11.

A Material Definition Properties - Standard

General | Display Properties

Display Representations	Display Property Source	Style Override
General	Material Definition Override - Standard	☑
General High Detail	Material Definition Override - Standard	☑
General Low Detail	Material Definition Override - Standard	☑
General Medium Det...	**Material Definition Override - Standard**	☑
General Presentation	Material Definition Override - Standard	☑
General Reflected	Material Definition Override - Standard	☑
General Reflected Scre...	Material Definition Override - Standard	☑
General Screened	Material Definition Override - Standard	☑

Click on the override button.

12.

Layer/Color/Linetype | Hatching | Other

Surface Hatch Placement
☑ Top   ☑ Bottom
☑ Left   ☑ Right
☑ Front   ☑ Back

Surface Rendering
Render Material: Wall Texture - Salmon
Mapping: Face Mapping

Live Section Rendering
Cut Surface Render Material: *NONE*
Sectioned Body Render Material: *NONE*

2D Section/Elevation Rules

Set the Render Material to **Wall Texture – Salmon**.

Click **OK**.

Close all the dialogs.

Click ESC to release the selection.

You should see the new material on the walls.

If you don't see the material change, verify that your display is set to **Realistic**.

13. Click on a window.
On the ribbon:
Select **Edit Style**.

14. Highlight the Frame Component.
Click on **New Material**.

15. Create a new material called **sand paint**.

New Name: Sand Paint

OK

Click **OK**.

16. The Frame is now assigned the new material.

Component	Material Definition
Frame	Sand Paint
Sash	Doors & Windows.Metal Doors & Frames.
Glass	Doors & Windows.Glazing.Glass.Clear
Muntins	Standard

17. Highlight the Glass Component.
Click on **New Material**.

18. Create a new material called **Glass – Clear Light**.

New Name: Glass - Clear Light

OK

Click **OK**.

19. The Glass is now assigned the new material.

Component	Material Definition
Frame	Sand Paint
Sash	Doors & Windows.Metal
Glass	Glass - Clear Light
Muntins	Standard

20. Highlight the Frame and select **Edit Material**.

21.

Place a Check next to the General Medium Detail to enable Style Override.

22.

Click on the Other tab.
Set the Render Material to the **Sand** material.

Click **OK**.

Close the Display Properties dialog.

23.

Highlight the Glass and select **Edit Material**.

24.

Place a Check next to the General Medium Detail to enable Style Override.

25.

Click on the Other tab.
Set the Render Material to the **Clear - Light** material.

Click **OK**.

Close the Display Properties dialog.

26.

Verify that:

Set the Frame to **sand paint**.

Set the Glass to **Glass – Clear Light**.

Close all the dialogs.

Click ESC to release the selection.

27. Select the floor slab.

28. On the ribbon:
Select **Edit Style**.

29. On the Components tab:

    Click **Add component**.

30. Rename **wood flooring**.

31. Switch to the Materials tab.

    Highlight the wood flooring
    Component.
    Click on **New Material**.

32. Name the new material **beechwood floor**.

    Click **OK**.

33. Highlight the wood flooring
    component and select **Edit
    Material**.

34. Place a Check next to the General
    Medium Detail to enable Style Override.

35. Click on the Other tab.
    Set the Render Material to the
    Beechwood - Honey material.

Click **OK**.

Close the Display Properties dialog.

36.   Click ESC to release the selection.

37.   Switch to the Render tab.

Enable **Sun Status**.

38.   Click on **Keep the default lighting turned on.**

→ Turn off the default lighting (recommended)

→ Keep the default lighting turned on
The default lighting will stay turned on when you add user lights. To see the effect of user lights, turn off the default lights manually.

39.   Click on **Adjust exposure settings**.

→ Adjust exposure settings (recommended).

→ Keep exposure settings.

40.   Turn the Environment **On**.

Environment:	On
Image Based Lighting:	Sharp Highlights
Rotation:	0
○ Use IBL Image as Background	
● Use Custom Background	Background...

Enable **Use Custom Background.**

Click on **Background...**

41.

Set Type to **Image**.

Click **Browse**.

Select the *Beach.jpg* file in the downloaded exercise files.

Click **Open**.

Click on **Adjust Image**.

42.

Select **Stretch** for Image position.

Enable **Scale**.

Click **OK**.

Close the dialogs.

43.

Orbit, pan and zoom to position the model on the beach so it appears proper.

44.

Switch to the View tab.

Launch the **View Manager**.

45.   New...   Click **New**.

46.   Save the view as **Beach**.

Enable **Save sun properties with view**.

Click OK.

47.   Click **OK**.

48.   Type **RENDER**.

The preview window will appear and the view will render.

Save as *ex8-10.dwg*.

Exercise 8-11:
Applying Materials to Furniture

Drawing Name: Wicker chair and sofa.dwg
Estimated Time: 15 minutes

This exercise reinforces the following skills:

- ❑ Navigate the Materials Browser
- ❑ Apply materials to model components
- ❑ Customize materials

1.
   Open the *Wicker chair and sofa* file in the exercises folder.

2.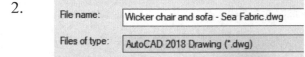
   Save the file with a new name - *Wicker chair and sofa – Sea Fabric.*

3.
   Use explode to explode the blocks until you see solids when you hover over the elements.

4.
   Switch to the Render tab on the ribbon.

   Click on **Materials Browser**.

5.
   Locate **Pebbled – Mauve** and load into the drawing.

   This is for the chair fabric.

6. Locate **Chrome - Satin** and load into the drawing.

This is for the chair frame.

7. 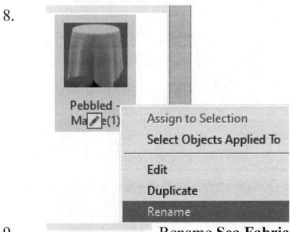 Highlight the Pebbled – Mauve fabric.

Right click and select **Duplicate**.

8. Right click on the duplicate material.

Select **Rename**.

9. Rename **Sea Fabric**.

10. Select the Sea Fabric material.

Right click and select **Edit**.

11.

Click on the image name and set to *sea fabric.jpg*.

This file is available as part of the exercise downloads.

Close the Materials Editor.

12.

Select one of the cushions.

Right click and select **Properties**.

13.

On the Properties palette:

Note the color is set to **92, 179,150**.

Click **ESC** to release the selection.

14.

Type **QS** for quickselect.

Set the Object type to **3D Solid**.

Set the Color Equals to **92, 179, 150**.

Click **OK**.

All the chair cushions are selected.

15.

Highlight the Sea Fabric material.

Right click and select **Assign to Selection**.

Click ESC to release the selection.

If the view is set to Realistic, you should see the material as it is applied.

16.

Select one of the chair frame elements.

General		
Color	◥ White	
Layer	None	
Linetype	———————	Continuous
Linetype scale	1.0000	

The Color is set to White.

Click ESC to release the selection.

17.

Type **QS** for quickselect.

Set the Object type to **3D Solid**.

Set the Color Equals to **Black**.

Click **OK**.

The chair frames are selected.

18.

Highlight the **Chrome - Satin** material.

Right click and select **Assign to Selection**.

Click **ESC** to release the selection.

19.

The drawing has been redefined with new materials.

Save as *Wicker chair and sofa – Sea Fabric.dwg*

Exercise 8-12:
Replace a Block

Drawing Name: replace_block.dwg
Estimated Time: 5 minutes

This exercise reinforces the following skills:

    ❑   Replace a block
    ❑   Render

1.   Open *replace_block.dwg.*

2.   Type **INSERT**.

   Click ENTER.

3.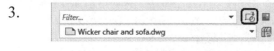
   Select the **Browse** button next to the Filter box.

4.
   Locate the *Wicker chair and sofa – Sea Fabric.dwg.*

   Click **Open**.

   Click a point in the view to place the block away from the room.

   Click ENTER when prompted for a rotation angle.

5.
   Type **BLOCKREPLACE**.

   Scroll down and select *Wicker chair and sofa.*

   Click **OK**.

6.

Select a block to replace Wicker chair and sofa

Group-3-1
Group-4-1
Group-5-1
Group-6-1
Group-7-1
Group-8-1
Group-9-1
Wicker chair and sofa
Wicker chair and sofa - Sea Fabric

Pick<   Wicker chair and sofa - Sea Fabric

OK   Cancel   Help

Scroll down and select the *Wicker chair and sofa – Sea Fabric* block.

Click **OK**.

7.

▾Purge unreferenced items when finished? <Y>:

Click ENTER.

8.

The block is replaced using the same location and orientation.

Delete the block that was inserted and isn't needed any more.

Note that you had to fully insert the new block into the drawing before you could replace the block.

9.

Type RENDER.

The preview window will appear and the view will render.

Save as *ex8-12.dwg*.

Exercise 8-13:
Using Artificial Light

Drawing Name: lights.dwg
Estimated Time: 15 minutes

This exercise reinforces the following skills:

  ❑ Add lights to a model
  ❑ Edit light properties

1.   Open *lights.dwg*.

2.   Switch to the Render tab.

      Select the **Point** light tool.

3.   Select the center of the circle on the left as the location for the point light.

      Click ENTER to accept all the default settings for the light.

      If you have difficulty placing the lights, freeze all the layers except for Light Locator.

4.   Select the point light.
      Right click and select **Properties**.

      Change the Name to **Dominant Light**.

      Change the Lamp intensity to **15.00 Cd**.

      Click ESC to release the selection.

5.   Enable **Full Shadows**.
      Enable **Sky Background and Illumination**.

6.

→ Adjust exposure settings (recommended).

→ Keep exposure settings.

Click on **Sun Status**.
Click on **Adjust exposure settings**.

7.

Set Environment to **On**.

Set the Image Based Lighting to **Warm Light**.

Enable **Use IBL Image as Background**.

Close the palette.

8.

Click **Render to Size** on the ribbon.

The Render Window will appear.

You will see a new rendering.

Close the Render Window.

9.

Select the **Point** light tool.

10.

Select the center of the circle in the middle of the room as the location for the point light.

Click ENTER to accept all the default settings for the light.

If you have difficulty placing the lights, freeze all the layers except for Light Locator.

11. 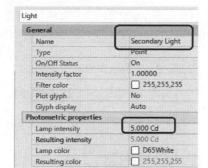 Select the point light.
Right click and select **Properties**.

Change the Name to **Secondary Light**.

Change the Lamp intensity to **5.00 Cd**.

Click ESC to release the selection.

12. Use Thaw All to thaw any frozen layers.

13. Switch to the Render tab.

Enable **Full Shadows**.
Enable **Sky Background**.

14. Click on **Sun Status**.

15. Click on **Adjust exposure settings**.

16. Set Environment to **Off**.

Set the Exposure to **8**.

Set the White Balance to **15000.**

Close the palette.

17. Click **Render to Size** on the ribbon.

The Render Window will appear.

You will see a new rendering.

Close the Render Window.

Save as *ex8-13.dwg*.

Exercise 8-14:
Mapping Materials

Drawing Name: medallion.dwg
Estimated Time: 15 minutes

This exercise reinforces the following skills:

- ❏ Create a material
- ❏ Apply material to a face.

1. Open *medallion.dwg*.

2. Switch to the Render tab.

    Click on Materials Browser.

3.   Select the **Create Material** tool at the bottom of the palette.

4.

Create the new material using the **Stone** template.

5.

Change the name to Medallion.

Change the Scene to **Canvas**.

Click on the image name.

6.

File name: stone medallion.JPG

Locate the *stone medallion* file in the downloaded exercise files.

Click **Open**.

7.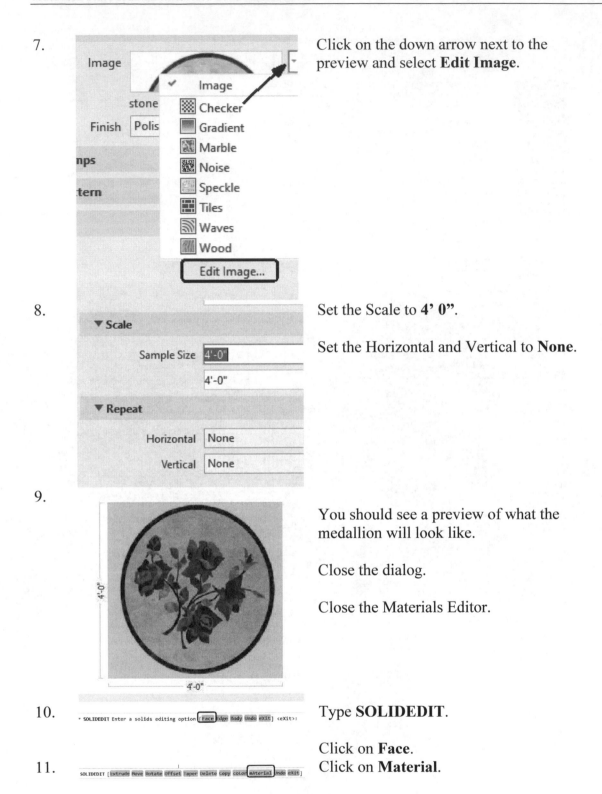
Click on the down arrow next to the preview and select **Edit Image**.

8. Set the Scale to **4' 0"**.

Set the Horizontal and Vertical to **None**.

9. You should see a preview of what the medallion will look like.

Close the dialog.

Close the Materials Editor.

10. Type **SOLIDEDIT**.

Click on **Face**.

11. Click on **Material**.

12.

Click on the disk.

SOLIDEDIT Select faces or [Undo Remove ALL]:

We only want the top face selected, so click **Remove**.

13.

Click on the bottom of the disk.

Click ENTER when only the top face is highlighted.

14. SOLIDEDIT Enter new material name <ByLayer>: Medallion

Type **Medallion** for the material to be applied.

15. [−][Top][Realistic] Change the display to **Top Realistic**.

16.

The material is placed, but it didn't map properly.

Double click on the material in the Material Browser to open the editor.

17. Select **Edit Image**.

✔ Image
▩ Checker
▦ Gradient
▩ Marble
▩ Noise
▩ Speckle
▦ Tiles
▧ Waves
▦ Wood
Edit Image...

18.

Adjust the Position and the Scale until the preview looks correct.

Close the dialogs.

19.

Save as *flower medallion.dwg*.

Extra: *Place the medallion in the beach scene you did in the previous exercise and see if you can create a nice rendering.*

QUIZ 8

True or False

1. When rendering, it is useful to save named views using the View Manager.

2. Sky illumination can be used to add extra light to a scene.

3. You can use an image or a color to change the background of a scene.

4. To change the material used in a wall, you need to modify the wall style.

5. When mapping a material, you can only use grips to adjust the placement.

Multiple Choice

6. Materials can be displayed in the following views: (select all that apply)

   A. plans
   B. sections
   C. elevations
   D. renderings

7. Surface Hatches can be displayed in the following views: (select all that apply)

   A. model
   B. plan
   C. section
   D. elevation

8. Identify the tool shown.

   A. Expand Render Window
   B. Expand Tea Kettle
   C. Scale
   D. Render to Size

9. When there are no lights placed in a scene, the scene is rendered using:

   A. Default lighting.
   B. Sun & Sky.
   C. Nothing, it is really dark.
   D. Sun only, based on location.

10. Spotlights and point lights are represented by:

    A. Glyphs (symbols used to indicate the position and direction of the light)
    B. Nothing
    C. Blocks
    D. Linework

11. When mapping a material, you can adjust: (select all that apply)

    A. The X position
    B. The Y position
    C. Rotation
    D. Scale

12. Once you place a camera, you can adjust the camera using: (select all that apply)

    A. Properties
    B. The Adjust tool on the Render tab
    C. Using the MOVE and ROTATE tools
    D. You can't modify a camera once it has been placed

ANSWERS:

1) T; 2) T; 3) T; 4) T; 5) F; 6) A, B, C, D; 7) A, C, D; 8) D; 9) A; 10) A; 11) A, B, C, D; 12) A, B, C

Lesson 9:
Documentation

Before we can create our construction drawings, we need to create layouts or views to present the design. AutoCAD Architecture is similar to AutoCAD in that the user can work in Model and Paper Space. Model Space is where we create the 3D model of our house. Paper Space is where we create or set up various views that can be used in our construction drawings. In each view, we can control what we see by turning off layers, zooming, panning, etc.

To understand paper space and model space, imagine a cardboard box. Inside the cardboard box is Model Space. This is where your 3D model is located. On each side of the cardboard box, tear out a small rectangular window. The windows are your viewports. You can look through the viewports to see your model. To reach inside the window so you can move your model around or modify it, you double-click inside the viewport. If your hand is not reaching through any of the windows and you are just looking from the outside, then you are in Paper Space or Layout mode.
You can create an elevation in your current drawing by first drawing an elevation line and mark, and then creating a 2D or 3D elevation based on that line. You can control the size and shape of the elevation that is generated. Unless you explode the elevation that you create, the elevation remains linked to the building model that you used to create it. Because of this link between the elevation and the building model, any changes to the building model can be made in the elevation as well.

When you create a 2D elevation, the elevation is created with hidden and overlapping lines removed. You can edit the 2D elevation that you created by changing its display properties. The 2D Section/Elevation style allows you to add your own display components to the display representation of the elevation and create rules that assign different parts of the elevation to different display components. You can control the visibility, layer, color, linetype, lineweight, and linetype scale of each component. You can also use the line work editing commands to assign individual lines in your 2D elevation to display components and merge geometry into your 2D elevation.

After you create a 2D elevation, you can use the AutoCAD BHATCH and AutoCAD DIMLINEAR commands to hatch and dimension the 2D elevation.

AutoCAD Architecture comes with standard title block templates. They are located in the Templates subdirectory under *Program Data \ Autodesk\ ACA 2022 \enu \Template.*

Many companies will place their templates on the network so all users can access the same templates. In order to make this work properly, set the Options so that the templates folder is pointed to the correct path.

Exercise 9-1:

Creating a Custom Titleblock

Drawing Name: Architectural Title Block.dwg
Estimated Time: 30 minutes

This exercise reinforces the following skills:

- ❑ Title blocks
- ❑ Attributes
- ❑ Edit Block In-Place
- ❑ Insert Image
- ❑ Insert Hyperlink

1.   Select the **Open** tool.

2. 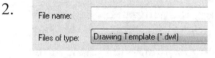 Set the Files of type to *Drawing Template*.

3.   Browse to *ProgramData\Autodesk\ACA 2022\enu\ Template\AutoCAD Templates*.

4.   Open the *Tutorial-iArch.dwt*.
Verify that *Files of type* is set to Drawing Template or you won't see the file.

5.   Perform a **File→Save as**.

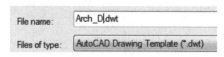

Save the file to your work folder.
Rename **Arch_D.dwt**.

6.   Enter a description and Click **OK**.

7. [Firm Name and Address] Zoom into the Firm Name and Address rectangle.

8.   Select the **MTEXT** tool from the **Annotation** panel on the Home tab on the ribbon.

    Multiline Text

    Draw a rectangle to place the text.

9. Set the Font to **Verdana**.

    Hint: If you type the first letter of the font, the drop-down list will jump to fonts starting with that letter.

    Set the text height to ⅛".
    Set the justification to **centered**.
    Enter the name and address of your college.

10. LANEY COLLEGE
    800 FALLON STREET
    OAKLAND, CA

    Extend the ruler to change the width of your MTEXT box to fill the rectangle.

    Click **OK**.

11. Firm Name and Address

    LANEY COLLEGE
    800 FALLON STREET
    OAKLAND, CA

    Use **MOVE** to locate the text properly, if needed.

12. Home Insert Annotate Render

    Attach Clip Adjust
    Underlay Layers
    Frames vary
    Snap to Underlays ON
    Reference

    Activate the **Insert** tab on the ribbon.

    Select the arrow located on the right bottom of the Reference panel.

13. 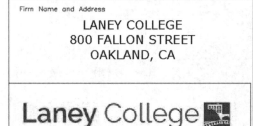 The External Reference Manager will launch.

Select **Attach Image** from the drop-down list.

14. Locate the image file you wish to use.
There is an image file available for use from the publisher's website called *college logo.jpg*.
Click **Open**.

15. Click **OK**.

16. Place the image in the rectangle.

FIRM Name and Address

**LANEY COLLEGE
800 FALLON STREET
OAKLAND, CA**

Laney College

Tips & Tricks

If you are concerned about losing the link to the image file (for example, if you plan to email this file to another person), you can use **INSERTOBJ** to embed the image into the drawing. Do not enable link to create an embedded object. The INSERTOBJ command is not available on the standard tab on the ribbon.

---

17. Select the image.
Right click and select **Properties**.

18.

Select the **Extended** tab.
Pick the Hyperlink field.

19.

Type in the name of the school in the Text to display field.

Type in the website address in the *Type the file or Web page name* field.

Click **OK**.
Close the Properties dialog.

20.

If you hover your mouse over the image, you will see a small icon. This indicates there is a hyperlink attached to the image. To launch the webpage, simply hold down the CTRL key and left click on the icon.

Tips & Tricks

If you are unsure of the web address of the website you wish to link, use the Browse for **Web Page** button.

21.
Firm Name and Address
LANEY COLLEGE
800 FALLON STREET
OAKLAND, CA

Laney College

To turn off the image frame/boundary, type **IMAGEFRAME** at the command line. Enter **0**.

IMAGEFRAME has the following options:

0: Turns off the image frame and does not plot
1: Turns on the image frame and is plotted
2: Turns on the image frame but does not plot

22. Select the titleblock.
Right click and select **Edit Block in-place**.

| Block Editor |
| Edit Block in-place... |
| Edit Attributes... |

23. Click **OK**.

24. Change the text for Project to **Drafter**.
To change, simply double click on the text and an edit box will appear.

25. Select the **Define Attribute** tool from the Insert tab on the ribbon.

26. Select the **Field** tool.

27. Highlight Author and Uppercase.

Click **OK**.

28. In the Tag field, enter **DRAFTER**.
In the Prompt field, enter **DRAFTER**.
The Value field is used by the FIELD property.
  In the Insertion Point area:
    In the X field, enter **2′ 6.5″**.
    In the Y field, enter **2-1/16″**.
    In the Z field, enter **0″**.
  In the Text Options area:
    Set the Justification to **Left**.
    Set the Text Style to **Standard**.
    Set the Height to **1/8″**.

Click **OK**.

29. Select the **Define Attributes** tool.

30. In the Tag field, enter **DATE**.
In the Prompt field, enter **DATE**.

In the Insertion Point area:
  In the X field, enter **2′ 6.5″**.
  In the Y field, enter **1-9/16″**.
  In the Z field, enter **0″**.
In the Text Options area:
  Set the Justification to **Left**.
  Set the Text Style to **Standard**.
  Set the Height to **1/8″**.

31. Select the Field button to set the default value for the attribute.

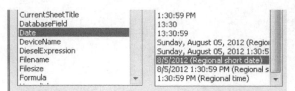

Select **Date**.
Set the Date format to **Regional short date**.

Click **OK**.

32.   Select the **Define Attributes** tool.

33.

In the Tag field, enter **SCALE**.
In the Prompt field, enter **SCALE**.
  In the Insertion Point area:
    In the X field, enter **2′ 6.5″**.
    In the Y field, enter **1-1/16″**.
    In the Z field, enter **0″**.
  In the Text Options area:
    Set the Justification to **Left**.
    Set the Text Style to **Standard**.
Set the Height to **1/8″**.

34.

Select the Field button to set the default value for the attribute.

Select **PlotScale**.
Set the format to **1:#**.

Click **OK**.

Click **OK** to place the attribute.

35.   Select the **Define Attributes** tool.

36.

In the Tag field, enter **SHEETNO**.
In the Prompt field, enter **SHEET NO**.
  In the Insertion Point area:
    In the X field, enter **2′ 8.25″**.
    In the Y field, enter **1-9/16″**.
    In the Z field, enter **0**.
  In the Text Options area:
    Set the Justification to **Left**.
    Set the Text Style to **Standard**.
    Set the Height to **1/8″**.

37. Select the Field button to set the default value for the attribute.

Select **CurrentSheetNumber**.
Set the format to **Uppercase**.

Click **OK**.

Click **OK** to place the attribute.

38. Select the **Define Attribute** tool.

Define Attributes

39. In the Tag field, enter **PROJECTNAME**.
In the Prompt field, enter **PROJECT NAME**.
In the Insertion Point area:
In the X field, enter **2' 7-9/16"**.
In the Y field, enter **4"**.
In the Z field, enter **0**.
In the Text Options area:
Set the Justification to **Center**.
Set the Text Style to **Standard**.
Set the Height to **1/8"**.

40. Select the Field button to set the default value for the attribute.

Select **AEC Project** for the field category.
Set the Field Name to **Project Name**.
Set the format to **Uppercase**.

Click **OK**.

A common error for students is to forget to enter the insertion point. The default insertion point is set to 0,0,0. If you don't see your attributes, look for them at the lower left corner of your title block and use the MOVE tool to position them appropriately.

Your title block should look similar to the image shown.

If you like, you can use the MOVE tool to reposition any of the attributes to make them fit better.

41. Select **Save** on the tab on the ribbon to save the changes to the title block and exit the Edit Block In-Place mode.

42. AutoCAD ✕ Click **OK**.

> ⚠ All references edits will be saved.
>
> - To save reference changes, click OK.
> - To cancel the command, click Cancel.
>
> [OK]   [Cancel]

43. Save the file and go to **File→Close**.

> ➢ Use templates to standardize how you want your drawing sheets to look. Store your templates on a server so everyone in your department uses the same titleblock and sheet settings. You can also set up dimension styles and layer standards in your templates.

> ➢ ADT 2005 introduced a new tool available when you are in Paper Space that allows you to quickly switch to the model space of a viewport without messing up your scale. Simply select the **Maximize Viewport** button located on your task bar to switch to model space.

> ➢ To switch back to paper space, select the **Minimize Viewport** button.

You use the Project Navigator to create additional drawing files with the desired views for your model. The views are created on the Views tab of the Project Navigator. You then create a sheet set which gathers together all the necessary drawing files that are pertinent to your project.

Previously, you would use external references, which would be external drawing files that would be linked to a master drawing. You would then create several layout sheets in your master drawing that would show the various views. Some users placed all their data in a single drawing and then used layers to organize the data.

This shift in the way of organizing your drawings will mean that you need to have a better understanding of how to manage all the drawings. It also means you can leverage the drawings so you can reuse the same drawing in more than one sheet set.

You can create five different types of views using the Project Navigator:

❑ Model Space View – a portion that is displayed in its own viewport. This view can have a distinct name, display configuration, description, layer snapshot and drawing scale.
❑ Detail View – displays a small section of the model, i.e. a wall section, plumbing, or foundation. This type of view is usually associated with a callout. It can be placed in your current active drawing or in a new drawing.
❑ Section View – displays a building section, usually an interior view. This type of view is usually associated with a callout. It can be placed in your current active drawing or in a new drawing.
❑ Elevation View – displays a building elevation, usually an exterior view. This type of view is usually associated with a callout. It can be placed in your current active drawing or in a new drawing.
❑ Sheet View – this type of view is created when a model space view is dropped onto a layout sheet.

Note: Some classes have difficulty using the Project Navigator because they do not use the same workstation each class or the drawings are stored on a network server. In those cases, the links can be lost and the students get frustrated trying to get the correct results.

As we start building our layout sheets and views, we will be adding schedule tags to identify different building elements.

Schedule tags can be project-based or standard tags. Schedule tags are linked to a property in a property set. When you anchor or tag a building element, the value of the property displays in the tag. The value displayed depends on which property is defined by the attribute used by the schedule tag. ACA comes with several pre-defined schedule tags, but you will probably want to create your own custom tags to display the desired property data.

Property sets are specified using property set definitions. A property set definition is a documentation object that is tracked with an object or object style. Each property has a name, description, data type, data format, and default value.

To access the property sets, open the Style Manager. Highlight the building element you wish to define and then select the Property Sets button. You can add custom property sets in addition to using the default property sets included in each element style.

To determine what properties are available for your schedules, select the element to be included in the schedule, right click and select Properties.

Tags and schedules use project information. If you do not have a current project defined, you may see some error messages when you tag elements.

Exercise 9-2:

Creating Elevation Views

Drawing Name: elevation.dwg
Estimated Time: 15 minutes

This exercise reinforces the following skills:

- ❑ Creating an Elevation View
- ❑ Named Views

1.   Open *elevation.dwg.*

2.   Switch to the Model tab.

3.   Activate the **Top** view by clicking the top plane on the view cube. *You can also use the shortcut menu in the upper left corner of the display window to switch views.*

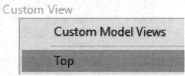

4.   Verify using the View cube that North is oriented on top.

5.   [–][Top][2D Wireframe]   Set the view to **2D Wireframe** mode by selecting the View Display in the upper left corner of the window.

6.   Zoom Window / Zoom Extents / Zoom Previous   Use **Zoom Extents** to view the entire model.

7.

Thaw the **A-Roof-Slab** and **A-Roof** layers.

8.

Activate the **Annotate** tab on the ribbon.

Select the **Elevation** tool on the Callouts panel.

9.

Place the elevation mark below the model.
Use your cursor to orient the arrow toward the building model.

10.

Set your view name to **South Elevation**.

Enable **Generate Section/Elevation**.

Enable **Place Titlemark**.

Set the Scale to **1/8″ = 1′-0″**.

Click the **Current Drawing** button.

11. Window around the entire building to select it.
    Select the upper left corner above the building and the lower right corner below the building.

12. Place the elevation to the right of the view.

    Zoom into the elevation view, so you can inspect it.

13. Switch to the View tab.

    Note that the elevation view you just created is listed.

14. Save as *ex9-2.dwg*.

Exercise 9-3:
Creating Layouts

Drawing Name: layouts.dwg
Estimated Time: 25 minutes

This exercise reinforces the following skills:

- ❑ Create Layout
- ❑ Adding a View to a Layout
- ❑ Control Visibility of elements using Layers

1.   Open *layouts.dwg*.

2.   Right click on the command line and select **Options**.

                                     You can also type OPTIONS.

3.
Layout elements
☑ Display Layout and Model tabs
☑ Display printable area
☑ Display paper background
☑ Display paper shadow
☐ Show Page Setup Manager for new layouts
☑ Create viewport in new layouts

                           Activate the **Display** tab.

                           Enable **Display Layout and Model tabs**.

                           Click **OK**.

                           These can also be enabled on the View tab on the ribbon.

4.   Right click on the Work tab.

                  Select **From template**.

New Layout
From Template...
Select All Layouts
Activate Previous Layout
Page Setup Manager...
Plot...
Drafting Standard Setup...
Dock above Status Bar

Model   Work   +

5. Browse to your exercise folder.

Select the *Arch_D* template.
Click **Open**.

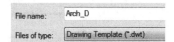

| File name: | Arch_D |
| Files of type: | Drawing Template (*.dwt) |

6.

Layout name(s):   OK

D-Size Layout   Cancel

Click **OK**.

7. Model / Work \ D-Size Layout /   Activate the **D-Size Layout**.

8.

From Template...

Delete

Rename

Move or Copy...

Select All Layouts

Activate Previous Layout

Activate Model Tab

Page Setup Manager...

Plot...

Drafting Standard Setup...

Import Layout as Sheet...

Export Layout to Model...

Dock above Status Bar

Size Layout

Right click on the **D-Size Layout** tab.

Select **Rename**.

9. \ Floorplan /   Rename **Floorplan**.
Activate/Open the **Floorplan** layout.

10.

Misc	
On	Yes
Clipped	No
Display locked	No
Annotation scale	1'-0" = 1'-0"
Standard scale	1/4" = 1'-0"

Select the viewport.
*If the Properties dialog doesn't come up, right click and select **Properties**.*

Set Display locked to **No**.

11.

Resize the viewport to only show the floor plan.

Double click inside the viewport to activate model space.

Pan the model to position inside the viewport.

12.

Activate the Home tab on the ribbon.

Freeze the layer assigned to roof slabs in the current viewport.

13.

The view updates with no roof.

14.

Freeze the **G-Elev-Line** layer assigned to the section in the current viewport.

Freeze the **I-Furn** and **I-Furniture** layer in the current viewport.

15. To turn off the display of the camera, type **CAMERADISPLAY**, and then **0.**

16.

Double click outside the viewport to return to paper space.

Observe how the floor plan view has changed.

17.

Launch the Layer Manager.

18.

Scroll down to the Viewport layer.
Set the Viewport layer to DO NOT PLOT.

The viewports can be visible so you can adjust them but will not appear in prints.

19.

Click on **Layer States**.

20.
Click **New**.

21.
Name the new layer state **Floor Plan**.

Click **OK**.

22.
Close the dialog.

Close the Layer Manager dialog.

23.

Layer	Viewport
Display locked	Yes
Annotation scale	1/4" = 1'-0"
Standard scale	1/4" = 1'-0"
Custom scale	1/32"
Layer property o...	No
Visual style	2D Wireframe
Shade plot	Hidden

Select the viewport.
On the Properties palette,
set the Annotation scale to **1/4″ = 1′-0″**,
set the standard scale to **1/4″ = 1′-0″**,
set the Shade plot to **Hidden**, and
set the Display locked to **Yes**.

24. Save as *ex9-3.dwg*.

Exercise 9-4:
Copy a Layout

Drawing Name: copy_layout.dwg
Estimated Time: 15 minutes

This exercise reinforces the following skills:

    ❑ Layouts
    ❑ Viewports

1. Open *copy_layout.dwg*.

2.
Right click on the Floorplan layout.

Select **Move or Copy**.

3.
Highlight **move to end**.

Enable **Create a copy**.

Click **OK**.

4. Right click on the copied layout.

   Select **Rename**.

5. Rename **South Elevation**.

6. Activate/Open the South Elevation layout.
   Select the viewport.
   Right click and set the Display locked to **No**.

7. Double click inside the viewport to activate model space.

8. Left click inside the viewport and then position the elevation view inside the viewport.

   Use PAN to move the view over in the model.

9. Select the viewport.
   Set the Annotation scale to **1/4″ = 1′-0″ [1:100]**.
   Set the Standard scale to **1/4 ″= 1′-0″ [1:100]**.

   Set the Shade plot to **Hidden**.

You may need to re-center the view in the viewport after you change the scale. Use PAN to do this so the scale does not change.

Lock the display.

10. Save the file as *ex9-4.dwg*.

➢ By locking the Display you ensure your model view will not accidentally shift if you activate the viewport.

➢ The Annotation Plot Size value can be restricted by the Linear Precision setting on the Units tab. If the Annotation Plot Size value is more precise than the Linear Precision value, then the Annotation Plot Size value is not accepted.

Most projects require a floorplan indicating the fire ratings of the building walls. These are submitted to the planning department for approval to ensure the project is to building code. In the next exercises, we will complete the following tasks:

- Load the custom linetypes to be used for the exterior and interior walls
- Apply the 2-hr linetype to the exterior walls using the Fire Rating Line tool
- Apply the 1-hr linetype to the interior walls using the Fire Rating Line tool
- Add wall tags which display fire ratings for the walls
- Create a layer group filter to save the layer settings to be applied to a viewport
- Apply the layer group filter to a viewport
- Create the layout of the floorplan with the fire rating designations

Exercise 9-5:
Loading a Linetype

Drawing Name: linetypes.dwg
Estimated Time: 10 minutes

This exercise reinforces the following skills:

❑   Loading Linetypes

FIRE RATED, SMOKE BARRIER WALLS, 1 HOUR

FIRE RATED, SMOKE BARRIER WALLS, 2 HOUR

FIRE RATED, SMOKE BARRIER WALLS, 3 HOUR

FIRE RATED, SMOKE BARRIER WALLS, 4 HOUR

These are standard line patterns used to designate different fire ratings.

I have created the linetypes and saved them into the firerating.lin file included in the exercise files. You may recall we used the ExClick Tools Make Linetype tool to create custom linetypes.

1.   Open *linetypes.dwg*.

2.   Activate the Model tab.

3.   Type **LINETYPE** to load the linetypes.
4.   Select **Load**.
5.   Select the **File** button to load the linetype file.

6.   Locate the *fire rating.lin* file in the exercise files.

     Click **Open**.

     This is a txt file you can open and edit with Notepad.
7.   Hold down the control key to select both linetypes available.

     Click **OK** to load.
8.   The linetypes are loaded.

     Click **OK** to close the dialog box.
9.   Save as *ex9-5.dwg*.

Exercise 9-6:
Applying a Fire Rating Line

Drawing Name: fire rating.dwg
Estimated Time: 25 minutes

This exercise reinforces the following skills:

- ❑   Adding a Layout
- ❑   Layers
- ❑   Edit an External Reference In-Place
- ❑   Adding Fire Rating Lines

1.   Open *fire rating.dwg*.

2.   Right click on the + layout tab.

     Select **From Template**.

3.   Select the **Arch_D** template from the
     exercise folder.

     Click **Open**.

4.   Highlight the Layout name.

     Click **OK**.

5.   Right click on the D-Size Layout.

     Select **Rename**.

     Rename to **Floorplan with Fire Rating**.

6.   Open/activate the **Floorplan with Fire Rating** layout.

7.

Double click inside the layout to activate model space.

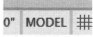

0"   MODEL   ⊞

Note the viewport is bold when model space is activated. You also see MODEL on the status bar.

8.

Unsaved Layer State

Floor Plan

Set the Layer State to **Floor Plan**.

This will freeze the roof and furniture layers.

9.

Launch the **Design Tools** palette from the Home tab on the ribbon if it is not available.

10.

Design

✓ Document

Detailing

Visualization

All Palettes

Right click on the Design Tools palette title bar.

Enable **Document**.

11.

Plan Elevation Label (1)

Anno_Elevation_A2

Anno_Title_A1

North Arrow

Datum Point

Match Line

Bar Scale

Fire Rating Line

Select the Annotation tab.

Locate and select the **Fire Rating Line** tool.

12.

Right click and select **LType** to assign a linetype.

13. `ANNORATINGLINEADD Specify polyline linetype or [?]<Aec_Rating_4Hr>: 2-hr`

Type **2-hr.**
Click **Enter.**

14.

Right click and select **Width**.

15. `ANNORATINGLINEADD Specify polyline width<6">: 11.125"`

Type **11.125"** for the width.

Click **Enter.**

16.

Select the end points of the exterior walls and trace around the building to place the fire rating line.

Go slowly and wait for the preview to place each line segment. You can't undo if you make a mistake on a segment selection.

17.

Set the Display Configuration to **Low Detail.**

This is on the status bar.

18.

Select the polyline that is the fire rating line.

Right click and select **Properties**.

Note that the line is placed on the F-Wall-Fire-Patt layer.

Change the linetype scale to **5.**

Click **ESC** to release the selection.

You should be able to see the hatch pattern of the fire rating line.

19.

Select the **Fire Rating Line** tool.
Right click and select **Copy**.

20.

Right click on the palette.

Click **Paste**.

21.

Select the duplicate Fire Rating Line tool.

Right click and select **Rename**.

22.

Rename **1-hr Fire Rating Line**.

23.

Highlight the **1-hr Fire Rating Line**.

Right click and select **Properties.**

24.

BASIC	
General	
Layer key	▦ WALLFIRE
Layer overrid...	▦ --
Line width	6 1/2"
Linetype	Aec_Rating_1Hr

Set the Linetype to **Aec_Rating_1Hr.**

Set the Linewidth to **6.5".**

Click **OK.**

25.

—— Fire Rating Line

—— 1-hr Fire Rating Line

⬭ Revision Cloud & Tag

Select the **1-hr Fire Rating Line**.

26.

Enter
Cancel

Width
Color
LType

Right click and select **LType** to assign a linetype.

27.

or [?]<Aec_Rating_1Hr>: |

*Notice the default is set to the **Aec_Rating_1Hr.***

Click **ENTER.**

28.

Enter
Cancel
Recent Input

Width
Color
LType

Right click and select **Width.**

29.

Specify polyline width<6 1/2">:

*Notice the default is set to **6.5".***

Click **Enter.**

30.

Place the 1-hr polyline on all the interior walls.

You will need to place more than one polyline as the interior walls are not all connected.

31.

Type **qslelect.**

Select **Polyline** from the Object Type drop-down list.

Highlight **Linetype** in Properties.

Set the Value to **1-hr.**

Click **OK.**

32.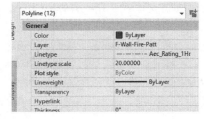

Right click and select **Properties**.

Set the Linetype scale to **20.00**.

33. Click outside the viewport to return to paper space.

34. Save as *ex9-6.dwg*.

Exercise 9-7:
Assigning Fire Ratings to Wall Properties

Drawing Name: fire rating walls.dwg
Estimated Time: 10 minutes

This exercise reinforces the following skills:

    ❑   Wall Properties

1.   Open *fire rating walls.dwg*.

2.   Activate the *Floor Plan with Fire Rating* layout.

    Double click inside the viewport to activate model space.

3.   Activate the Manage tab on the ribbon.

    Select the **Style Manager**.

4.   Locate and select the **Stud-4 Rigid-1.5 Air-1-Brick-4** Wall Style.

Wall Styles
- Brick_Block
- Standard
- Stud-4 GWB-0.625 2 Layers Each Side
- Stud-4 Rigid-1.5 Air-1 Brick-4

5.   On the General tab:

    Select **Property Sets**.

    Property sets control the values of parameters which are used in schedules and tags.

6. 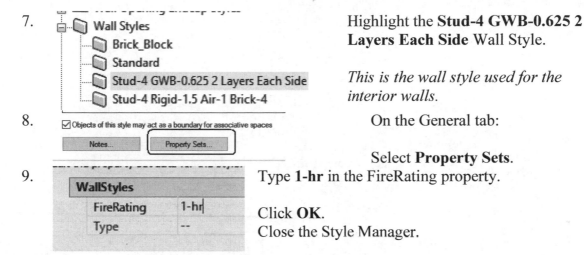 Type **2-hr** in the FireRating property.

Click **OK**.

When defining the attribute to use this value, we use the format WallStyles:FireRating. The first word is the property set and the second word is the property.

7. Highlight the **Stud-4 GWB-0.625 2 Layers Each Side** Wall Style.

This is the wall style used for the interior walls.

8. On the General tab:

Select **Property Sets**.

9. Type **1-hr** in the FireRating property.

Click **OK**.
Close the Style Manager.

10. Double click outside the viewport to return to paper space.

Save the file as *ex9-7.dwg*.

Exercise 9-8:
Creating a Schedule Tag

Drawing Name: wall schedule_tag.dwg
Estimated Time: 15 minutes

This exercise reinforces the following skills:

- ❑ Wall Tags
- ❑ Attributes
- ❑ Create a Schedule Tag

1.   Open *wall schedule tag.dwg*.

2.   **Model**   Activate the **Model** layout.

3.   1'-0" = 1'-0"   Set the view scale to **1'-0" = 1'-0"**.

4.   Unsaved Layer State
     0
     0
     A-Anno-Wall-Iden
     A-Anno-Wall-Iden

     Set the **A-Anno-Wall-Iden** layer current.

     This is the layer to be used by the new wall tag.

5.   Draw an 8" x 8" square.

     Hint: *Use the Rectangle tool. Click one corner and for the second corner, type @ 8", 8".*

6.   Select the square.
     Right click and select **Basic Modify Tools→Rotate**.

     When prompted for the base point, right click and select **Geometric Center**.

     Then select the center of the square.

     Type **45** for the angle of rotation.

7. Activate the Insert ribbon.

Select the **Define Attributes** tool.

8. Type
WALLSTYLES:FIRERATING for the tag.
This is the property set definition used for this tag.
Type **Fire Rating** for the prompt.
Type **2-hr** for the Default value.

Set the Justification for the **Middle center**.
Set the Text style to **RomanS**.
Disable **Annotative**.
Set the Text Height to **1"**.

Enable **Specify on-screen**.

Click **OK**.

9. Select the Geometric Center of the Square to insert the attribute.

WALLSTYLES:FIRERATING

10. *In order to use annotative scales, we need to re-size these elements.*

Use the modify tools to scale the square and the attribute by a factor of 10.67.

11. Activate the Annotate ribbon.

Select the **Create Tag** tool from the Scheduling panel in the drop-down area.

12.

Select the square and the attribute you just created.

Press **ENTER**.

13.

Name the new tag **Wall Fire Rating - Imperial**.

You should see a preview of the tag and you should see the Property Set and Property Definition used by the tag based on the attribute you created.

Click **OK**.

14.

You will be prompted for the insertion point for the tag.

Select the bottom vertex of the rectangle.

15.

The tag will convert to a block and you will see the default attribute.

Notice that when it converts, the size will change.

If you don't see the tag, check that the Display Property is set to Medium Detail on the status bar.

16. Save the drawing as *ex9-8.dwg*.

Exercise 9-9:
Creating a Schedule Tag Tool on the Document Palette

Drawing Name: palette tools.dwg
Estimated Time: 10 minutes

This exercise reinforces the following skills:

     ❑   Wall Tags
     ❑   Create a Tool on the Tool Palette
     ❑   Property Sets

1.   Open *palette tools.dwg*.

2.   Locate the **Wall Tag (Leader) tool** on the Document tool palette.

Right click and select **Copy**.

3.   Move the cursor to a blank space on the palette.

Right click and select **Paste**.

4.   Highlight the copied Wall Tag tool.

Right click and select **Rename**.

5.   Rename it **FireRating Wall Tag (Leader)** and move it below the original wall tag.

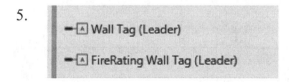

6.

Apply Tool Property Set Data to Ot
Re-import 'Aec6_Wall_Tag' Multi-\
Multi-View Block Definitions...

Cut
Copy

Delete
Rename

Specify Image...
Set Image from Selection...

Properties...

Highlight the **FireRating Wall Tag.**

Right click and select **Properties**.

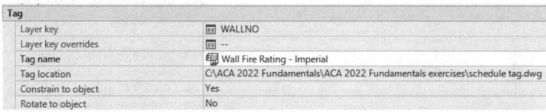

Tag	
Layer key	WALLNO
Layer key overrides	--
Tag name	Wall Fire Rating - Imperial
Tag location	C:\ACA 2022 Fundamentals\ACA 2022 Fundamentals exercises\schedule tag.dwg
Constrain to object	Yes
Rotate to object	No

7. Set the Tag Location as *schedule_tag.dwg*.
Set the Tag Name to **Wall Fire Rating - Imperial**.

You may want to create a drawing to store all your custom schedule tags and then use that drawing when setting the tag location.

Click **OK**.

8. Floorplan with Fire Rating

Select the **Floorplan with Fire Rating** layout.

Activate **Model** space by clicking inside the viewport.

9. Medium Detail ▾

Set the Display to **Medium Detail**.

10.

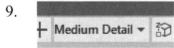
FireRating Wall Tag (Leader)

Select the **FireRating Wall Tag** tool and tag an exterior wall.

11.

Left click to place the tag and then click **OK** to accept the properties.

You should see the updated tag.

12.

Go through the floor plan to tag all the walls.

Double click outside the viewport to switch to paper space.

13. Save as *ex9-9.dwg*.

Layer States

Layer states are used to save configurations of layer properties and their state (ON/OFF/FROZEN/LOCKED). For example, you can set a layer to be a different color depending on the state. Instead of constantly resetting which layers are on or off, you can save your settings in layer states and apply them to layouts.

Layer States are saved in the drawing. To share them across drawings, you need to export them. Each layer state has its own LAS file. To export a layer state, select it in the Layer States Manager and choose Export.

To import a layer state, open the Layer States Manager and click the Import tool. Then select the *.las file you wish to import.

You can save layer states in your drawing template.

Exercise 9-10:

Modify a Dimension Style

Drawing Name: dim_style.dwg
Estimated Time: 15 minutes

This exercise reinforces the following skills:

❑   Dimension Styles
❑   AEC Dimensions

1.   Open *dim_style.dwg*.

2.   Activate the Annotate tab on the ribbon.

     Select the **Dimension Style Editor** on the Dimensions panel.

3.   Highlight **Annotative**.

4.   Select **Modify**.

5.   On the Lines tab,
     set the Baseline spacing to **6″**.

6.   Set Extend beyond dim lines to **2″**.
     Set Offset from origin to **1″**.

7.   On the Symbols and Arrows tab,

     Select **Architectural** tick for the arrowheads.
     Set the Arrow size to **6″**.

8. On the Text tab,
set the Text height to **6″**.

9. Set the Offset from dim line to **1/8″**.

10. Set the Text alignment to **Horizontal.**

11. Activate the Primary Units tab.

Set the Unit format to **Architectural.**
Set the Precision to **1/4″**.

12. Click **OK** and **Close**.

13. Save as *ex9-10.dwg*.

Exercise 9-11:

Dimensioning a Floor Plan

Drawing Name: dim1.dwg
Estimated Time: 30 minutes

This exercise reinforces the following skills:

- ❑ Drawing Setup
- ❑ AEC Dimensions
- ❑ Title Mark
- ❑ Attributes
- ❑ Layouts

1. Open *dim1.dwg*.

2. 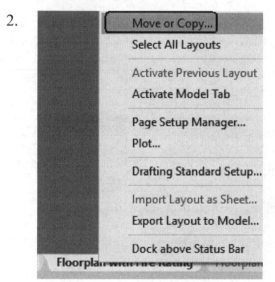 Highlight the **Floor Plan with FireRating** layout tab.

    Right click and select **Move or Copy**.

3. Enable **Create a copy**.

    Highlight **(move to end)**.

    Click **OK**.

4.

Rename	
Move or Copy...	
Select All Layouts	
Activate Previous Layout	
Activate Model Tab	
Page Setup Manager...	
Plot...	
Drafting Standard Setup...	
Import Layout as Sheet...	
Export Layout to Model...	
Dock above Status Bar	

Floorplan with fire rating (2)

Highlight the copied layout tab.

Right click and select **Rename**.

5. A102 02 FLOOR PLAN

Modify the layout name to **A102 02 FLOOR PLAN**.

6.

Activate model space for the new layout.

Activate the Home tab on the ribbon.

7.

ENTCTR_VCR_SLOT

F-Wall-Fire-Patt

Locate the **F-Wall-Patt** layer on the layer drop-down list.

Select **Freeze in Viewport** to turn off the fire rating polylines.

8.

Viewport	
Layer	Viewport
Display locked	No
Annotation scale	1/4" = 1'-0"
Standard scale	1/4" = 1'-0"
Custom scale	1/32"
Layer property o...	No
Visual style	2D Wireframe
Shade plot	Wireframe

Select the viewport.

Unlock the display.

Set the Annotation scale to **¼" = 1'-0"**.

Lock the display.

9. 0" PAPER +

Note that you are in **PAPER** space on the layout.

10.

Activate the Annotate tab on the ribbon.

Select the **Title Mark** tool.
Pick below the view to place the title mark.

11.

VIEWTITLE

ViewportScale

Pick two points to indicate the start and end points of the title mark.

Place the title mark below the view.

12.

Double click to edit the attributes.
In the Title field, enter **FLOOR PLAN**.
In the SCALE field, enter **¼″ = 1′-0″**.

Click **Apply**.

Click **OK**.

The view title updates.

FLOOR PLAN
1/4″ = 1′-0″

13.

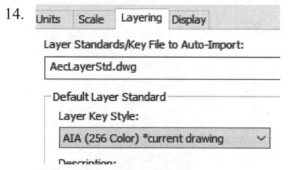

Activate the Home tab on the ribbon.

In the Layers panel drop-down,
select **Select Layer Standard**.

14.

Set the Layer Key Style to **AIA (256 Color)**.

Click **OK**.

15.

On the Status Bar: Set the Global Cut Plane to 3′6″.

That way you see the doors and windows in the floor plan.

16.

Left click on the Global Cut Plane icon.

Set the Cut Height to **3'6"**.

Click **OK**.

17.

Verify that the **Add Annotative Scales** is enabled on the status bar.

18.

for use current <"use current">: A-Anno-Dims

Type **DIMLAYER**.

Type **A-Anno-Dims**.

This ensures any dimensions are placed on the A-Anno-Dims layer, regardless of which layer is current.

19.

Zoom out to see how the layout sheet appears.

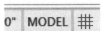

Activate MODEL space in the viewport on the A102 02 FLOOR PLAN layout tab.

20.

Set the Dimension Style to **AEC**.

21.

Select the **Linear Dimension** tool on the Home tab on the ribbon.

22.

H▼ DIMLINEAR Specify first extension line origin or <select object>:

Click **ENTER** to select an object.

23.

Select the right side of the building.

24.

Drag and place the dimension away and to the right of the building.

25.

Select the **Linear Dimension** tool on the Home tab on the ribbon.

26. Select the upper right corner of the building.

Select the midpoint of the window.

Drag and place the dimension away and to the right of the building.

27. Select **DIMCONTINUE**.

28. Select the endpoint of the wall below the window.

Endpoint

29. Select the midpoint of the wall below the door.

Midpoint

30. Select the endpoint of the wall below the door.

Endpoint

31.   Select the midpoint of the sectional door.

32.   Select the south exterior wall.

33.   Click **ENTER** to complete the dimension.

Click **ENTER** to exit the dimension command.

34.   Hover over a dimension.

The dimension should automatically be placed on A-Anno-Dims because the DIMLAYER system variable was set to that layer.

35. Switch back to Paper space.

36. Save as *ex9-11.dwg*.

![Tips & Tricks]

You can insert blocks into model or paper space. Note that you did not need to activate the viewport in order to place the Scale block.

Exercise 9-12:

Create a Wall Section

Drawing Name: wall section.dwg
Estimated Time: 15 minutes

This exercise reinforces the following skills:

❑ Wall Section
❑ Layouts

Most building documents include section cuts for each wall style used in the building model. The section cut shows the walls from the roof down through the foundation. Imagine if you could cut through a house like a cake and take a look at a cross section of the layers, that's what a wall section is. It shows the structure of the wall with specific indication of materials and measurements. It doesn't show every wall, it is just a general guide for the builder and the county planning office, so they understand how the structure is designed.

1.   Open *wall section.dwg*.

2.   Activate the Model layout tab.

3.   Apply the Floor Plan layer state.

      This layer state freezes several layers.

4.   Activate the **Annotate** tab on the ribbon.

      Select the **Section (Sheet Tail)** tool.

5.   Draw the section through the south wall of the garage area.

      Select a point below the wall.
      Select a point above the wall.
      Right click and select ENTER.
      Left click to the right of the section line to indicate the section depth.

6.

Type Exterior Wall Section in the View Name field.

Enable Current Drawing.

Enable Generate Section/Elevation.

Enable Place Title mark.
Set the Scale to 1/8″ = 1′-0″.

7.

Place the view to the right of the South Elevation view.

8.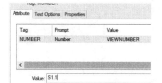

Double click on the view title for the wall section to bring up the attribute editor.

Type **1/8″ = 1′-0″** for the SCALE.

Type **Exterior Wall Section** for the TITLE.

Click ESC to release and update.

9.

Select the View title bubble.

Type **S1.1** for the NUMBER.
Click **OK**.

Click **ESC** to release and update.

10.

Highlight the **Floorplan** layout tab.

Right click and select **Move or Copy**.

11. Enable **Create a copy**.

Highlight **(move to end)**.

Click **OK**.

12. Select the copied layout.

13. Highlight the second layout tab.

Right click and select **Rename**.

14. Modify the layout name to **S1.2 Details**.

15. Unlock the viewport.
Position the Exterior Wall Section in the viewport.

Hint: Use the Named View that was created to adjust the view.

Adjust the size of the viewport.

16.

Layer	Viewport
Display locked	Yes
Annotation scale	1/8" = 1'-0"
Standard scale	1/8" = 1'-0"
Custom scale	0"
Layer property o...	No
Visual style	2D Wireframe
Shade plot	Realistic

Select the viewport.
Set the Annotation scale to **1/8″ = 1′0″**.
Set the Standard scale to **1/8″ = 1′0″**.

Set the Shade plot to **Realistic**.

Lock the display.

The title bar will not display unless the view is set to the correct scale.

17. Click ESC to release the viewport.

18. Save as *ex9-12.dwg*.

EXTRA: Create a section view for the interior wall.

Keynotes

Keynotes are used to standardize how materials are called out for architectural drawings. Most keynotes use a database. The database is created from the Construction Specifications Institute (CSI) Masterformat Numbers and Titles standard. ACA comes with several databases which can be used for keynoting or you can use your own custom database. The database ACA uses is in Microsoft Access format (*.mdb). If you wish to modify ACA's database, you will need Microsoft Access to edit the files.

Exercise 9-13:
Add Keynotes

Drawing Name: add_keynotes.dwg
Estimated Time: 25 minutes

This exercise reinforces the following skills:

- ❑ Keynote Database
- ❑ Adding Keynotes

1. Open *add_keynotes.dwg*.

2. **S1.2 Details** +   Activate the **S1.2 Details** layout tab.

   Double click inside the wall section viewport to activate model space.

   If you add the keynotes inside the viewport on the sheet, they will automatically use the annotative scale of that viewport and will be visible.

3.

Detail Component Databases: Add/Remove...

Keynote Databases: Add/Remove...

☑ Display Edit Property Data Dialog During Tag Insertion

Verify that the keynote database is set properly in Options.

Type **OPTIONS** to launch the Options dialog.

Select the AEC Content tab.

Select the Add/Remove button next to **Keynote Databases**.

4.

Path
. C:\ProgramData\Autodesk\ACA 2020\enu\Details\Details (UK)
. C:\ProgramData\Autodesk\ACA 2020\enu\Details\Details (Global)
C:\ProgramData\Autodesk\ACA 2020\enu\Styles\Imperial
C:\ProgramData\Autodesk\ACA 2020\enu\Styles\Metric
C:\ProgramData\Autodesk\ACA 2020\enu\Details\Details (US)

Verify that the paths and file names are correct.

Click **OK**.

Many companies set up their own keynote files.

Close the Options dialog.

5.

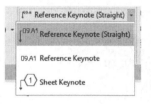

Activate the Annotate tab on the ribbon.

Select the **Reference Keynote (Straight)** tool on the Keynoting panel.

6.

Select the outside component of the wall section.

The Keynote database dialog window will open.

7.

Keynote Database:

C:\ProgramData\Autodesk\ACA 2020\enu\Details\Details (UK)\AecKeynotes (UK NBS).mdb

☐☐ Aec Keynote Database (UK NBS)
☐☐ C - Demolition/Alteration/Renovation
☐☐ D - Groundwork
☐☐ E - In Situ Concrete/Large Precast Concrete
☐☐ F - Masonry
☐☐ F10 - Brick/Block Walling
F10/110 - Clay facing brickwork
F10/170 - Calcium silicate facing brickwork
F10/210 - Concrete facing brickwork

Locate the keynote for the **Clay/facing brickwork**.

Highlight and Click **OK**.

8.

Select the outside component to start the leader line.
Left click to locate the text placement.
Click ENTER to complete the command.

9.

Select the **Reference Keynote (Straight)** tool on the Keynoting panel.

10.

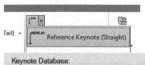

Keynote Database:

C:\ProgramData\Autodesk\ACA 2020\enu\Details\Details (US)\AecKeynotes (US).mdb

Select the (US)AecKeynotes (US).mdb database from the drop-down list.

11.

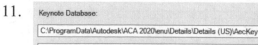

Keynote Database:

C:\ProgramData\Autodesk\ACA 2020\enu\Details\Details (US)\AecKeynotes (US).mdb

- Aec Keynote Database (US)
  - Division 07 - Thermal and Moisture Protection
    - 07 26 00 - Vapor Retarders
      - 07 26 00.A1 - Moisture Barrier
      - 07 26 00.A2 - Building Felt
      - 07 26 00.A3 - 6 Mil Polyethylene
      - 07 26 00.A4 - Vapor Retarder
      - 07 26 00.A5 - Air Barrier
  - Division 26 - Electrical
    - 26 56 00 - Exterior Lighting
      - 26 56 00.A3 - Mercury Vapor Light

Locate the air barrier keynote.

Highlight and Click **OK**.

You can use the Filter tool at the bottom of the dialog to search for key words.

12.

Left click to place the leader and text.

13.

07 26 00.A5 - AIR BARRIER

F10/110 - CLAY FACING BRICKWORK

To turn off the shading on the keynotes, turn off the field display.

Type **FIELDDISPLAY** and then **0**.

14.

Select the **Reference Keynote (Straight)** tool on the Keynoting panel.

15.

Select the top of the wall.

In the Filter text field, type **insulation**.
Left click on the Filter icon.

16.

- Aec Keynote Database (UK NBS)
  - E - In Situ Concrete/Large Precast Concrete
  - F - Masonry
    - F30 - Accessories/Sundry Items for Brick/Block/Stone Walling
      - F30/150 - Cavity insulation
      - F30/151 - Cavity insulation
  - H - Cladding/Covering

Locate the keynote for the rigid insulation and add to the view.

Note that if you select the component on the wall section, ACA will automatically take you to the correct area of the database to locate the proper keynote.

17.

Left click to place the leader and the text.

18.

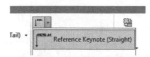

Select the **Reference Keynote (Straight)** tool on the Keynoting panel.

19.

Select the top of the wall.

In the Filter text field, type **stud**.
Left click on the Filter icon.

20.

Details\Details (US)\AecKeynotes (US).mdb

Select the *AecKeynotes (US).mdb.*

21.

Division 06 - Wood, Plastics, and Composites
    06 11 00 - Wood Framing
        06 11 00.A3 - Existing Studs
        06 11 00.D7 - 2x4 Studs
        06 11 00.D8 - 2x4 Studs @ 16" O.C.
        06 11 00.D9 - 2x4 Studs @ 24" O.C.
        06 11 00.F6 - 2x6 Studs
        06 11 00.F7 - 2x6 Studs @ 16" O.C.
        06 11 00.F8 - 2x6 Studs @ 24" O.C.

Locate the keynote for the 2x4 Studs.

22.

Left click to place the leader and the text.

23.

Select the **Reference Keynote (Straight)** tool on the Keynoting panel.

24.

Select the top of the wall.

In the Filter text field, type gypsum.
Left click on the Filter icon.

25.

    09 29 00.C1 - 1/2" Gypsum Wallboard
    09 29 00.C2 - 1/2" Type "X" Gypsum Wallboard
    09 29 00.C3 - 1/2" M.R. Gypsum Board
    09 29 00.D1 - 5/8" Gypsum Wallboard
    09 29 00.D2 - 1 Layer 5/8" Gypsum Board
    09 29 00.D3 - 1 Layer 5/8" Gypsum Board On Each Side
    09 29 00.D4 - Add 1 Layer 5/8" Gypsum Board To Existing Wall

Locate the keynote for the **1 Layer 5/8" Gypsum Board.**

Click **OK.**

26.

Save as *ex9-13.dwg*.

EXTRA: If you created a section view of the interior wall, add keynotes to that section view.

Exercise 9-14:

Add Keynote Legend

Drawing Name: keynote_legend.dwg
Estimated Time: 25 minutes

This exercise reinforces the following skills:

- ❑ Keynote Legend
- ❑ Keynote display
- ❑ View Manager
- ❑ Layouts

1.   Open *keynote_legend.dwg*.

2.   **Model**   Activate the Model layout tab.

3.   Switch to the View tab on the ribbon.

Activate the **Exterior Wall Section** named view.

Notice the keynote numbers and text.

4.

Switch to the Annotate tab on the ribbon.

Locate the **Reference Keynote Display** tool and select it.

5.

Enable **Reference Keynote – Key only**.

Enable **Uppercase**.

Click **OK**.

The keynotes update to display keys only.

6.

Select the **Reference Keynote Legend** tool from the Keynotes panel on the Annotate tab.

7.

You will be prompted for the keynotes to be included in the legend.

Window around to select all the keynotes.

Click ENTER to complete the selection.

8.

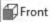

Click to place the keynote legend.

There will be a slight pause before the legend is placed while ACA compiles the data.

REFERENCE KEYNOTES		
DIVISION 04 - MASONRY		
04 21 00 - CLAY UNIT MASONRY		
04 21 00.A1	--	STANDARD BRICK - 3/8" JOINT
DIVISION 06 - WOOD, PLASTICS, AND COMPOSITES		
06 11 00 - WOOD FRAMING		
06 11 00.D9	--	2X4 STUDS @ 24" O.C.
DIVISION 07 - THERMAL AND MOISTURE PROTECTION		
07 21 00 - THERMAL INSULATION		
07 21 00.B3	--	1 1/2" RIGID INSULATION
07 26 00 - VAPOR RETARDERS		
07 26 00.A5	--	AIR BARRIER
DIVISION 09 - FINISHES		
09 29 00 - GYPSUM BOARD		
09 29 00.D1	--	5/8" GYPSUM WALLBOARD

9.

Switch to the View tab.

Launch the **View Manager**.

10.

Click **New**.

11.

Type **Exterior Wall Keynotes Legend**.

Enable **Define Window**.

Click the window icon.

Window around the keynotes legend.

Click **ENTER**.

Click **OK**.
The new named view is listed.

12.

You can see a preview in the preview window.

Click **OK**.

13.

| Model |
| Work |
| Floorplan |
| Door & Window Tags |
| Schedules |
| South Elevation |
| Floorplan with Fire Rating |
| S1.2 Details |
| Master Bath Layout |
| E1.2 Door Details |
| A102 03 ROOM PLAN |

Fire Rating +

Click the double arrows to the right of the layout tabs to bring up the list of available layouts.

Select **S1.2 Details**.

14.

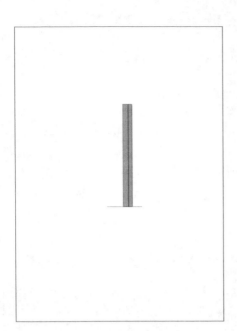

We don't see the keynotes which are visible on the Model layout.

This is because the keynotes do not have the correct annotation scale available.

Check the viewport scales and you will see it is set to **1/8" = 1'-0"**.

Clipped	No
Display locked	Yes
Annotation scale	1/8" = 1'-0"
Standard scale	1/8" = 1'-0"
Custom scale	0"

15. **Model**   Activate the Model layout tab.

16.

If you hover over one of the keynotes, you will see only one annotative scale.

You also will see the keynote information and the assigned layer.

17.

Select one of the keynotes.
Right click and select **Select Similar**.

This will select all the keynotes.

Right click and select **Properties**.

18.

Click on the **Annotative scale** button.

19.

Click **Add**.

20.

Highlight **1/8" = 1'0"**.

Click **OK**.

21.

The **1/8" = 1'0" scale** is added to the list.

Click **OK**.

Close the Properties palette.

Click **ESC** to release the selection.

22.

If you hover over one of the keynotes, you will see more than one annotative scale.

23. **S1.2 Details**

Select the **S1.2 Details** layout.

24.

The keynotes are now visible.

This is because we added an annotative scale that matches the viewport.

Adjust the size of the viewport so you can see the keynotes properly.

25.

Activate model space to adjust the position of the keynotes.

You can adjust the keynotes by clicking on a keynote, select the text grip and positioning the text into the desired location.

Return to PAPER space.

26.

Switch to the Layout tab on the ribbon.

Select **Rectangular** viewport.

27.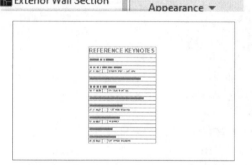

Draw a rectangular viewport on the layout sheet.

Double click inside the viewport to activate model space.

28.

Switch to the View tab on the ribbon.

Activate the **Exterior Wall Keynotes Legend** named view.

29.

The view in the viewport will adjust to display the keynote legend.

Select the viewport.

Right click and select **Properties**.

30.

Misc	
On	Yes
Clipped	No
Display locked	Yes
Annotation scale	1:25
Standard scale	1:25
Custom scale	1/32"

General	
Color	ByLayer
Layer	Viewport

Place the viewport on the Viewport layer.

Set the Annotation scale to **1:25**.
Set the Standard scale to **1:25**.

Set the Display locked to **Yes**.

Click ESC to release the selection.

31.

Save as *ex9-14.dwg*.

Extra: The Title for the Exterior Wall Section needs to have an annotative scale added so it is visible on the S1.2 Details sheet. Add the necessary annotative scale.

Exercise 9-15:

Copy and Paste between Drawings

Drawing Name: target.dwg, source.dwg
Estimated Time: 10 minutes

This exercise reinforces the following skills:

❑ Copy
❑ Paste

1. Open *target.dwg*.
   Open *source.dwg*.

2.   In the *target.dwg*:

Open the Floorplan layout tab.

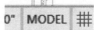

Double left click inside the viewport to activate MODEL space.

Zoom into the bathroom area.

3.

In the *source.dwg*:

[−][Top][Hidden]

Switch to a **Top Hidden** view.

Zoom into the bathroom area.

4.

Select the blocks located in the bathrooms.

5.

Right click and select **Clipboard→Copy with Base Point**.

6.

Select the top right corner of the master bathroom as the base point.

7.

Switch to *target.dwg*.

8.

Right click and select **Copy→Paste to Original Coordinates**.

Paste to Original Coordinates only works if you are using similar floorplans/coordinate systems. If there is a difference between the two drawings, use Copy with Base Point and

9.

then select an insertion point in the target drawing.

Save as *ex9-15.dwg*.

Section Views

Section views show a view of a structure or building as though it has been sliced in half or along an imaginary plane. This is useful because it gives a view through spaces and can reveal the relationships between different parts of the building which may not be apparent on the plan views. Plan views are also a type of section view, but they cut through the building on a horizontal plane instead of a vertical plane.

Exercise 9-16:
Create a Section View

Drawing Name: section.dwg
Estimated Time: 20 minutes

This exercise reinforces the following skills:

- Sections
- Elevations
- Layouts
- Viewports
- View Titles

1.   Open *section.dwg*.

2.   Activate the **Model** layout tab.

3. Restore the **Floor Plan** layer state.

4. Activate the Annotate tab on the ribbon.

Select the **Section (Sheet Tail)** tool on the Callouts panel.

5. Draw a horizontal line through the master bathroom walls as shown.

6. Name the View **Master Bath Elevation**.
Enable **Generate Section/Elevation**.
Enable **Place Titlemark**.
Set the Scale to **1/2″ = 1′-0″**.

Click **Current Drawing**.

Place the view in the current drawing to the right of the building.

7. Right click on the + layout tab.

Select **From Template**.

8.

File name: Arch_D.dwt

Files of type: Drawing Template (*.dwt)

Select the **Arch_D** template from the classwork folder.

Click **Open**.

9.

Layout name(s):

D-Size Layout

OK

Cancel

Select the **D-size Layout**.

Click **OK**.

10.

Rename
Move or Copy...
Select All Layouts
Activate Previous Layout
Page Setup Manager...
Plot...
Drafting Standard Setup...
Import Layout as Sheet...
Export Layout to Model...
Dock Inline with Status Bar

D-Size Layout

Highlight the layout tab.

Right click and select **Rename**.

11.

Details \ Master Bath Elevation /

Rename the layout name to **Master Bath Elevation**.

12.

Maximize Viewport
Viewport Clip
Display Viewport Objects ▸
Display Locked ▸
Shade Plot ▸
Add Selected

Yes
No

Unlock the viewport display.
Select the Viewport, right click and set Display Locked to No.

13.

Activate Model space by double clicking inside the viewport.

Position and resize the viewport to show the Master Bath Elevation.

14.

Misc	
On	Yes
Clipped	No
Display locked	Yes
Annotation scale	1/2" = 1'-0"
Standard scale	1/2" = 1'-0"
Custom scale	1/32"

Select the viewport and set the scales to ½" = **1'-0"**.

Hint: You will not see the title bar unless the annotation scale matches the viewport scale and is set correctly. Remember this is the scale you selected when you created the view.

Set the Display Locked to **Yes**.

15.

Return to the Model tab.
Zoom into the Master Bath Elevation.

16.

Change the values of the view title attributes as shown.

17.

Adjust the position of the view title to be below the elevation.

18.

Use the double arrows on the layout bar to access the Master Bath Elevation and make it active.

19.

Adjust the viewport so the view title is visible using the grips.

20. Save as *ex9-16.dwg*.

To create an elevation view with different visual styles, create a camera view.

Exercise 9-17:
Add a Door Elevation

Drawing Name: door elevation.dwg
Estimated Time: 20 minutes

This exercise reinforces the following skills:

- ❑ Elevations
- ❑ View Titles
- ❑ View Manager
- ❑ Named Views

1. Open *door elevation.dwg*.

2. Activate the **Model** tab.

| Model | Work |

3. Zoom into the laundry room area.

We will create an elevation for the interior door frame.

4. Activate the Annotate tab on the ribbon.

Select the **Elevation (Sheet No)** tool.

5.

Left click to the left of the door to place the elevation marker.

Orient the marker so it is pointing toward the door.

6.

Name the view **Single Interior Door**.
Enable **Generate Section/Elevation**.
Enable **Place Titlemark**.
Set the Scale to **1/2″ = 1′-0″**.

Click **Current Drawing**.

7.

Draw a rectangle around the door to define the scope of the elevation.

8.

Left click to the right of the floor plan to place the elevation view.

9.

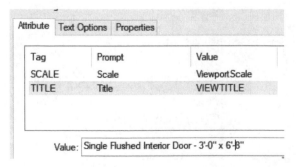

Double click on the title attribute.

Change the title to
**Single Flushed Interior Door - 3'-0"
x 6'-8".**

10.

Change the Scale to **½" = 1'-0"**.

Click **OK.**

11.

Double click on the view number attribute.

Change the View Number to **D1.1.**

This is what the view should look like.

12.

Activate the View tab on the ribbon.

Notice that the door elevation view was added to the view list.

13. Save as *ex9-17.dwg*.

Exercise 9-18:

Add a Door Details Layout

Drawing Name: door detail.dwg
Estimated Time: 45 minutes

This exercise reinforces the following skills:

- ❑ Layouts
- ❑ Named Views
- ❑ Annotation Scales

1.   Open *door detail.dwg.*

2.   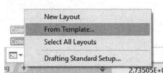   Right click on the + add layout tab.
     Select **From Template**.

3.   Select the **Arch_D** template from the classwork folder.

    File name: Arch_D.dwt

    Files of type: Drawing Template (*.dwt)

    Click **Open**.

4.   Layout name(s):   OK

    D-Size Layout   Cancel

    Select the **D-size Layout**.

    Click **OK**.

5.   Highlight the layout tab.

    Right click and select **Rename**.

6.   **E1.2 Door Details**   Rename the layout name to **E1.2 Door Details**.

    Activate this layout.

7.

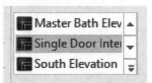

Resize the viewport.

Unlock the display.

Double click inside the viewport to activate MODEL space.

8.

Activate the View tab on the ribbon.

Select the **Single Door Interior** view.

Position inside the viewport.

9.

Viewport		
Layer	Viewport	
Display locked	Yes	▼
Annotation scale	1/2" = 1'-0"	
Standard scale	1/2" = 1'-0"	
Custom scale	1/32"	
Layer property o...	No	
Visual style	2D Wireframe	
Shade plot	Hidden	

Set the Viewport scale to **1/2" = 1'-0"**.
Set the Annotation scale to **1/2" = 1'-0"**.
Set the Shade Plot to **Hidden.**

Set the Display Locked to **Yes.**

10.

Adjust the size of the viewport.

11.

Save as *ex9-18.dwg*.

Callouts

Callouts are typically used to reference drawing details. For example, builders will often reference a door or window call-out which provides information on how to frame and install the door or window. Most architectural firms have a detail library they use to create these call-outs as they are the same across building projects.

Exercise 9-19:
Add a Callout

Drawing Name: callout.dwg
Estimated Time: 45 minutes

This exercise reinforces the following skills:

- ❏ Callouts
- ❏ Viewports
- ❏ Detail Elements
- ❏ Layouts
- ❏ Hatching

1. Open *callout.dwg*.

2. **Model**   Activate **Model** space.

3.   Zoom into the door elevation view.

    We will create a callout for the interior door frame.

4. Activate the Annotate tab on the ribbon.

    Turn ORTHO **ON**.

    Locate and select the **Detail Boundary (Rectangle)** tool on the Detail drop-down list on the Callouts panel.

5.

Draw a small rectangle to designate the callout location around the top of the door.

Select the midpoint of the left side of the rectangle for the start point leader line.
Left click to the side of the callout to place the label.

Click **ENTER** or right click to accept.

6.

Type **HD1** in the View Name field.

Enable **Generate Section/Elevation**.

Enable **Place Titlemark**.

Set the Scale to **1″ = 1′-0″**.

Click on the **Current Drawing** button.

7.

Place the view to the right of the elevation.

8.

Activate the **S1.2 Details** layout tab.

9.

Activate the Layout tab on the ribbon.

Select the **Rectangular** viewport tool.

10.

Draw a rectangle by selecting two opposite corners to place the viewport.

11.

Set the Viewport scale to **1" = 1'-0"**.
Set the Annotation scale to **1" = 1'-0"**.
Set the Shade Plot to **Hidden.**

12.
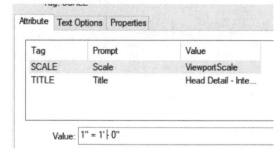

Adjust the size of the viewport.

Position the door view in the viewport.

Hint: Use the Named View list to bring up the view.

Lock the display.

13.

Place the viewport on the viewport layer.

14.

Double click inside the viewport to activate model space.

Select the view title for the door callout.

Type **1" = 1'-0"** for the SCALE.

Type **Head Detail – Interior Door** for the TITLE.

15.

Select the View title bubble.

Type **HD1** for the NUMBER.

Click **ESC** to release and update.

16. Use the grips to position the text and the title line so it looks correct.

17. Launch the **Document** tool palette from the Annotate tab on the ribbon.

18. 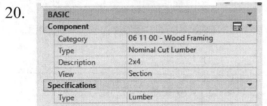 Right click on the Tool palette's bar.

Enable the Detailing palette.

19. Select the **06- Woods, Plastics % Composites** detail tool on the Basic tab.

20. Select 2x4 from the Description list on the Properties palette.

21. Right click and select Rotate to rotate the detail.

22. Place the stud in the upper door frame location.

23.

Geometry	
Position X	394'-9 25/32"
Position Y	20'-6 7/8"
Position Z	0"
Scale X	-1.30000
Scale Y	3.50000
Scale Z	1.00000

Select the stud detail.

Right click and select Properties.
Change the X scale to **1.3**.
Change the Y scale to **3.5**.

The stud size will adjust to fit the frame.

To get those values, I took the desired dimension 12" and divided it by the current dimension 3.5 to get 3.5. I took the desired dimension of 2.0 and divided it by the current dimension of 1.5 to get 1.3. To determine the dimensions, simply measure the current length and width and the desired length and width.

24.

Copy and place the stud to the other side of the door.

25.

Unsaved Layer State

A-Detl-Wide

Layers ▼

Activate the Home tab on the ribbon.

Set the layer **A-Detl-Wide** current.

26.

Draw a rectangle in the header area.

27.

Line

Match Propertie

Draw

Hatch

Select the **Hatch** tool.

28.

ANSI31

Select the **ANSI31** hatch.

29.

Place a hatch inside the rectangle.

30.   Select **Close Hatch Creation** on the tab on the ribbon.

31.   Activate the Annotate tab on the ribbon.

Select the **Text (Straight Leader)** tool.

32.   Text should read:

ADD RETURN ON FRAME WHERE
DRYWALL FINISH IS REQUIRED

33.   Select the text.
Right click and select **Add Leader**.

34.   Add a second leader to the other side of the door frame.

Click **ESC** to release the selection.

35.

Hover over the leader that was just placed.

Notice that it is on the **G-Anno-Note** layer. *This layer was created automatically when you placed the leader.*

Multileader

Color	ByLayer
Layer	G-Anno-Note
Linetype	ByLayer

36. Select the Linear Dimension tool on the Annotate tab on the ribbon.

37. _____ Place a dimension in the opening.

38.

Text

Fill color	None
Fractional type	Horizontal
Text color	ByBlock
Text height	3/32"
Text offset	1/8"
Text outside align	Off

Select the dimension.
Right click and select **Properties**.

Change the Text height to **3/32"**.

39.

Text rotation	0.00
Text view direction	Left-to-Right
Measurement	2'-10 3/4"
Text override	THROAT OPENING = PARTITION WIDTH + 1/8" MIN.

Modify the text to read:

THROAT OPENING = PARTITION WIDTH + 1/8" MIN.

40. Double click outside of the viewport to return to paper space.

This is what the view should look like.

41. Save as *ex9-19.dwg*.

Space Styles

Depending on the scope of the drawing, you may want to create different space styles to represent different types of spaces, such as different room types in an office building. Many projects require a minimum square footage for specific spaces – such as the size of bedrooms, closets, or common areas – based on building code. Additionally, by placing spaces in a building, you can look at the traffic flow from one space to another and determine if the building has a good flow pattern.

You can use styles for controlling the following aspects of spaces:

• Boundary offsets: You can specify the distance that a space's net, usable, and gross boundaries will be offset from its base boundary. Each boundary has its own display components that you can set according to your needs.

• Name lists: You can select a list of allowed names for spaces of a particular style. This helps you to maintain consistent naming schemes across a building project.

• Target dimensions: You can define a target area, length, and width for spaces inserted with a specific style. This is helpful when you have upper and lower space limits for a type of room that you want to insert.

• Displaying different space types: You can draw construction spaces, demolition spaces, and traffic spaces with different display properties. For example, you might draw all construction areas in green and hatched, and the traffic areas in blue with a solid fill.

• Displaying different decomposition methods: You can specify how spaces are decomposed (trapezoid or triangular). If you are not working with space decomposition extensively, you will probably set it up in the drawing default.

Space Styles are created, modified, or deleted inside the Style Manager.

Exercise 9-20:
Creating Space Styles

Drawing Name: spaces.dwg
Estimated Time: 10 minutes

This exercise reinforces the following skills:

- ❑ Style Manager
- ❑ Space Styles

1.   Open *spaces.dwg*.

2.   Activate the **Manage** tab on the ribbon.

       Select the **Style Manager**.

3.   Locate the *Space Styles* inside the drawing.

       Note that there is only one space style currently available in the spaces.dwg.

4.   Select the **Open Drawing** tool.

5.   Browse to the exercise folders for this text.
Change the files of type to **Drawing (*.dwg)**.
Open the *space styles.dwg*.

6.   Expand the *space styles.dwg* in the Style Manager.

Note several space styles have been defined.

7.   Highlight the **Space Styles** in the *space styles.dwg*.
Right click and select **Copy**.

8.   Scroll up to the *ex9-19.dwg*.

Highlight **Space Styles**.

Right click and select **Paste**.

9.   If this dialog appears advising of duplicate definitions,
enable **Overwrite Existing**.
Click **OK**.

10. The space styles are now copied into your project.

Close the Style Manager.

11. Save as *ex9-20.dwg*.

Exercise 9-21:
Adding Spaces

Drawing Name: add_space.dwg
Estimated Time: 15 minutes

This exercise reinforces the following skills:

❑ Layouts
❑ Spaces

1. Open *add_space.dwg*.

2. Right click on the Floorplan layout tab and select **Move or Copy**.

Enable **Create a copy**.

Highlight **(move to end)**.

Click **OK**.

3. Select the copied layout.

4.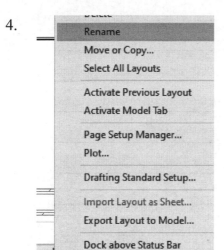

Right click and select **Rename**.

5. _etails ∖ A102 03 ROOM PLAN ／_

Modify the layout name to **A102 03 ROOM PLAN**.

6. 💡 ☀ 🔲 🔓 ⬛ G-Elev-Iden

💡 ☀ 🔲 🔓 ⬜ G-Elev-Line

💡 ☀ 🔲 🔓 ⬛ G-Sect-Iden

💡 ☀ 🔲 🔓 ⬛ G-Sect-Line

Double click inside the viewport to activate model space.

Freeze in Viewport the following layers:

G-Sect-Iden
G-Sect-Line
G-Elev-Line

7.

Unsaved Layer State

Floor Plan

New Layer State...

Manage Layer States...

Select **New Layer State** from the Home tab.

8. 🅰 New Layer State to Save

New layer state name:

Room Plan|

Type **Room Plan** as the new layer state name.

Click **OK**.

9.

Select the **Generate Space** tool from the Home tab on the ribbon on the Build panel.

10. On the Properties palette, select the space style to apply.

Left click inside the designated space to place the space.

11. If you hover over a space, you should see a tool tip with the space style name.

12. Select a space.

In the Properties palette select the Name for the SPACE using the drop-down list.

This is the name that will appear on the room tag.

13. Repeat for all the spaces.
Click ESC to release the selection of each space before moving on to the next space.

Verify that only one space is selected to be renamed each time or you may assign a name to the wrong space unintentionally.

14. Save as *ex9-21.dwg*.

Exercise 9-22:
Modifying Spaces

Drawing Name: space_modify.dwg
Estimated Time: 15 minutes

This exercise reinforces the following skills:

❑   Spaces

1.   Open *space_modify.dwg.*

2.   Open A102 03 ROOM PLAN layout.

3.   Double click inside the viewport to activate MODEL space.

Select the space located in the living room area.

4.   On the Space contextual tab on the ribbon, select **Divide Space**.

5.   *Turn off Object Snap to make selecting the points easier.*

Place points to define a kitchen area.

6.

Repeat the Divide Space command to place lines to define the den and dining room areas.

Make sure each divided space is a closed polygon.

7.

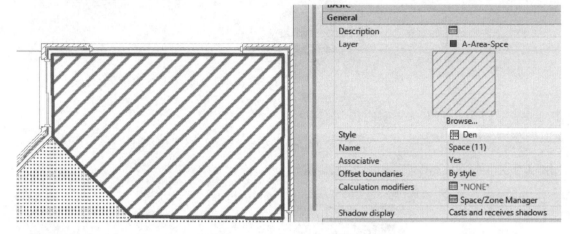

Select the den area space.

Right click and select **Properties**.

Change the Style to **Den**.
Change the Name to **Den.**

Click **ESC** to release the selection.

8.

Select the kitchen area space.

Right click and select **Properties**.

Change the Style to **Kitchen**. Change the Name to **Kitchen**.

Click **ESC** to release the selection.

9.

Select the dining room area space.

Right click and select **Properties**.

Change the Style to **Dining Room**.
Change the Name to **Dining Room**.

Click **ESC** to release the selection.

10.

Select the Living room space.
Right click and select Properties.
On the Design tab,
change the name to **Living Room**.

Repeat for the remaining spaces. Verify that
each space has been assigned the correct
style and name.

11.

Inspect the floor plan to verify that all
spaces have been placed.

Note that different space styles use
different hatch patterns.

12. Save as *ex9-22.dwg*.

Property Set Definitions

Property set definitions are used to assign properties to AEC objects. These properties can then be used in tags and schedules.

Exercise 9-23:

Create a Room Tag

Drawing Name: schedule tag updated.dwg
Estimated Time: 45 minutes

This exercise reinforces the following skills:

- ❑ Spaces
- ❑ Property Set Definitions
- ❑ Style Manager
- ❑ Property Set Formats
- ❑ Attributes
- ❑ Add/Delete Scales
- ❑ Tags
- ❑ Palettes
- ❑ Blocks

1.   Open *schedule tag updated.dwg.*

2.   `1'-0" = 1'-0" ▾ ⚙ ▾ ┼ Medium Detail ▾`   Click on the **Model** tab.
Verify that the scale is set to **1'-0"-1'-0"**.
Set the Display to **Medium Detail**.

3.   Launch the Document tools palette.

Click on the Tags tab.

Locate the Room Tag (w/Dimensions).

Place on the top space in the drawing.

Click **ENTER** to accept placing in the center of the space.

4. The available properties will display.

Click **OK**.

Repeat to tag the lower space.

5. If you zoom in, you see the tag is using mm units, not Imperial.

 The tag is also quite small.

 Select the tag.

6. 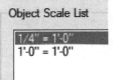 On the ribbon:

Click **Add/Delete Scales**.

7. Click **Add**.

8. Highlight **¼" = 1'-0"**.

Click **OK**.

9. *There are now two annotative scales available for the tag.*

Click **OK**.

Click ESC to release the selection.

10.

Zoom out.

Set the view scale to ¼" = 1'-0".

11.

Both space tags now look OK.

We are going to create a space tag using imperial units.

Select the two room tags that were placed and delete.

12.

Set the scale to **1'-0"-1'-0"**.
Set the Display to **Medium Detail**.

13.

Switch to the Manage tab on the ribbon.

Click on **Style Manager**.

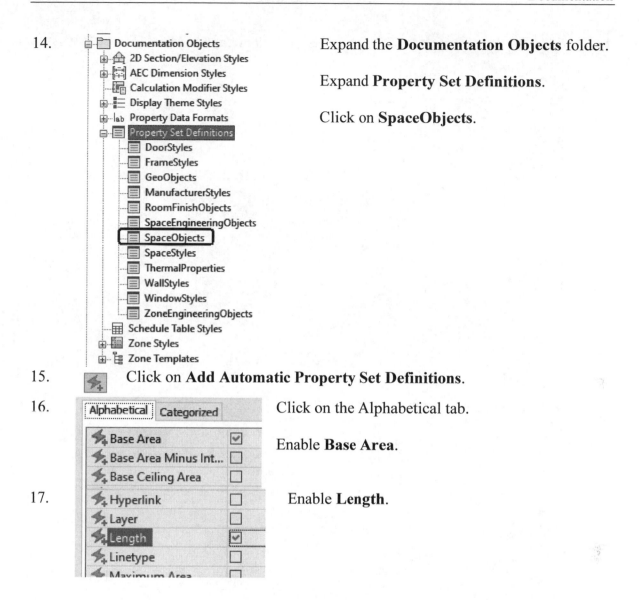

14. Expand the **Documentation Objects** folder.

Expand **Property Set Definitions**.

Click on **SpaceObjects**.

15. Click on **Add Automatic Property Set Definitions**.

16. Click on the Alphabetical tab.

Enable **Base Area**.

17. Enable **Length**.

18.

Enable **Name** and **Style**.

19.

Enable **Width**.

Click **OK**.

20.

You can see a list of properties which will be applied to space objects.

Click **Apply** to save your changes.

21.

Set the Format for the Property Set Definitions.

Set BaseArea to **Area**.
Set Length to **Length – Short**.
Set Name to **Case – Sentence**.
Set Style to **Case – Sentence**.
Set Width to **Length – Short**.
Click **Apply**.

22.

Property Data Formats
- Area
- Case - Sentence
- Case - Upper
- Costing
- Length - Long
- Length - Nominal
- Length - Short
- Number - Object
- Standard
- Unit Suffix – Flow Cubic feet per minu
- Unit Suffix – Power Watts
- Unit Suffix – Temperature Fahrenheit
- Volume

Expand the **Property Data Formats** category.

23.

Real Numbers

Unit Type:	Area
Units:	Square feet
Unit Format:	Decimal
Precision:	0.0
Fraction Format:	Not Stacked

Highlight **Area** in the list.

Set the Precision to **0.0**.

Verify that the other fields are set correctly.

24.

General | Formatting

General

Prefix:	
Suffix:	SF
Undefined:	?
Not Applicable:	NA

Verify that the Suffix is set to **SF**.

Click **Apply**.

25.

Real Numbers

Unit Type:	Length
Units:	Inches
Unit Format:	Architectural
Precision:	0'-0 1/4"
Fraction Format:	Not Stacked

Highlight Length – Short.

Set the Precision to ¼".

Click **Apply**.

Click **OK** to close the Style Manager.

26.

Define Attributes

Switch to the Insert tab on the ribbon.

Click **Define Attributes**.

27.

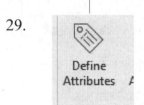

In the Tag field:
Type **SPACEOBJECTS:STYLE**.
In the Prompt field:
Type **Style**.
In the Default field:
Type **Living Room**.
Set the Justification to **Center**.
Set the Text style to **RomanS**.
Disable **Annotative**.
Set the Text height to **1"**
Enable **Specify on-screen** for the insertion point.
Click **OK**.

28.

SPACEOBJECTS.STYLE

Click to place the attribute in the drawing.
Zoom into the attribute.

29.

Switch to the Insert tab on the ribbon.

Click **Define Attributes**.

30.

In the Tag field:
Type **SPACEOBJECTS:BASEAREA**.
In the Prompt field:
Type **Area**.
In the Default field:
Type **00.0 SF**.
Set the Justification to **Center**.
Set the Text style to **RomanS**.
Disable **Annotative**.
Set the Text height to **1"**

31.

Enable **Align below previous attribute definition**
for the insertion point.
Click **OK**.

The attribute is placed.

SPACEOBJECTS:STYLE
SPACEOBJECTS:BASEAREA

32. SPACEOBJECTS:STYLE
     SPACEOBJECTS:BASEAREA
     10' — 0" X 10' — 0"

Place some text below the existing attributes to help you locate the length and width attributes.

You can then modify the text to only show the X.

33.

Switch to the Insert tab on the ribbon.

Click **Define Attributes**.

34.

In the Tag field:
Type **SPACEOBJECTS:LENGTH**.
In the Prompt field:
Type **Length**.
In the Default field:
Type **10'- 0"**.
Set the Justification to **Left**.
Set the Text style to **RomanS**.
Disable **Annotative**.
Set the Text height to **3/4"**

35.

Insertion Point

☑ Specify on-screen

X: 0"

Y: 0"

Z: 0"

Enable **Specify on-screen** for the insertion point.
Click **OK**.

36. SPACEOBJECTS:STYLE
     SPACEOBJECTS:BASEAREA
     SPACEOBJECTS:LENGTH — 0"

Place below and slightly left of the previous attributes.

Use the text to help you locate the attribute.

37. SPACEOBJECTS:STYLE
     SPACEOBJECTS:BASEAREA
     SPACEOBJECTS:LENGTH SPACEOBJECTS:LENGTH

Copy the length attribute and place to the right.

38. Tag: SPACEOBJECTS:WIDTH
     Prompt: Width
     Default: 10'-0"
             OK   Cancel

Double click on the copied attribute.
Change the tag to **SPACEOBJECTS:WIDTH**.
Change the prompt to **Width**.
Click **OK**.
Click **ENTER** to exit the command.

39.   Double click on the text and edit to leave only the X.

40.   Activate the Annotate ribbon.

Select the **Create Tag** tool from the Scheduling panel in the drop-down area.

41. Select the attributes and the text.

42. Type **Room Tag – Imperial** for the name.

Verify that the property sets and definitions have been assigned correctly.

If the property definitions are not correct, you may need to double check your attribute definitions.

43. Click **OK**.

Select the center of the attribute list to set the insertion point for the tag.

44. The attributes will be converted into a block.

If the position of the attributes need to be adjusted, insert the Room Tag – Imperial block into the drawing.

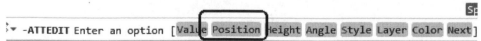

45. Type **-attedit** to modify the block.

Click ENTER until you are prompted to select an attribute.

Click on the attribute to be re-positioned.

Click ENTER to accept your selection.

Click on POSITION to change the attribute position.

Move the attribute to the desired location.

46.   To change the position of the text, select the block.
       Right click and select Edit Block In Place.
       Adjust the position of the text.
       Save the changes.

47.   Save as *ex9-23.dwg*.

Exercise 9-24:

Create a Room Tag Tool

Drawing Name: palette tools.dwg
Estimated Time: 5 minutes

This exercise reinforces the following skills:

- ❏ Spaces
- ❏ Property Set Definitions
- ❏ Style Manager
- ❏ Property Set Formats
- ❏ Attributes
- ❏ Add/Delete Scales
- ❏ Tags
- ❏ Palettes
- ❏ Blocks

1.   Open *palette tools.dwg*.

2.   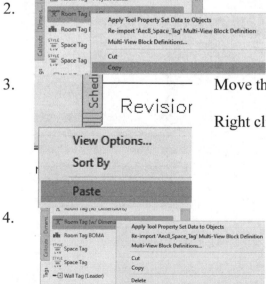   Locate the **Room Tag (w/Dimensions)** tool
       on the Document tool palette.

       Right click and select **Copy**.

3.   Move the cursor to a blank space on the palette.

      Right click and select **Paste**.

4.   Highlight the copied Room Tag tool.

      Right click and select **Rename**.

5. 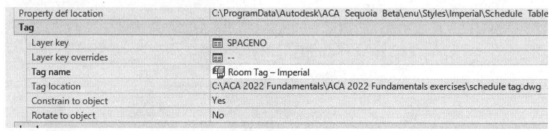 Rename it **Room Tag (w/Dimensions) - Imperial** and move it below the original wall tag.

6.

> Apply Tool Property Set Data to Ot
> Re-import 'Aec6_Wall_Tag' Multi-V
> Multi-View Block Definitions...
>
> Cut
> Copy
>
> Delete
> Rename
>
> Specify Image...
> Set Image from Selection...
>
> Properties...

Highlight the **Room Tag (w/Dimensions) - Imperial.**

Right click and select **Properties**.

Property def location	C:\ProgramData\Autodesk\ACA Sequoia Beta\enu\Styles\Imperial\Schedule Table
Tag	
Layer key	SPACENO
Layer key overrides	--
Tag name	Room Tag – Imperial
Tag location	C:\ACA 2022 Fundamentals\ACA 2022 Fundamentals exercises\schedule tag.dwg
Constrain to object	Yes
Rotate to object	No

7. Set the Tag Location as *schedule_tag.dwg*.
   Set the Tag Name to **Room Tag - Imperial**.

   You may want to create a drawing to store all your custom schedule tags and then use that drawing when setting the tag location.

   Click **OK**.

8. Save as *ex9-24.dwg*.

Exercise 9-25:

Adding Room Tags

Drawing Name: room_tags.dwg
Estimated Time: 20 minutes

This exercise reinforces the following skills:

- ❑ Tags
- ❑ Tool Palette
- ❑ Content Browser

1.   Open *room_tags.dwg*.

2.   Activate the **A102 03 Room Plan** layout.
Double click inside the viewport to activate model space.

3.   Select the **Room Tag (w/Dimensions) – Imperial** on the tool palette.

4.   Select the family room space.
Click **ENTER** to place the tag centered in the room.

5.   A small dialog will appear showing all the data attached to the space.

You can modify any field that is not grayed out.

Click **OK**.

6.   Zoom in to see the tag.

Right click and select **Multiple** and then window around the entire building.

Click ENTER to complete the selection.

This will add space tags to every space.

7.

2 objects were already tagged with the same tag.
Do you want to tag them again?

You will be asked if you want to re-tag spaces which have already been tagged.
Select **No**.

8.

The small dialog will appear again.

Click **OK**.

All the spaces are now tagged.

Click ENTER to exit the command.

9.

Select the Hallway tag.

Right click and select Properties.

10.

On the Properties palette,
select **Anchor**.

11.

Set the Rotation angle to **90**.
Click **OK**.

12. Click ESC or left click outside the building model to release the selected tag.

13. Thc tag is rotated 90 degrees.

14.   Save as *ex9-25.dwg*.

Exercise 9-26:
Adding Door Tags

Drawing Name: door_tags.dwg
Estimated Time: 15 minutes

This exercise reinforces the following skills:

❑   Tags

1.   Open *door_tags.dwg*.

2.   Activate the **Door & Window Tags** layout tab.

3.   Activate model space by double-clicking inside the viewport.

4.   Activate the Annotate tab on the ribbon.
     Select the **Door Tag** tool.

5.   Select a door.

     Click ENTER to center the tag on the door.

6.   Click **OK**.

Some students may be concerned because they see the Error getting value next to the Room Number field.

If you tag the spaces with a room tag assigning a number, you will not see that error.

7. Right click and select **Multiple**. Window around the entire building.

   All the doors will be selected.

   Click **ENTER**.

8.   Click **No**.

   1 object was already tagged with the same tag. Do you want to tag it again?

9.   Click **OK.**

   Edit the property set data for the objects:

10.

All the doors are tagged.

11. Save as *ex9-26.dwg*.

Extra: *Tag all the windows in the building.*

Schedule Styles

A schedule table style specifies the properties that can be included in a table for a specific element type. The style controls the table formatting, such as text styles, columns, and headers. To use a schedule table style, it must be defined inside the building drawing file. If you copy a schedule table style from one drawing to another using the Style Manager, any data format and property set definitions are also copied.

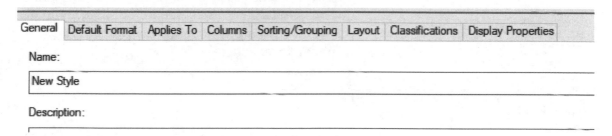

When you create a new Schedule Table Style, there are eight tabs that control the table definition.

Name: New Style Description:	**General** This is where you provide a name and description for your schedule table style.

Default Format

Allows you to set the text style, text height, and cell size.

Applies To

Specify which object types you want to be included in the schedule. You can create a multi-category schedule, such as a Doors & Windows schedule.

Columns

Select which property set definitions to be included in the schedule. You can determine the order of the columns as well as the data format and use formulas.

Sorting/Grouping

Specify the sort order or use filters to control which elements are included in the schedule. This tab also allows you to group elements and create sub-totals on counts.

Layout

Specify the title of the schedule and the text style to be applied to the title, column headers, and data cells.

Classifications

Assign a group of named properties to different object types. They can be used to control how objects are displayed and grouped.

Display Properties

Controls the visibility and color of different components of the schedule table.

Exercise 9-27:

Create a Door Schedule

Drawing Name: door schedule.dwg
Estimated Time: 25 minutes

This exercise reinforces the following skills:

  ❏ Schedules
  ❏ Named Views

1. Open *door schedule.dwg.*

2. Activate the **Model** layout tab.

3.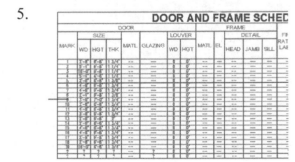

   Activate the Annotate tab on the ribbon.

   Select the **Door Schedule** tool.

4. Window around the building model.

   ACA will automatically filter out any non-door entities and collect only doors.

   Click **ENTER**.

5.

   Left click to place the schedule in the drawing window.

   Click **ENTER**.

6. *A ? will appear for any doors that are missing tags. So, if you see a ? in the list go back to the model and see which doors are missing tags.*

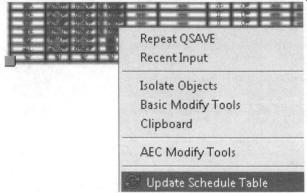

Once you add door tags, you need to update the schedule. Select the schedule, right click and select Update Schedule Table.

7. Activate the **Schedules** layout tab.

Double click inside the viewport to activate model space.

8. Rectangular · Activate the Layout tab on the ribbon.
Select the **Rectangular** viewport tool.

9.   Draw a rectangular viewport next to the floor plan viewport.

Position the door schedule in the viewport.

10.

Layer	Viewport
Display locked	Yes
Annotation scale	1/8" = 1'-0"
Standard scale	Custom
Custom scale	0"
Visual style	2D Wireframe
Shade plot	Hidden

Select the viewport.

Verify that it is on the Viewport layer.

Set the Standard scale to **Custom.**

Set the Display locked to **Yes**.

11. Switch to the MODEL layout.

12.　　Zoom into the Door Schedule.

13.
　Top
　Bottom
　Left
　Right
　Front
　Back
　SW Isometric
　SE Isometric
　NE Isometric

　View Manager...

Activate the View tab on the ribbon.

Launch the **View Manager.**

14.　New...　Select **New**.

15.

View name: Door Schedule

View category: <None>

View type: Still

Boundary
　● Current display
　○ Define window

Type **Door Schedule** for the name.

Enable **Current display**.

Click **OK**.

Close the dialog.

16.　Save as *ex9-27.dwg*.

Exercise 9-28:

Create a Door Schedule Style

Drawing Name: schedule_styles.dwg
Estimated Time: 30 minutes

This exercise reinforces the following skills:

- ❑ Schedules
- ❑ Style Manager
- ❑ Text Styles
- ❑ Update Schedule

1.   Open *schedule_styles.dwg.*

2.   Open the **MODEL** tab.

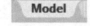

3.   Activate the View tab on the ribbon.

Restore the **Door Schedule** view.

4.   Select the door schedule.

Right click and select **Copy Schedule Table Style and Assign….**

This will create a new style that you can modify.

5.   Select the **General** tab.

Rename **Custom Door Schedule**.

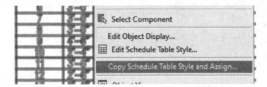

6.   Select the **Columns** tab.

7. Highlight Louver, WD, and HGT.

8. [Delete...]   Click **Delete**.

9. A Remove Columns/Headers   You will be asked to confirm the deletion.

☑ HGT(DoorStyles:LouverHeight)   Click **OK**.
☑ LOUVER
☑ WD(DoorStyles:LouverWidth)

[OK]   [Cancel]

10. Highlight the columns under Hardware.

Click **Delete**.

HARDWARE

NG...   SET NO   KEYSIDE RM...   NOTES

ts   DoorObjects   DoorObjects   DoorObjects
g   SetNumber   KeySideRoom...   Remarks
er   Case - Upper   Case - Upper   Case - Senten...
       --   --   --
       No   No   No
       No   No   No
       No   No   No

antity Column

[Modify...]   [Delete...]

11.

Click **OK**.

12.

Highlight **MARK**.

Click the **Add Column** button.

13.

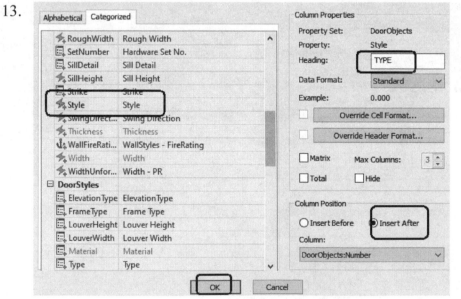

Scroll down until you see Style.

Highlight **Style**.

Confirm that the Column Position will be inserted after the DoorObjects: Number. Change the Heading to **TYPE**.

Click **OK**.

14. The new column is now inserted.

	MARK	TYPE	
Property Set	DoorObjects	DoorObjects	Doo
Property	Number	Style	
Format	Standard	Standard	Leng
Example	0.000	0.000	(
Total	No	No	
Hide	No	No	
Matrix	No	No	
Max Cols.			

15. Select the Layout tab.

General | Default Format | Applies To | Columns | Sorting | **Layout** | Classificati

Table Title: DOOR SCHEDULE

Format

Title: ☑ Override Cell Format...

Column Headers: ☑ Override Cell Format...

Matrix Headers: ☐ Override Cell Format...

Change the Table Title to **DOOR SCHEDULE**.

16.

	SIZE			MATL
le	WD	HGT	THK	
jects	DoorObjects	DoorObjects	DoorObjects	DoorStyles
le	Width	Height	Thickness	Material
lard	Length - Long	Length - Long	Length - Short	Case - Upper
	0	0	0	--
)	No	No	No	No
)	No	No	No	No
)	No	No	No	No

☐ Include Quantity Column

Formula Column... | Add Header... | Modify... |

Activate the Columns tab.

Highlight the **WD** column.

Select **Modify**.

17.

Column Properties

Property Set: DoorObjects
Property: Width
Heading: WIDTH
Data Format: Length - Long
Example: 0.000

Change the Heading to **WIDTH**.

Click **OK**.

18.

SIZE	
HGT	THK
DoorObjects	DoorObject
Height	Thickness
Length - Long	Length - Shc
0.000	0.0000
No	No
No	No
No	No

Quantity Column

Modify...

Highlight the **HGT** column.

Select **Modify**.

19.

Change the Heading to **HEIGHT**.

Click **OK**.

20.

Delete the THK column.

21.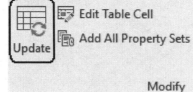

Click **OK**.

22. Click **OK** to close the dialog.

23.

The schedule updates.

If there are question marks in the schedule, that indicates doors which remain untagged.

24.

Select the schedule.
Select **Update** from the tab on the ribbon.
Click **ESC** to release the selection.

25.

Activate the Home tab on the ribbon.

Select the **Text Style** tool on the Annotation panel.

26. 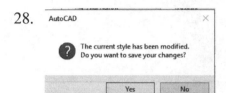 Notice there are text styles set up for schedules. Highlight each one to see their settings.

27. Highlight **Schedule-Data.**
Set the Font Name to **Arial Narrow**.
Enable **Annotative**.

Click **Apply**.

28. If this dialog appears, Click **Yes.**

29. Highlight Schedule-Header.
Set the Font Name to **Arial**.
Set the Font Style to **Bold**.
Enable **Annotative**.

Click **Apply**.

30. 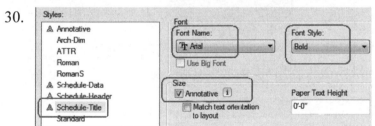 Highlight Schedule-Title.
Set the Font Name to **Arial**.
Set the Font Style to **Bold**.
Enable **Annotative**.

Click **Apply** and **Close**.

31. Note that the schedule automatically updates.

DOOR SCHEDULE

	DOOR		
		SIZE	
MARK	TYPE	WIDTH	HEIGHT
1	Hinged - Single	2'-6"	6'-8"
2	Cased Opening - Halfround	3'-0"	6'-8"
3	Cased Opening - Halfround	2'-6"	6'-8"
4	Pocket - Single	2'-4"	6'-8"
5	Pocket - Single	2'-4"	6'-8"
6	Sliding - Double - Full Lite	10'-0"	6'-8"
7	Sliding - Double - Full Lite	6'-4"	6'-8"
8	Sliding - Double - Full Lite	5'-4"	6'-8"
9	Overhead - Sectional	16'-0"	6'-8"
10	Hinged - Single - Exterior	2'-6"	6'-8"
11	Hinged - Single	2'-6"	6'-8"
12	Hinged - Single	2'-6"	6'-8"
13	Hinged - Single	2'-6"	6'-8"
14	Hinged - Single	2'-6"	6'-8"
15	Hinged - Single - Exterior	3'-0"	6'-8"
16	Bifold - Double	4'-0"	6'-8"
17	Bifold - Single	3'-0"	7'-0"
18	Bifold - Double	4'-6"	6'-8"
19	Bifold - Double	4'-6"	6'-8"
20	Bifold - Double	4'-6"	6'-8"
21	Bifold - Double	4'-6"	6'-8"

32. Save as *ex9-28.dwg*.

Exercise 9-29:

Create a Room Schedule

Drawing Name: room_schedule.dwg
Estimated Time: 30 minutes

This exercise reinforces the following skills:

- ❑ Schedules
- ❑ Tool Palettes
- ❑ Creating Tools
- ❑ Schedule Styles
- ❑ Property Set Definitions

1. Open *room_schedule.dwg*.

2.   Activate the Manage tab on the ribbon.

    Select **Style Manager**.

3.   Locate the Schedule Table Styles category under Documentation.

4.   Highlight the Schedule Table Styles category.

    Right click and select **New**.

5.   On the General tab:

    Type **Room Schedule** for the Name.

    Type **Uses Space Information** for the Description.

6. Select the Applies To tab.

Enable **Space**.

Note that Spaces have Classifications available which can be used for sorting.

7. Select the Columns tab.

Select **Add Column**.

8. Select **Style**.

Change the Heading to **Room Name**.

Set the Data Format to **Case – Sentence**.

Click **OK**.

If your property set definitions have not been modified, you will not be able to access these properties.

9. Select **Add Column**.

10. Select the Alphabetical tab to make it easier to locate the property definition.

Locate and select **Length**.

Click **OK**.

11. Select **Add Column**.

12. Select the Alphabetical tab to make it easier to locate the property definition.

Locate and select **Width**.

Click **OK**.

13. Select Add Column.

14.

Select the Alphabetical tab to make it easier to locate the property definition.

Select **BaseArea**.

Change the Heading to **Area**.

Click **OK**.

15.

	Room Name	Length	Width	Area
Property Set	SpaceObjects	SpaceObjects	SpaceObjects	SpaceObjects
Property	Style	Length	Width	BaseArea
Format	Case - Senten...	Length - Short	Length - Short	Area
Example				SF
Total	No	No	No	No
Hide	No	No	No	No
Matrix	No	No	No	No
Max Cols.				

The columns should appear as shown.

16.

General | Default Format | Applies To | Columns | Sorting/Grouping | Layout | Cl

Table Title: Room Schedule

Format

Title: ☐ Override Cell Format...

Column Headers: ☐ Override Cell Format...

Matrix Headers: ☐ Override Cell Format...

Select the Layout tab.

Change the Table Title to **Room Schedule.**

17.

Add... Remove

Sort Order

Sort
Group
Display Subtotals For Group

Select the **Sorting/Grouping** tab.
Highlight **Sort**.
Select the **Add** button.

18.

SpaceObjects:BaseArea
SpaceObjects:Length
SpaceObjects:Style
SpaceObjects:Width

OK

Select **SpaceObjects: Style** to sort by Style name.
Click **OK**.

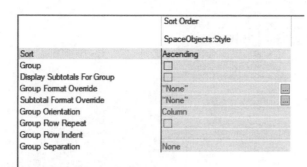

The panel should fill in with the sort information.

19. Place a check next to **Group**.

Place a check next to **Display Subtotals for Group.**

Note: To enable subtotals modify at least one column on the columns tab to include a total.

A small red note will appear at the bottom of the dialog.

20. Select the Columns tab.

Highlight **Area** and select **Modify**.

21. Enable **Total.**

Click **OK** to close the dialog.

Click **OK** to close the Style Manager dialog.

22. Launch the Annotation Tools palette from the Annotate tab on the ribbon.

23. Select the Schedules tab.

24. 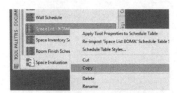 Highlight the Space List – BOMA.

Right click and select Copy.

25. Move the mouse off the tool.

Right click and select **Paste**.

26. 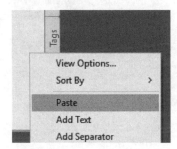 Select the copied tool.

Right click and select **Rename**.

27. 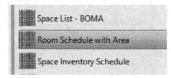 Type **Room Schedule with Area** for the name.

28. 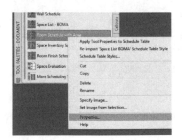 Highlight the new tool.

Right click and select **Properties**.

29.

In the Style field, select the **Room Schedule** style which you just created.

Click **OK**.

30.

Activate the Model tab.

Thaw the **G-Area-Spce** layer if it is not thawed.

31.

Select the Room Schedule with Area tool.

Window around the building.

Click ENTER.

Pan over to an empty space in the drawing and left pick to place the schedule.

Click ENTER.

Room Schedule			
Room Name	Length	Width	Area
?	?	?	? SF
	?	?	? SF
	?	?	? SF
Bathroom	11'-5 1/2"	5'-11"	60.5 SF
	15'-0"	5'-2 1/2"	69.2 SF
			129.7 SF
Bedroom	15'-0"	16'-4 3/4"	246.9 SF
	11'-5 1/2"	12'-7"	144.2 SF
	15'-0"	13'-3 3/4"	168.4 SF
			559.5 SF
Closet	5'-1 3/4"	1'-11 3/4"	10.2 SF
	5'-5 1/4"	1'-11 1/2"	10.7 SF
	5'-0 1/4"	1'-11 1/2"	9.9 SF
	3'-9"	2'-11 1/4"	11.1 SF
	5'-9 1/4"	1'-11 3/4"	11.4 SF
			53.2 SF
Den	20'-0"	13'-7"	250.1 SF
			250.1 SF
Dining room	21'-2 1/2"	10'-3 3/4"	178.7 SF
			178.7 SF
Garage	20'-8"	19'-11 1/2"	412.5 SF
			412.5 SF
Hallway	3'-0"	15'-11 1/4"	47.8 SF
			47.8 SF
Kitchen	13'-0 3/4"	13'-1"	85.4 SF
			85.4 SF
Laundry room	20'-8"	7'-7"	156.7 SF
			156.7 SF
Livingroom	25'-5 1/2"	27'-6 1/2"	597.5 SF
			597.5 SF
			2471.2 SF

If there are any ? symbols in the table, you have some spaces which are unassigned.

You may have placed duplicate spaces or empty spaces.

It may be easier to select all the spaces using QSELECT and delete them and then replace all the spaces.

32.

Activate the **A102 03 ROOM PLAN** layout tab.

Double click inside the viewport to activate model space.

33.

Adjust the size and position of the viewport.

34.

Activate the viewport and freeze the G-Area-Spce layer in the viewport.

If you don't see the space tags, it is because you need to add the correct annotative scale for the tags.

Double click outside the viewport to deactivate.

35.

Activate the Layout tab on the ribbon.

Place a rectangular viewport for the room schedule.

36.

Use Zoom Extents and Zoom Window to center the schedule in the viewport.

37.

Save as *ex9-29.dwg*.

Extra: Place the new rectangular viewport on the viewport layer.

Create a named view for the room schedule.

Add the correct annotative scale to the space tags so they are visible on the sheet.

Sheet Set Manager

The Sheet Set Manager provides a list of layout tabs available in a drawing or set of drawings and allows you to organize your layouts to be printed.

The Sheet Set Manager allows you to print to a printer as well as to PDF. Autodesk does not license their PDF creation module from Adobe. Instead, they have a partnership agreement with a third-party called Bluebeam. This means that some fonts may not appear correct in your PDF print.

Exercise 9-30:
Creating a PDF Document

Drawing Name: pdf.dwg
Estimated Time: 15 minutes

This exercise reinforces the following skills:

❑   Printing to PDF
❑   Sheet Set Manager

1.   Open *pdf.dwg*.

2.   Type **SSM** to launch the Sheet Set Manager.

3.   Select the drop-down arrow next to Open and select **New Sheet Set**.

4.   Enable **Existing drawings**.

     Click **Next**.

5.   Type **Brown Project**.

     Click **Next**.

6.   Browse...   Select the **Browse** button.

7.   Locate the pdf drawing file.

pdf.dwg
- Work
- ☑ Floorplan
- South Elevation
- ☑ Floorplan with Fire Rating
- S1.2 Details
- Master Bath Layout
- E1.2 Door Details
- ☑ A102 03 ROOM PLAN
- Door & Window Tags
- Schedules

Uncheck all the files.

Place a check next to the three floor plan layouts:

Floorpln
Floor Plan with Fire Rating
A102 03 ROOM PLAN

8.   Import Options...   Select **Import Options**.

9.   ☐ Prefix sheet titles with file name   Uncheck Prefix sheet title with the file name.

Click **OK**.

Click **Next.**

10. Sheet Set Preview:

Brown Project
- 1 Floorplan
- 2 Floorplan with Fire Rating
- 3 A102 03 ROOM PLAN

The sheets to be included in the sheet set are listed.

Click **Finish**.

11. Sheets

Brown Project
- 1 - Floorplan
- 2 - Floorplan with Fire Rating
- 3 - A102 03 ROOM PLAN

You should see the sheet set list in the Sheet Set Manager.

If you don't, select Open and select the SSM file.

12. Sheets

Brown Pr...
- 1 - Flo
- 2 - Flo
- 3 - A1

Close Sheet Set
New Sheet...
New Subset...
Import Layout as Sheet...
Resave All Sheets
Archive...
Publish   >
eTransmit...
Transmittal Setups...
Insert Sheet List Table...

Publish to DWF
Publish to DWFx
Publish to PDF
Publish to Plotter

Highlight the SSM file name.

Right click and select **Publish→Publish to PDF**.

13. File name: Brown Project.pdf

Files of type: PDF Files (*.pdf)

Browse to your classwork folder.

Save the pdf file.

14.

Browse to where the file was saved using Windows File Explorer.

Open the PDF file and review.

Save as *ex9-30.dwg*.

Legends

Component legends are used to display symbols that represent model components, such as doors and windows. Some architectural firms may already have tables with these symbols pre-defined. In which case, you can simply add them to your drawing as an external reference or as a block. However, if you want to generate your own legends using the components in your ACA model, you do have the tools to do that as well.

Exercise 9-31:
Create Door Symbols for a Legend

Drawing Name: legend.dwg
Estimated Time: 40 minutes

This exercise reinforces the following skills:

- ❑ Doors
- ❑ Images
- ❑ Object Viewers

1. Open *legend.dwg*.

2.

Select the **A102 03 Floor Plan** layout.

Activate **MODEL** space in the floor plan viewport. Hover over the interior door in the laundry room.

3.

Note that it is a Single hinged door.

4.

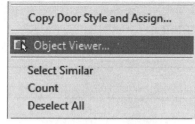

Select the interior door in the laundry room.

Right click and select **Object Viewer**.

5.

Use the arrows above the view cube to rotate the view so the door appears to be horizontal.

6.

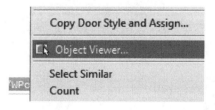

Select the **Save** button in the upper left.

7.

Browse to your work folder.

Type **single-hinged** for the file name.

Click **Save**.
Close the Object Viewer.

8.

Hover over the exterior door in the laundry room.

Note that it is a Single exterior hinged door.

9.

Select the exterior door in the laundry room.

Right click and select **Object Viewer**.

10.

Use the arrows above the view cube to rotate the view so the door appears to be horizontal.

11. Select the **Save** button in the upper left.

12. Browse to your work folder.

    Type **single-exterior** for the file name.

    Click **Save**.
    Close the Object Viewer.

13. Hover over the sectional overhead door in the garage.

    Note that it is an Overhead-Sectional door.

14. Select the door.

    Right click and select **Object Viewer**.

15. Use the arrows above the view cube to rotate the view so the door appears to be horizontal.

16. Select the **Save** button in the upper left.

17. Browse to your work folder.

    Type **overhead-sectional** for the file name.

    Click **Save**.
    Close the Object Viewer.

18. Hover over the closet door near the home entrance.

    Note that it is a Bifold-single door.

19.

Copy Door Style and Assign...

Object Viewer...

Select Similar
Count

Select the door.

Right click and select **Object Viewer**.

20.

3D Hidden

Plan Only

Select the **Save** button in the upper left.

21.

File name: bifold-single

Files of type: PNG (*.png)

Browse to your work folder.

Type **bifold-single** for the file name.

Click **Save**.
Close the Object Viewer.

22.

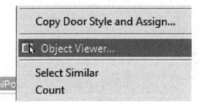

Hover over the closet door in the bedroom.

Note that it is a Bifold-Double door.

23.

Copy Door Style and Assign...

Object Viewer...

Select Similar
Count

Select the door.

Right click and select **Object Viewer**.

24.

3D Hidden

Plan Only

Select the **Save** button in the upper left.

25.

File name: bifold-double

Files of type: PNG (*.png)

Browse to your work folder.

Type **bifold-double** for the file name.

Click **Save**.
Close the Object Viewer.

26.
Hover over the pocket door below the master bedroom.

Note that it is a Single Pocket door.

27.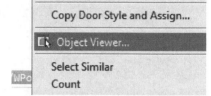
Select the door.

Right click and select **Object Viewer**.

28.
Select the **Save** button in the upper left.

29.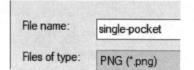
Browse to your work folder.

Type **single-pocket** for the file name.

Click **Save**.
Close the Object Viewer.

30.
Hover over the sliding door in the master bedroom.

Note that it is a Sliding-Double-Full Lite door.

31.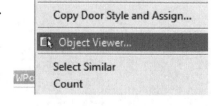
Select the door.

Right click and select **Object Viewer**.

32.
Use the arrows above the view cube to rotate the view so the door appears to be horizontal.

33.

Select the **Save** button in the upper left.

34.

File name: Sliding-Double-Full Lite

Files of type: PNG (*.png)

Browse to your work folder.

Type **Sliding-Double-Full Lite** for the file name.

Click **Save**.
Close the Object Viewer.

35. Hover over the Cased Opening below the master bedroom.

Closet

Door
Layer   A-Wall-Open
Style Name   Cased Opening - Halfround
Style Description   Cased halfround opening

Note that it is a Cased halfround Opening.

36.

Copy Door Style and Assign...

Object Viewer...

Select Similar
Count

Select the opening.

Right click and select **Object Viewer**.

37.

3D Hidden

Plan Only

Select the **Save** button in the upper left.

38.

File name: cased-opening-halfround

Files of type: PNG (*.png)

Browse to your work folder.

Type **cased-opening-halfround** for the file name.

Click **Save**.
Close the Object Viewer.

39. Save as *ex9-31.dwg*.

Exercise 9-32:
Convert Images to Blocks

Drawing Name: blocks.dwg
Estimated Time: 45 minutes

This exercise reinforces the following skills:

- ❑ Images
- ❑ Blocks
- ❑ Attach

1. Open *blocks.dwg.*

2. Activate the **MODEL** layout tab.

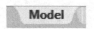

3. Activate the Insert tab on the ribbon.

    Select **Attach**.

4. Locate the **bifold-double** image file.
    Click **Open**.

    File name: bifold-double.png

    Files of type: All image files

5.

    Enable **Specify Insertion point**.
    Disable **Scale**.
    Disable **Rotation**.

    Click **OK**.

    Left click to place in the display window.

6. Select **Create Block** from the Insert tab on the ribbon.

7.

Type **bifold-double** for the Name.

Select a corner of the image as the base point.
Select the image.
Enable **Delete.**
Enable **Scale Uniformly**.
Disable **Allow Exploding**.
Click **OK**.

8.

Activate the Insert tab on the ribbon.

Select **Attach**.

9.

Locate the **bifold-single** image file.
Click **Open**.

10.

Enable **Specify Insertion point**.
Disable **Scale**.
Disable **Rotation**.

Click **OK**.

Left click to place in the display window.

11.

Select **Create Block** from the Insert tab on the ribbon.

12.

Type **bifold-single** for the Name.

Select a corner of the image as the base point.
Select the image.
Enable **Delete.**
Enable **Scale Uniformly**.
Disable **Allow Exploding**.

Click **OK**.

13.

Activate the Insert tab on the ribbon.

Select **Attach**.

14. Locate the **Sliding-Double-Full Lite** image file. Click **Open**.

15. Enable **Specify Insertion point**.
Disable **Scale**.
Disable **Rotation**.

Click **OK**.

Left click to place in the display window.

16. Select **Create Block** from the Insert tab on the ribbon.

17. Type **Sliding-Double-Full Lite** for the Name.

Select a corner of the image as the base point.
Select the image.
Enable **Delete.**
Enable **Scale Uniformly**.
Disable **Allow Exploding**.

Click **OK**.

18. Activate the Insert tab on the ribbon.

Select **Attach**.

19. 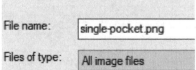 Locate the **Single Pocket** image file. Click **Open**.

20. Enable **Specify Insertion point**.
Disable **Scale**.
Disable **Rotation**.

Click **OK**.

Left click to place in the display window.

21. Select **Create Block** from the Insert tab on the ribbon.

22. Type **Single Pocket** for the Name.

   Select a corner of the image as the base point.
   Select the image.
   Enable **Delete.**
   Enable **Scale Uniformly**.
   Disable **Allow Exploding**.

   Click **OK**.

23. Activate the Insert tab on the ribbon.

   Select **Attach**.

24.
   File name: single-hinged.png

   Files of type: All image files

   Locate the **single-hinged** image file.
   Click **Open**.

25.
   Name: single-hinged

   Preview

   Path type: Full path

   Insertion point
   ☑ Specify on-screen
   X: 0"
   Y: 0"
   Z: 0"

   Enable **Specify Insertion point**.
   Disable **Scale**.
   Disable **Rotation**.

   Click **OK**.

   Left click to place in the display window.

26. Select **Create Block** from the Insert tab on the ribbon.

27.
   Name: single-hinged

   Base point
   ☐ Specify On-screen
   Pick point
   X: -119'-3 89/128"
   Y: 23'-8 29/128"
   Z: 0"

   Objects
   ☐ Specify On-screen
   Select objects
   ○ Retain
   ○ Convert to block
   ● Delete
   1 object selected

   Behavior
   ☐ Annotative
   ☐ Match block orientation to layout
   ☑ Scale uniformly
   ☐ Allow exploding

   Type **single-hinged** for the Name.

   Select a corner of the image as the base point.
   Select the image.
   Enable **Delete.**
   Enable **Scale Uniformly**.
   Disable **Allow Exploding**.

Click **OK**.

28. Activate the Insert tab on the ribbon.

Select **Attach**.

29. Locate the **single-exterior** image file.
Click **Open**.

File name: single-exterior.png

Files of type: All image files

30. Enable **Specify Insertion point**.
Disable **Scale**.
Disable **Rotation**.

Name: single-exterior

Click **OK**.

Left click to place in the display window.

31. Select **Create Block** from the Insert tab on the ribbon.

32. Type **single-exterior** for the Name.

Select a corner of the image as the base point.
Select the image.
Enable **Delete.**
Enable **Scale Uniformly**.
Disable **Allow Exploding**.

Click **OK**.

33. Activate the Insert tab on the ribbon.

Select **Attach**.

34. Locate the **overhead-sectional** image file.
Click **Open**.

File name: overhead-sectional.png

Files of type: All image files

35.

Enable **Specify Insertion point**.
Disable **Scale**.
Disable **Rotation**.

Click **OK**.

Left click to place in the display window.

36.

Select **Create Block** from the Insert tab on the ribbon.

37.

Type **overhead-sectional** for the Name.

Select a corner of the image as the base point.
Select the image.
Enable **Delete.**
Enable **Scale Uniformly**.
Disable **Allow Exploding**.

Click **OK**.

38.

Activate the Insert tab on the ribbon.

Select **Attach**.

39.

File name: cased-opening-halfround.png

Files of type: All image files

Locate the **cased-opening-halfround** image file.
Click **Open**.

40.

Enable **Specify Insertion point**.
Disable **Scale**.
Disable **Rotation**.

Click **OK**.

Left click to place in the display window.

41.

Select **Create Block** from the Insert tab on the ribbon.

42.

Type **cased-opening-halfround** for the Name.

Select a corner of the image as the base point.
Select the image.
Enable **Delete.**
Enable **Scale Uniformly**.
Disable **Allow Exploding**.

Click **OK**.

43. Save as *ex9-32.dwg*.

Exercise 9-33:

Create a Door Legend

Drawing Name: legend2.dwg
Estimated Time: 30 minutes

This exercise reinforces the following skills:

- ❑ Legends
- ❑ Tables
- ❑ Blocks
- ❑ Text Styles
- ❑ Viewports
- ❑ Layouts

1. Open *legend2.dwg.*

2. Activate the **MODEL** layout tab.

Model

3.

Activate the Home tab on the ribbon.

Select the **Table** tool located in the drop-down on the Annotation panel.

4.

Set the Columns to **2**.
Set the Data rows to **9.**

Click **OK**.

5.

Left click to place the table next to the door schedule.

Type **DOOR LEGEND** as the table header.

6.

Highlight the second row, first cell.
Right click and select **Insert Block**.

7.

Select **bifold-double** from the drop-down list.
Enable **Auto-fit**.
Set the Overall cell alignment to **Middle Center**.
Click **OK**.

8.

The image appears in the cell.

9.

Type **Bifold Double** in the second cell, second row.

Change the text height to **1/16"**.

Adjust the width of the columns.

10.

Highlight the third row, first cell.
Select **Insert Block** from the ribbon.

11.

Select **bifold-single** from the drop-down list.
Enable **Auto-fit**.
Set the Overall cell alignment to **Middle Center**.
Click **OK**.

12.

The image appears in the cell.

13.

Type **Bifold Single** in the second cell, third row.

Change the text height to **1/16"**.

14.

Highlight the fourth row, first cell.
Right click and select **Insert Block**.

15.

Select **single-hinged** from the drop-down list.
Enable **Auto-fit**.
Set the Overall cell alignment to **Middle Center**.
Click **OK**.

16.

The image appears in the cell.

17.

Type **Single Hinged** in the second cell, fourth row.

Change the text height to **1/16".**

18.

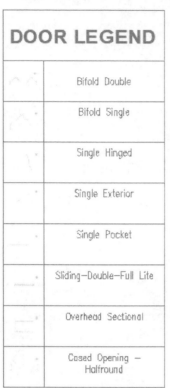

Continue inserting the blocks and text until the door legend is completed as shown.

Place the table on the **A-Anno-Schd** layer.

Type IMAGEFRAME and then 0 to turn off the border around the images.

19. Go to the View tab on the ribbon.

Launch the **View Manager**.

20. Select **New**.

21. Type **Door Legend** in the View name field.
Enable **Define window**.

Window around the legend table.
Click **ENTER**.
Click **OK**.
Close the View Manager.

22. Activate the **E1.2 Door Details** layout.

23.

Activate the Layout tab on the ribbon.

Select the **Rectangular** viewport tool.

24.

Draw the rectangle to place the viewport on the layout sheet.

Double click inside the viewport to activate MODEL space.

25.

Activate the View tab on the ribbon.

Double click on the **Door Legend** view.

The display in the viewport updates with the door legend.

26.

Select the viewport.

On the Properties palette:
Assign the viewport to the **viewport** layer.
Set Display locked to **Yes**.

Click ESC to release the selection.

27.

Save as *ex9-33.dwg*.

Extra:

1) Update the view titles with the correct sheet numbers based on the sheets where the views are placed.

2) Create additional elevation and section views for the kitchen, the second bathroom, the exterior elevations, and windows.

3) Add the new views to existing sheets or new sheets.

4) Add window tags to all the windows.

5) Create a window schedule.

6) Create a window legend.

7) Create a detail view for window framing.

8) Create a callout to the window framing detail view.

9) Create a section elevation view of an interior wall.

10) Add keynotes to the interior wall section elevation view.

11) Update the attributes on each title block with the correct sheet number and title information.

QUIZ 9

True or False

1. Images cannot be converted to blocks.

2. You can control the size and shape of any elevation view you create.

3. Once you create an elevation view, it cannot be updated.

4. Property set definitions are used in schedules and tags.

5. Property set definitions cannot be used by attributes.

6. You can only place one viewport on a layout.

Multiple Choice

7. You can perform the following in a 2D elevation view: (select all that apply)

    A. Assign a material to individual components
    B. Modify the linework
    C. Render
    D. Change the scale

8. A Live Section View: (select all that apply)

    A. is a 3D view
    B. plan
    C. section
    D. elevation

9. Identify the tool shown.

    A. Expand Window
    B. New Viewport
    C. Rectangle
    D. Paper space

10. If you do not see annotations in a viewport, but they are visible in the Model layout: (select all that apply)

    A. The layer they are on is probably frozen in that viewport.
    B. The annotations require an annotation scale added.
    C. They were deleted.
    D. They are hidden.

11. To add an annotative scale to a tag: (select all that apply)

    A. Select the tag and then use the Add/Delete Scale tool on the ribbon.
    B. Select the tag, right click and select Properties.
    C. Set the tag to be annotative.
    D. Select the tag and use the annotative scale tool on the status bar.

12. To create a custom schedule, you can:

    A. Use a table
    B. Create a schedule style
    C. Use lines and text
    D. Use rectangles and mtext

13. Schedule Table Styles control: (select all the apply:)

    A. Objects that are included in the schedule
    B. Sequence and format of the columns
    C. Property data that can be included
    D. Images of the components

14. Property Data Formats control: (select all the apply:)

    A. Whether a property set definition uses text or numerical data
    B. The units and precision of numerical data
    C. Whether text is upper, lower, or sentence case
    D. The property sets used by different objects, such as doors, windows, or spaces

ANSWERS:

1) F; 2) T; 3) F; 4) T; 5) F; 6) F; 7) A, B, C, D; 8) A; 9) B; 10) B; 11) A; 12) B; 13) A, B, C; 14) A, B, C